UKRAINE

WHAT EVERYONE NEEDS TO KNOW®

UKRAINE
WHAT EVERYONE NEEDS TO KNOW®

Second Edition

SERHY YEKELCHYK

OXFORD
UNIVERSITY PRESS

OXFORD

UNIVERSITY PRESS

Oxford University Press is a department of the University of Oxford. It furthers the University's objective of excellence in research, scholarship, and education by publishing worldwide. Oxford is a registered trade mark of Oxford University Press in the UK and certain other countries.

"What Everyone Needs to Know" is a registered trademark of Oxford University Press.

Published in the United States of America by Oxford University Press 198 Madison Avenue, New York, NY 10016, United States of America.

© Oxford University Press 2015, 2020

Library of Congress Control Number: 2020940800
ISBN 978-0-19-753211-9 (pbk.)
ISBN 978-0-19-753210-2 (hbk.)

5 7 9 8 6 4

Paperback printed by LSC Communications, United States of America
Hardback printed by Bridgeport National Bindery, Inc., United States of America

To the memory of
Anna I. Yeremina

CONTENTS

5 The Orange Revolution and the EuroMaidan 78

ACKNOWLEDGMENTS

I wrote the text of what became this book's first edition during a difficult year for Ukraine, when war seemed to rip the country apart. Both Ukrainian citizens and international specialists on Ukraine found themselves engaged in emotional arguments about people's power, political legitimacy, nationalism, and foreign involvement. Above all, they struggled to make sense of the war suddenly exploding in the heart of Eastern Europe decades after the collapse of communism, when the region should have been well on its way to prosperity and democracy. As I was writing this book, I was both worried and hopeful. I was concerned about family members and friends in Ukraine, who often held opposite views on the conflict but suffered from its consequences in much the same way. At the same time, I was hoping to see an end to the death and dislocation that the war had brought, and to catch a glimpse of a peaceful and democratic Ukraine emerging from the conflict.

That difficult year included four trips to Ukraine, and I must start by thanking my hosts there: the Lviv Center for Urban History of East-Central Europe, Laurus Publishers, and my family in Kyiv. I am also deeply grateful to the following institutions that invited me to deliver lectures about the conflict in Ukraine, thereby helping to formulate this book's main arguments: Agnes Scott College, Canadian Institute of Ukrainian Studies, Canadian International Council (Victoria Branch), Center for Urban History of East-Central Europe, University of Alberta, University of Ottawa, University of Toronto, and University of Tübingen. At my home institution, the University of Victoria, I gave talks on Ukraine twice in the Faculty of Continuing Studies and once in connection with the History Department's series "World Affairs in Historical Perspective." I wish to thank my colleagues who invited me to these forums and provided valuable commentary: Dominique Arel, Greg Blue, Elizabeth Bowman, Alan Breakspear, Penny Briden, Martin Bunton, Sofia Dyak, Mayhill C. Fowler, Madina Goldberg, Oleh Ilnytzkyj, Bohdan Klid, Volodymyr Kravchenko, Thomas Lahusen, Janet McDonald, Iryna Matsevko, Don Nightingale, Natalia Pylypiuk, and Schamma Schahadat. In addition, Derek Fraser and Michael Moser kindly shared with me some of their formidable diplomatic and linguistic expertise, respectively.

Special thanks are owed to two online periodicals that are run by academics but are aimed at a wider audience of policymakers and the general public: *Origins: Current Events in Historical Perspective* at Ohio State University and *Perspectives on Europe*, a publication of the Council on Foreign Relations. Both published my articles on the conflict in Ukraine, and the process of writing and revising them did much to clarify my thinking on this issue. I greatly appreciate the time and effort that Nicholas Breyfogle of *Origins* and Neringa Klumbytė of *Perspectives* took to help improve my texts and the invitation to contribute in the first place.

The many media interviews and texts that I wrote for a general audience since the crisis began helped greatly in honing the ideas in this book. Some of these media contacts provided inspiration as much as an opportunity to formulate my thoughts—in particular, a surprise invitation from Lisa M. Bonos to write an op-ed for the *Washington Post* and the dozens of telephone interviews with Terry Moore of C-FAX radio in Victoria, who joked about having my number on speed dial. Over the years, Stuart Williams of the AFP and Peter O'Neil of Postmedia asked a number of penetrating questions about Ukraine, and Pierre Heumann of *Die Weltwoche* published my longest-ever interview in a Western weekly. In Ukraine, I am grateful above all to Tetiana Teren for the lengthy, thought-provoking interview for *Ukrainska Pravda* and Ostap Drozdov for an inspiring conversation on his television show *Direct Quote* on ZIK channel.

Stephen Ejack, a graduate student at the University of Victoria and my industrious research assistant, has done a great job helping prepare the chapters for publication. My Montreal copyeditor, Marta D. Olynyk, was as always a paragon of efficiency in polishing them.

This is the third consecutive book I am publishing with Oxford University Press USA, which excels in highlighting connections between academic research and a better understanding of today's world. I am grateful to Angela Chnapko, who first approached me about this project and worked with me to make this book a reality. Anonymous readers for the press helped improve the book's structure and argument.

I was hoping that this book would need no new editions because the international community would help Ukraine end the war and the occupation of its territories. Yet, five years later the publisher has asked me for an update. By now, the ongoing armed conflict in Ukraine has become the new normal, and among some American politicians, the country has also acquired the dubious reputation of a Klondike for dirt-digging. The wider focus of the significant revisions I undertook necessitated the new title. In the second edition, the book is called *Ukraine* and it deals with much more than Russia's aggression.

This book is dedicated to the memory of my mother-in-law, Anna I. Yeremina (1937–2014), an ethnic Russian patriot of Ukraine, who died in Kyiv after a long illness as the war in the east of the country raged on. Until her very last days, she eagerly followed the news about the situation in Ukraine and, as she was a Russian speaker, served as a reminder that this was not a clear-cut ethnic conflict, but also—or perhaps even primarily—a clash of different political models and concepts of citizenship masquerading as ethnic strife. Talking to her and other ethnic Russian friends and family members, those who came to embrace the notion of a European Ukraine and those skeptical about it, helped me make sense of Ukraine's complex national and civic identity, the main focus of this book.

CHRONOLOGY

9th century	Formation of Kyivan Rus
980–1050	Reign of Prince Volodymyr
988	Adoption of Christianity
1240	Kyiv destroyed by the Mongols
1362	Kyiv annexed by Lithuania
1492	First documentary mention of the Cossacks
1569	Union of Lublin between Poland and Lithuania
1596	Creation of the Uniate (Ukrainian Greek Catholic) Church
1648	Uprising against Polish rule
1648–1657	Bohdan Khmelnytsky's tenure as a Cossack hetman
1654	Treaty of Pereiaslav brings the Cossacks under Muscovite rule
1709	Tsar Peter I defeats separatist Hetman Ivan Mazepa
1772	Galicia becomes part of the Habsburg Empire
1783	The Russian Empire annexes the Crimean Khanate
1876	Literature in Ukrainian banned in the Russian Empire
1890	First Ukrainian political party established in Austria-Hungary
1898	Mykhailo Hrushevsky publishes the first volume of *History of Ukraine-Rus*

1917	Revolution in the Russian Empire; the Central Rada convenes in Kyiv
1918	Founding of the independent Ukrainian People's Republic
1920	The Bolsheviks establish control over eastern Ukraine
1922	The Ukrainian Socialist Soviet Republic joins the Soviet Union
1923	The Allies approve Poland's annexation of eastern Galicia
1923–1933	Ukrainization campaign in Soviet Ukraine
1929	Founding of the Organization of Ukrainian Nationalists
1932–1933	The Ukrainian Famine (Holodomor)
1938–1949	Nikita Khrushchev's tenure as Communist Party boss in Ukraine
1939–1940	The Soviet Union annexes western Ukrainian lands from Poland and Romania
1941–1944	Nazi occupation of Ukraine
1944	Deportation of Crimean Tatars from the Crimea
1954	The Crimea is transferred from the Russian Federation to Ukraine
1976	The Ukrainian Helsinki Group is founded
1986	Chernobyl nuclear catastrophe
1990	Student protests in Kyiv
1991	The Soviet Union collapses; Ukraine proclaims independence
1991–1994	Presidency of Leonid Kravchuk
1994	The Budapest Memorandum on Security Assurances; Ukraine gives up its nuclear arsenal
1994–2004	Presidency of Leonid Kuchma
1997	Russia and Ukraine divide the Black Sea Fleet
2004	The Orange Revolution

2005–2010	Presidency of Viktor Yushchenko
2009	Ukraine's "gas war" with Russia
2010–2014	Presidency of Viktor Yanukovych
2011	Former Prime Minister Yulia Tymoshenko is imprisoned
2013–2014	The EuroMaidan Revolution
2014	Russia annexes the Crimea
2014	War in the Donbas begins
2014–2019	Presidency of Petro Poroshenko
2015	Second Minsk Agreement establishes shaky cease-fire in the Donbas
2018	Strait of Kerch incident
2019	Volodymyr Zelensky sworn in as president

UKRAINE

RUSSIAN FEDERATION

RUSSIAN FEDERATION

BELARUS

POLAND

SLOVAKIA

HUNGARY

ROMANIA

REP. OF MOLDOVA

BULGARIA

Chernobyl

Kyiv

Lviv

Galicia

Uzhhorod

Chernivtsi

Kharkiv

Dnipropetrovsk

Dnipro River

Donbas

Luhansk

Donetsk

Rostov-on-Don

Odesa

TRANSNISTRIA

SEA OF AZOV

Kerch

AUTONOMOUS REP. OF CRIMEA

Sevastopol

BLACK SEA

Site of July 17, 2014 Malaysia Airlines crash

National capital
Provincial capital
City, town
International boundary
Boundary of oblasts and of the Autonomous Republic of Crimea
Boundary of separatist-controlled territories as of May 2020
Site of July 17, 2014 Malaysia Airlines crash

0   50   100 150 200 250 300 km
0   50   100   150   200 mi

UKRAINE

WHAT EVERYONE NEEDS TO KNOW®

1

WHY UKRAINE?

Why did Ukraine become a key reference point of American political struggles?

In recent years, Ukraine has emerged as the most prominent test case of American support for democracy and liberal economic reforms worldwide. A combination of several factors has made Ukraine and the United States mutually important political symbols.

As the second most populous and economically important Soviet republic after Russia, Ukraine's geopolitical choice after the Soviet collapse in 1991 held major significance. It took American policymakers some time to orient themselves in the confusing world of post-Soviet politics and to realize Ukraine's strategic importance. Once they understood, by the mid-1990s, that an independent Ukraine was crucial for preventing an increasingly assertive Russia from reclaiming its Soviet-era control of East-Central Europe, they made Ukraine the focus of American attention in the region.

However, the United States helped to conclude one important international agreement before this "rediscovery" of Ukraine was complete. Because Ukraine had inherited from the Soviet Union the world's third-largest nuclear arsenal, over which it had no operational control, the United States and other major nuclear powers applied pressure to have the Ukrainian authorities surrender it to Russia, where it would be dismantled under Western supervision. In Budapest in 1994, the United States, the United Kingdom, and Russia signed the Budapest Memorandum on Security Assurances, which guaranteed the security and territorial integrity of Ukraine, the latter in turn committing to the destruction of its nuclear stockpiles and the policy of nuclear non-proliferation. Subsequently, France and China also endorsed the Budapest Memorandum. Thus, the United States became a guarantor of Ukrainian sovereignty.

Once American economic assistance to Ukraine began in earnest in the mid-1990s, it always had bipartisan support and was pursued by Democratic and Republican administrations alike. Already by the late 1990s, Ukraine, which was still struggling with the transition to a market economy, had become one of the world's top recipients of US financial aid. The Ukrainian authorities well understood the utility of their geopolitical position, although at the time they focused on enriching their cronies while balancing carefully between Russia and the West.

The developments in Ukraine at the start of the new millennium changed this unhealthy equilibrium of the United States supporting, for strategic reasons, yet another corrupt regime. The birth of a mass protest movement in Ukraine against the muzzling of the press and parliamentary manipulations made it impossible for the West to keep talking about the promotion of democracy there without taking a stand. With the public release of secret recordings made in the president's office, the Ukrainian leadership lost face and no longer had the credibility to sit at the same table with its Western partners. Now dealing with a Ukraine enveloped by social discontent and its government drifting in the direction of authoritarianism—and Russia—American policymakers had no choice but to side with the opposition. The moment to make a stand came in 2004, when the government's flagrant attempt to steal the election resulted in massive non-violent rallies in the Ukrainian capital. The Americans' refusal to recognize the falsified results and the efforts of international intermediaries contributed greatly to the peaceful resolution of the conflict.

This also meant that the United States and the West, in general, now also played an important symbolic role in Ukraine as both promoters and models of democracy and economic transparency. Their failure to live up to this example would undermine the reformist forces in Ukraine and push the Ukrainian elites in the direction of the authoritarian and corrupt regime in Russia that presents itself as opposed to Western values. American administrations, even when they seemed aware of this symbolic role, did not do enough to support their diplomats in Ukraine, nor did they push strongly enough for political and economic reforms in the country.

In 2013, when another Ukrainian president tried, in a stunning political U turn, to reverse the country's course on cooperation with the European Union and the West, a popular revolution unfolded once again in the center of the Ukrainian capital. Sensing support from Russia, this time the authorities did not give up easily until the escalating violence resulted in a significant number of casualties, the overwhelming majority of them on the protesters' side. With the officials of the old regime making off to Russia, the Ukrainian parliament installed a new government, which the United States and their Western partners supported. But Russia took this opportunity to annex the Crimean Peninsula from Ukraine and to start a war in the borderland region of the Donbas, which it tried to present as an internal Ukrainian conflict, the involvement of Russian tanks, artillery, and soldiers notwithstanding.

With the outbreak of Russian aggression in 2014, Ukraine became, for the United States and their Western partners, something more than a strategically important country whose security the West guaranteed and where they supported, albeit insufficiently, democratic and market reforms. The Russian annexation of the Crimea and the Russian-sponsored war in the Donbas highlighted Russia's brazen violation of international treaties and an open challenge to a world order based on the rule of law rather than the right of the strong. The American response would not only strongly influence the conduct of international politics but would also reflect on America's own commitment to transparency and due process in supporting its allies, such as Ukraine.

Instead, the reaction in Washington was mixed. Although the Trump administration reversed the ban on the delivery of lethal weapons to Ukraine instituted under Obama, it has also tried to embroil the Ukrainian authorities in precisely the kind of political deals they wanted to leave behind. These Ukrainian authorities were also new, because the Ukraine that emerged from the revolution and ongoing war in the Donbas proved its capacity for democratic renewal by holding free and fair elections. With the support of its Western partners, the country has also made significant advances with reforms, only to be labeled by some American politicians and media outlets as a corrupt place, where one could find compromising material on any Westerner who ever visited.

This unfair perception has caused Ukraine to become a metaphor in American politics rather than a real country needing America's positive example and support as it fights for its sovereignty and the well-being of its citizens. In the decades since the collapse of communism, Ukraine has been important for the West for a variety of reasons and its importance has only increased in the new millennium. But the West has also stood for something in the Ukrainian political imagination: the rule of law, observance of human rights, struggle against corruption, and political transparency. It can inspire Ukrainians—and the rest of the world—only if it stays true to these principles.

What is the Maidan, and what made it top news around the world?

"Maidan" is how the residents of the Ukrainian capital, Kyiv, usually abbreviate the name of their city's main plaza, Maidan Nezalezhnosti (Independence Square). In recent times this name has also come to connote a space of popular protests and people power in general. "Maidan" is a Turkic word for a square, and Ukrainians likely borrowed it from the Crimean Tatars or other Turkic-speaking people. The Maidan is centrally located in downtown Kyiv, straddling the city's main thoroughfare, Khreshchatyk Boulevard. There are no government buildings in the vicinity, with the exception of City Hall, where no major political decisions are made. However, in Soviet times Khreshchatyk Boulevard served as a parade ground and the Maidan, then named after the (Bolshevik) October Revolution, as a place for political rallies. Because of this, Kyivites came to perceive it not just as the capital's central plaza, but also as a space for political expression. The square acquired this reputation after hosting three rounds of mass political protests: in 1990, 2004–2005, and 2013–2014.

During the late Soviet period, the Maidan was dominated at its eastern end by an impressive October Revolution monument depicting Lenin leading revolutionary workers and soldiers. It was on the granite steps under this sculpture that several dozen students declared a hunger strike in October 1990, demanding the government's resignation and other reforms. Ukraine was then a republic within the Soviet Union. The Soviet leader Mikhail Gorbachev had initiated political liberalization, which led to an increased push for democracy and national assertiveness in the union republics. In Ukraine, the party leadership remained conservative, and it took a student hunger strike in the center of the capital to remove the unpopular head of the Cabinet of Ministers. In the process, the students achieved something even more important. By setting up their small pup tents on the granite steps in what was subsequently dubbed the "Revolution on the Granite," they asserted the public's right to political protest and established the capital's central square as a protest venue.[1] The authorities did not dare to crack down on the students' peaceful protest, which had widespread public sympathy among Kyivites. By then, the Soviet Union was on its last legs; it would be dissolved the following year.

Some of the student participants of the Revolution on the Granite went on to organize the Orange Revolution in the winter of 2004–2005. Once again, the Maidan served as a focal point of popular protests, with a greater number of much larger surplus army tents set up on the square itself and along Khreshchatyk Boulevard, which obstructed traffic on this normally busy central avenue. Unlike in 1990, however, the revolution's main action was not a hunger strike, but a nonstop mass protest rally on the Maidan and the peaceful occupation of the square and the adjacent area. The cause was also different. Instead of targeting diehard communist apparatchiks, the protesters (many of them Kyivites who demonstrated for several hours every day, as well as people arriving from the provinces, who camped out on the Maidan or stayed elsewhere in Kyiv) took up the battle against the corrupt and manipulative post-communist elites. The rigged presidential election and the poisoning of the oppositional candidate, Viktor Yushchenko, served as catalysts, but the protesters' demands were broader: true democracy, political transparency, the rule of law, and the reining in of corruption. Leonid Kuchma, the outgoing president, did not use force against the Maidan protesters, and the West condemned the rigged elections, offering mediation. In the end, the regime agreed to repeat the run-off, which the official candidate went on to lose. The Maidan thus not only affirmed its reputation as a premier Ukrainian protest space but also became known worldwide as a symbol of popular democracy.

However, the victors of the Orange Revolution (named after the opposition's campaign colors) quarreled among themselves instead of pursuing much-needed reforms. The intended beneficiary of the rigged election that prompted the revolution, Viktor Yanukovych, remained in control of the Party of Regions with an electoral base in the eastern, predominantly Russian-speaking regions, where the Maidan was portrayed as a Western intrigue. Taking advantage of the divisions in the Orange camp, Yanukovych was able to return to the government, first as prime minister and, in 2010, as president. However, the return to pre-Orange kleptocracy did not last long. In November 2013 mass protests on the Maidan erupted again after the government suddenly backed out of the Association Agreement with the European Union. In addition to the tents, makeshift barricades went up on and around the Maidan. This time the authorities ordered the deployment of riot police and, eventually and covertly, the use of firepower. The protesters threw Molotov cocktails at the police. Facing escalating casualties, smaller "maidans" in other cities, and expressions of concern from the West, in February 2014 President Yanukovych escaped to Russia and the parliament formed an interim government. The Maidan had won, but it became marked with crosses and makeshift memorials erected in honor of those who had been killed in the clashes. With the appearance of these memorials, its name acquired a new and tragic connotation—that of an urban battlefield, where protesters lost their lives during what is now called the EuroMaidan Revolution or the Revolution of Dignity.

How and why did Russia annex the Crimea from Ukraine?

The EuroMaidan's victory frustrated Russia's political leaders, who had just forced the Yanukovych regime to turn its back on the West. The Kremlin could not undo the overthrow of its ally in Kyiv, but it could cripple the new Ukraine while at the same time asserting Russia's greater geopolitical role. Annexing Ukraine's southernmost region, the Autonomous Republic of the Crimea, presented a seemingly perfect way of achieving both aims. With such a thorn in its side, Ukraine would be prevented from joining the European Union or NATO, neither of which organizations accept members with active territorial conflicts. At the same time, "returning" the Crimea to Russia was bound to be popular with the Russian public, which by and large remained nostalgic for the larger great-power polity that was the Soviet Union and, before it, the Russian Empire. The Crimea holds a special place in Russian military mythology that has arisen around its defense during the Crimean War (1853–1855) and World War II. Present-day Russia could also advance a better claim to the Crimea than to the other parts of the empire that were lost in 1917 or 1991 because this region had belonged to the Russian Soviet Federative Socialist Republic (SFSR) between 1920 and 1954, before being transferred to the Ukrainian Soviet Socialist Republic (SSR) in an internal Soviet territorial rearrangement.

The Crimea was also a low-dangling fruit. The only region of Ukraine with an ethnic Russian majority, the Crimean Peninsula was for decades after the Soviet collapse the political bailiwick of parties cultivating an alternative to modern Ukrainian identity— first the Communist Party and, more recently, Yanukovych's Party of Regions. The local elites were likely to defect because the Russian authoritarian system was more to their liking, as well as for cultural and economic reasons. The Russian Black Sea Fleet kept a major naval base in the Crimea, in Sevastopol, with commandos easily available for any military operation on the peninsula. They were unlikely to face any serious opposition locally.

Within days of the change of power in Kyiv, starting on February 27, 2014, commandos in unmarked uniforms (later revealed as Russian soldiers) began taking over government buildings, airports, and military installations in the Crimea. The local legislature scheduled a hurried (and unconstitutional, under Ukrainian law) referendum on the Crimea's independence from Ukraine and on joining Russia, which took place on March 16, 2014. According to the official results, which many analysts questioned, 96.77 percent of the Crimean population was in favor, with a voter turnout of 83.1 percent. The Crimean authorities declared independence the next day and signed an accession treaty with Russia on March 18, 2014.

On March 27, 2014, the UN General Assembly passed a resolution condemning the referendum and the annexation as illegal. Only Russia and 10 of its allies, including North Korea, Syria, and Venezuela, voted against it. Beginning in April, Western countries introduced the first round of diplomatic and economic sanctions against Russia in connection with its violation of Ukraine's territorial integrity. Within Russia, however, President Vladimir Putin's approval rating soared to a record-high 83 percent. He apparently managed to strike a deep nationalist chord by "returning" the Crimea and standing up to the West.

Why did fighting break out in eastern Ukraine in the spring of 2014?

The fighting in eastern Ukraine or, to be precise, in Donetsk and Luhansk provinces combines features of a covert foreign invasion with those of a civil conflict. Accordingly, it has both external and internal causes, even if these happen to be closely connected.

On the one hand, Ukraine's powerful neighbor and former imperial master, Russia, refuses to accept the political order that has emerged in Ukraine after the 2014 Maidan victory. Russia's position is not surprising, because President Vladimir Putin's regime has fought for many years to keep Ukraine in Russia's economic and political orbit. It was the threat of Russian economic sanctions that forced the fateful decision of the Yanukovych administration to reject a political and trade agreement with the European Union in November 2013, starting the revolution. The Russian state-run media have portrayed the Maidan as pro-Western and pro-Nazi at the same time, a curious combination necessitated by Russia's idiosyncratic self-image as an anti-Western great power that was the principal victor of World War II. However, Russia similarly took the side of the old regime in Ukraine during the Orange Revolution of 2004–2005, which the Russian media also presented as a Western conspiracy. More generally, such a stand reflects Russia's difficulty in coming to terms with its own post-imperial complex and the "loss" of Ukraine—as painful an issue for many Russians today as it was in 1918 and 1991, when Ukraine declared its independence after the collapse of the Russian Empire and the Soviet Union, respectively.

An increasingly important component in the ideology of the Putin regime is Russia's alleged right to protect ethnic Russians and Russian speakers abroad. The latter are citizens of other countries who could be of non-Russian ethnic background but who identified with Russian culture when their present-day nation-states were part of the Soviet Union. Both of these categories are imprecise and can serve as a convenient human-rights cover for imperial-restoration policies. The Russian authorities justified their annexation of the

Crimea from Ukraine in March 2014 by the need to protect their "compatriots," thus defined, from the threat of a Western-supported coup in Ukraine. Similarly, the official Russian line on the conflict in the Donbas (i.e., the Donets Basin, an industrial region on the Russian border comprising Donetsk and Luhansk provinces) is that ethnic Russians and Russian speakers are fighting to protect their cultural rights. However, the armed conflict there would not have started without the Crimean precedent and other encouraging signals from Moscow, as well as the weapons and military personnel coming from Russia. It became clear very quickly that the "volunteers" from Russia comprised a significant proportion of the separatist rebels and that many of their leaders were also Russian citizens, who had come to Ukraine only recently. By the summer of 2014, evidence had mounted of the transfer of heavy weapons from the Russian army to the rebels. Reports were also coming in about regular Russian army units covertly shelling Ukrainian positions from across the border and even operating on Ukrainian territory. All this amounted to Russia's undeclared involvement in the conflict.

Yet it is undeniable that native inhabitants of the Donbas are also present among the separatist rebels. It is not that the volunteers from Russia are fighting on behalf of the locals totally without the latter's support. Rather, it is that the idea of "greater Russia" appeals to both the Russian nationalist newcomers and some part of the local population. A significant proportion of both local and outside fighters can also be classified as mercenaries in that they are being paid to fight. At the same time, however, opinion polls in the Donbas both before and after the start of fighting never showed majority support for separation from Ukraine; indeed, unlike in the Crimea, ethnic Ukrainians constitute the majority population in the Donbas.

Still, the prolonged conflict there has roots in both the region's cultural identity and recently instilled fears. Rather than being a "Russian" region of Ukraine, the Donbas is a "Soviet" industrial region, uncertain of its place in the new Ukraine. Originally migrants from Russia or Ukrainian peasants assimilated by Russophone factory life, Donbas workers identified with the glory of their Soviet-built but now inefficient mines and smokestack industries. For nearly a decade marked by its political domination in the Donbas, Yanukovych's Party of Regions strengthened its hold over voters by fueling their anxieties about the "nationalists" in Ukraine's west potentially encroaching on the region's Russophone cultural space. After the victory of the Maidan, it was relatively easy for the local political elite to stir discontent in the Donbas. The victorious revolutionaries provided perfect pretexts with their misguided attempts to abolish a language law seen as protecting Russian as a regional language and abortive symbolical "occupations" of some administrative buildings in the east. A violent clash in the southern city of Odesa (not in the Donbas) between young radicals from both camps served as ultimate proof that "the nationalists were coming." The anti-Maidan hysteria in the Russian media, which were still influential in eastern Ukraine, and the hope that a Crimean-style incorporation into Russia would immediately increase living standards added to the explosive cocktail.

Still, it took the covert and eventually overt involvement of Russian political advisors and the military to translate the tensions in the Donbas into a violent conflict and, soon, a hybrid war blending irregular and conventional warfare.

Why did the Ukrainian crisis cause tensions between Russia and the West?

Putin's Russia and the West have fundamentally different views of the Soviet collapse and post-communist global political order. In 2005 President Putin famously referred to the breakup of the Soviet Union as the "greatest geopolitical catastrophe of the century."[2] The ideology of the Putin regime is devoid of communist elements, but it valorizes Russia's past as a great power, be it in tsarist or Soviet times. It is the loss of great-power status and empire that explains the Putin regime's negative view of the Soviet Union's dissolution. For similar reasons, the democratic reforms of President Boris Yeltsin in the 1990s are now dismissed in Russian official discourse as the chaotic and "lawless nineties." In contrast, Putin's Russia represents itself in revivalist mode as a state "rising from its knees."

In this historical mythology, the West is cast as the principal villain. Russian media claim that the West betrayed Russia by allegedly promising not to accept the former Soviet satellites in Eastern Europe as members of NATO, but doing just that in 1999–2004.

Russia had strongly opposed the acceptance of the former Soviet satellite states of Poland, Hungary, and the Czech Republic in 1999, but was even more offended in 2004, when the group of seven new NATO members included Estonia, Latvia, and Lithuania, which had been republics of the Soviet Union and thus part of the Soviet "inner empire." Russian state-run media have been fanning fears that Ukraine would become the next and final step in NATO's encroachment on the former Russian sphere of influence in Eastern Europe.

The Russian elites likewise saw the EuroMaidan Revolution in Ukraine, just like the 2004 Orange Revolution before that, as a Western-sponsored coup. In his speech on the occasion of the Crimea's annexation, President Putin spent much time accusing the United States of hypocrisy, disregard of international law, and harming Russia's interests. After enumerating a series of historical wrongs, from the 1999 intervention in Serbia and NATO's eastward expansion to the bombings of Libya, he concluded that "with Ukraine, our Western partners have crossed the line."[3] Clearly, Putin and his government see Ukraine as a crucial battleground in Russia's historical struggle with the West and as a place where Russia must take the last stand.

Ironically, the West does not share such a millenarian vision. It was only in the late 1990s that the United States realized the strategic importance of independent Ukraine as an impediment to a potential restoration of Russia's influence in Eastern Europe. NATO's relations with Ukraine have been very limited, functioning at a level of undefined "partnership," and the European Union has never offered Ukraine a clear accession path. Western backing for the two popular revolutions in Ukraine (2004–2005 and 2013–2014) came primarily in the form of moral support and diplomatic pressure on Russia, as well as humanitarian assistance and educational programs. The West started introducing meaningful economic sanctions only after the Russian annexation of the Crimea and began tightening them only once clear evidence of Russian complicity in the war in the Donbas had emerged. It is only gradually that the West has come to see the conflict over Ukraine as part of Russia's challenge to the post–Cold War global order and to Western concepts of democracy and human rights more generally.

Although Russian and Western interests have clashed in parts of the globe as distant as Venezuela and Syria, Ukraine's geographical location and its special place in Russian history have much to do with this country becoming the principal site of the escalating tensions between Russia and the West.

2

THE LAND AND THE PEOPLE

What is Ukraine's geographical location, and what natural resources and industry does it possess?

Ukraine is located in southeastern Europe. Its longest land border, in the east and north, is with Russia; another northern neighbor is Belarus, a post-Soviet state and Russia's close ally. Ukraine's western neighbors are Poland, Slovakia, Hungary, Romania, and Moldova. All of them, except Moldova, are now members of the European Union and NATO; Ukraine is thus "sandwiched" between Russia and the member countries of the Western political and military alliance. In the south, Ukrainian territory is washed by the Black Sea, which links Ukraine to Turkey and Bulgaria and, beyond the Straits, to the Mediterranean world. Although lacking a common land border with Ukraine, these Black Sea neighbors have played an important role in Ukrainian history.

Ukraine is Europe's second-largest country after Russia. Spanning 603,700 square kilometers, or 233,100 square miles (including the Crimea), it is a bit larger than France and approximately the size of Germany and Great Britain combined. Ukraine's terrain consists almost entirely of vast plains well suited for agricultural cultivation, with higher elevations only along the far edges of Ukrainian territory: the Carpathians in the west and the more impressive Crimean Mountains along the southern tip of the Crimean Peninsula. The most important Ukrainian river is the Dnipro (Dnieper), which traverses the entire country before emptying into the Black Sea.

For centuries Ukraine's most valuable resource was the large "black-earth" belt of humus-rich soil in the Dnipro basin. Dubbed the "breadbasket of Europe," the Ukrainian lands controlled by the Polish-Lithuanian Commonwealth and, later, the Russian Empire became a major area of commercial agriculture and a leading producer of grain and sugar beets. With the arrival of modern industry in the nineteenth century, rich deposits of coal and iron ore in eastern Ukraine led to the growth of mining and steel production, particularly in the Donbas. During the twentieth century, the mighty Ukrainian rivers became major sources of hydroelectric power, and a number of nuclear power stations were built, including in Chernobyl, situated just north of Kyiv.

Ukraine's once-important deposits of oil and gas were largely exhausted by the 1970s, making the republic a net importer of these fuels. However, in recent decades the arrival of new extraction technologies rejuvenated this sector and also led to the discovery of significant offshore liquefied gas deposits in the Black Sea, off the Crimean coast. The status of these natural riches is now uncertain because of Russia's annexation of the peninsula.

Some sectors of the Ukrainian economy weathered relatively well the crash triggered by the collapse of the Soviet economic system. The country remains among the world's leading producers of steel, cast iron, and pipes, as well as mineral fertilizers. Building on its Soviet legacy of developed military industry, Ukraine is still among the world's top 10 arms traders. However, other sectors did not fare so well in the new climate of global competition. Ukraine's once-thriving aircraft industry is nearly extinct, and production of an indigenous Ukrainian car brand, Zaporozhets (later, Tavriia and Slavuta), ceased in 2011. Ukrainian machine building is aimed primarily at Russia and other post-Soviet states because it would not be competitive in Western markets.

Agriculture, the traditional mainstay of Ukraine's economy, is still experiencing the pains of a slow and difficult transition from Soviet-era collective farms to market-oriented commercial agriculture. At the same time, however, the country has developed a modern service industry based to a large degree on the small-business model. The information technology sector is booming as well. Tourism is becoming an increasingly important part of the Ukrainian economy, especially in the western regions with their rich architectural heritage and new mountain resorts.

What is Ukraine's demography and ethnic composition?

The most recent population census, conducted in Ukraine in 2001, registered 48.4 million people, a notable decrease from the 51.5 million in 1989. Such a population decline reflects the general European trend of decreasing fertility rates, but it has been aggravated in Ukraine's case by the post-Soviet economic collapse and the lack of significant in-migration. In addition to the number of deaths consistently exceeding the number of births since the early 1990s, there has been considerable immigration from Ukraine to more economically developed countries during the same period. As a result, official estimates put the population totals for 2014 at 45.4 million, and the prognosis, even before the Donbas war and the related population dislocation, pointed to a continuing decline.

Throughout the post-communist period, the industrial regions of eastern and southern Ukraine registered the steepest population decline. At the same time, large urban centers and Kyiv in particular (current population estimate: 3.1 million) continue to grow at the expense of the countryside. After reaching a low point in 2001, when Ukraine produced the lowest fertility rate ever recorded in a modern European state (1.078 child per woman), the successive governments improved the trend somewhat with child payments and other pro-natalist measures.[1] Average life expectancy in Ukraine has also been increasing recently, although at 66 years for men and 76 for women, it still remains far below that of Western Europe.

According to the 2001 census, the population of Ukraine is composed of 77.8 percent ethnic Ukrainians and 17.3 percent Russians. Other ethnic groups are comparatively negligible, constituting less than one percent, but they can be quite visible in certain regions if settled compactly, as are Moldovans or Romanians (0.8 percent) and Hungarians (0.3 percent) in the southwest; Belarusians (0.6 percent) in the northwest; Bulgarians (0.4 percent) and Greeks (0.2 percent) in the south; and Crimean Tatars (0.5 percent) in the Crimea. Historically, Jews and Poles constituted significant minority groups in the Ukrainian lands, but the two world wars, the Holocaust, and forced population resettlements under Stalin reduced their respective proportions among Ukraine's population. Once a prominent presence in the regions west of the Dnipro River, Poles now number only 0.3 percent of the total population (144,000). Already decimated during the war, Ukraine's Jews have been emigrating en masse to Israel and the West since the late 1980s, reducing their share from 2 percent in 1959 to 0.2 percent (104,000) in 2001. Most German-speaking Mennonites left southern Ukraine in the 1920s and during World War II.

Historically a land of ethnic diversity, Ukraine has become a more homogenous East Slavic country since the late Soviet period, with a significant Russian minority and de facto Russian-Ukrainian bilingualism. Ethnic Russians in the Ukrainian SSR did not see themselves as a minority but, rather, as representatives of the Soviet Union's leading nation. After the emergence of independent Ukraine, such an ethnic landscape set the stage for the present conflict.

Who are the Ukrainians, and what is modern Ukrainian national identity?

In Eastern Europe, which was dominated for centuries by multinational dynastic empires, the concept of nationality developed differently from Western Europe and North America. Instead of referring to themselves as members of a state (e.g., Americans), the subjects of the Romanov and Habsburg empires entered the age of modern nationalism by identifying with their ethnic nationalities (e.g., Poles, Serbs, Ukrainians). As the empires collapsed at the end of World War I, some of these ethnic nations managed to obtain (they would often prefer to say "restore") statehood based on the principle of national self-determination. Yet, the concept of nationhood was based on ethnicity, and a necessary distinction had to be made between members of the new state's titular ethnic group and citizens of other ethnic backgrounds. Because Ukraine regained its independence relatively late, in 1991, the notion of "Ukrainians" or the "Ukrainian nation" is still understood there as referring to ethnic Ukrainians. When one wants to include all citizens of the Ukrainian state regardless of their ethnicity, one would typically speak of "citizens of Ukraine" or "people of Ukraine." The Constitution of Ukraine proclaims as the source of state sovereignty the "Ukrainian people—citizens of Ukraine of all nationalities" and distinguishes between this civic concept of the nation and the ethnic "Ukrainian nation."[2] In recent decades, however, speakers of the Ukrainian language have gradually come to accept a Western understanding of "Ukrainians" as all citizens of Ukraine. Such a linguistic change reflects the slow development of civic patriotism based on allegiance to the state rather than an ethnic nation.

But in order to answer the question, we first need to understand the nature of the Ukrainian ethnic nation, which is also changing. Nationalists believe in organic, primordial ethnic nations defined by blood, but modern scholars argue otherwise. They demonstrate that modern nations emerge when education and mass media help the masses "imagine" themselves as part of a nation. The folk culture of the peasantry served as the foundation of modern nations in Eastern Europe, but it took the effort of patriotic intellectuals to define ethnic nations within patchwork empires and to design from folk elements a modern high culture that could serve as a foundation of contemporary national identity.

Ukrainians are an excellent example of this process, because the nation's modern name took hold only in the late nineteenth century, thanks to the efforts of the patriotic intelligentsia. Of course, the ancestors of modern Ukrainians lived on the same territories since at least the fifth century and were known under various names. Originally called the *Rus* people (*Rusy*, or *Rusyny*), they later became known as "Little Russians" in the Russian Empire and "Ruthenians" in Austria-Hungary. Looking for a name that would clearly separate their people from the Russians, local activists began propagating the appellation "Ukrainians" in the late nineteenth century. It was derived from the name of the land, Ukraine, meaning "borderland" and by then sufficiently established as the geographical designation for present-day central Ukraine. The name "Ukrainians" really took hold in the 1920s, with the creation of the Ukrainian SSR within the Soviet Union and the national mobilization of Ukrainians in Poland. However, even today some enclaves of East Slavic populations in the Ukrainian southwest and in neighboring Slovakia have preserved the historical name "Rusyns." Scholars disagree on whether they are a branch of the Ukrainian people that did not develop a modern ethnic identity or a separate ethnic group.

Perhaps more important, the concept of ethnic Ukrainians as a group separate from the Russians was something Ukrainian activists had to fight for. The Russian Empire recognized "Little Russians" only as a "tribe" of the Russian people and banned education and publishing in Ukrainian. The Soviet Union acknowledged the existence of the Ukrainian nation and created the Ukrainian SSR as a national homeland for Ukrainians. However, in the long run, Soviet leaders emphasized the leading role of Russians in an East Slavic fraternal union of Russians, Ukrainians, and Belarusians within the Soviet Union. As a result, Russians were taught to see Ukrainians as their "younger brothers" rather than as equals. As for Ukrainians, during the postwar period in particular, the state encouraged them to identify with the Soviet Union in general, more than with their own republic, and to adopt the Russian language and culture. Creeping assimilation made considerable inroads in Ukraine by the end of the Soviet period. Since tsarist times, a share of ethnic Ukrainians identified themselves as native speakers of the Russian language, and this group grew in size during the postwar period. By the time of the 2001 census, 14.8 percent of self-identified ethnic Ukrainians in Ukraine claimed Russian as their native language. Although it was not recorded by census-takers, more subtle opinion polls in the 1990s revealed the presence of people, especially in eastern Ukraine, who preferred to identify as "Soviets" rather than as Ukrainians or Russians. Some 27 percent of respondents in a 1997 nationwide opinion poll selected the answer "both Ukrainian and Russian" when asked to identify their ethnicity.[3] Many self-identified Ukrainians also subscribed to the idea of a special connection to Russia.

Modern Ukrainian ethnic identity continued to evolve during the post-communist period. The state-run education system did much to consolidate popular identification with the concept of the Ukrainian ethnic nation, marked by the Ukrainian language and folk traditions. At the same time, politicians discovered the language issue to be a convenient mobilization tool. Incapable of solving the grave economic and social problems during the post-communist transition, political parties found it easier to fight over the "imposition" of Ukrainian on traditionally Russian-speaking or bilingual regions in eastern and southern Ukraine. The Russian state next door also found it advantageous for its own internal political reasons to fan political rhetoric about the protection of Russian speakers against forced Ukrainization. In reality, however, what the opposing sides often try to present as a clear-cut conflict between the Ukrainian and Russian national identities in Ukraine is actually the painful process of overcoming the ambivalent Soviet legacy in the region. Hidden beneath the surface of supposed ethnic strife, one finds a conflict between the new Western-style civil society and the strong paternalistic state, the latter representing not only the Soviet past and the Russian present but also the ideal to which the Yanukovych regime aspired.

The war in the Donbas, tragic as it is, has strengthened the concept of the Ukrainian civic nation identifying with the Ukrainian state, in part because the rebels identify so openly with Russia and are often Russian citizens. One can see from social media and footage from the war zone that Ukrainian volunteers and soldiers are more often than not also speaking Russian, meaning that they are fighting for a civic rather than an ethnic concept of Ukrainian identity. It is now up to the new Ukrainian authorities to cement this new civic patriotism with measures that link modern Ukrainian identity with democracy and inclusivity.

Is it true that Ukraine is split into pro-Western and pro-Russian halves?

Such a picture is a convenient simplification, often reproduced by mass media. In reality, there is no clear line dividing Ukraine on this or any other issue, although regional differences do exist and can be mobilized for political ends. It is important to understand that there is no ethnic "Russian" half of Ukraine. Ethnic Ukrainians constitute the majority of the population in all provinces except for the Autonomous Republic of the Crimea, where ethnic Russians are in the majority. Ukrainians predominate even in the two provinces of the Donbas region on the Russian border, where the conflict is raging. The religious divide between the Ukrainian Greek Catholic Church (recognizing the pope) and the three Orthodox churches in Ukraine does not provide a clear dividing line either, because Ukrainian Catholics are concentrated in the westernmost historical regions of Galicia and Transcarpathia, whereas the current conflict is taking place in traditionally Orthodox territory.

If this is so, what are the divisions one encounters in Ukraine, and how do they fuel the current conflict? As in many other countries, including the United States, there are regional voting patterns and cultural variances in Ukraine. However, these divisions are fluid and are not usually expressed in terms of a simple dichotomy of pro-Russian versus pro-Western. In order to understand them, we need to look at Ukraine's historical regions.

It is worth keeping in mind that prior to World War II, the region we now call western Ukraine was divided among Poland, Hungary, Romania, and Czechoslovakia. Before that, these lands were part of the Austro-Hungarian Empire. This westernmost region, which constitutes more like a quarter than a half of Ukrainian territory, only experienced Soviet rule for half a century and therefore underwent a much shorter indoctrination in "fraternal relations" with Russia. It was also there, and in Galicia in particular, that the Ukrainian national movement developed freely during the nineteenth century, while it was being suppressed in the Russian Empire. Patriotic intellectuals gained access to the peasantry early on through reading rooms, co-ops, and the educational system, resulting in a strong popular sense of Ukrainian identity by the early twentieth century. Ukrainian radical nationalism was also born in the region in the 1920s, after the Allies denied the Ukrainians the right of self-determination, and nationalist insurgents in Galicia fought against the Soviets for several years after the end of World War II. Assimilation into Russian culture was least advanced there. In the years leading up to the Soviet collapse, mass rallies and demands for independence also originated there.

With this in mind, perhaps one could call Galicia and, with lesser justification, all of western Ukraine a hotbed of anti-Russian Ukrainian nationalism. Yet, this in itself would not make the region "pro-Western." The immediate neighbor to the west, Poland, was to local Ukrainians a former imperial master just like Russia, and during the interwar period the Polish state was the main enemy of Ukrainian radical nationalists. The periods of Hungarian and Romanian rule did not leave warm memories either. However, western Ukraine could be seen as culturally "Western" in the sense of having experience with political participation and civil society, two phenomena that were sorely lacking on the Russian side of the border. Imperfect as they were, the Austrian models of parliamentary democracy and communal organization shaped western Ukrainian social life. This experience of political participation in a multinational empire and its successors also strengthened Ukrainian national identity.

But if only the westernmost quarter of the country can claim the longer tradition of European constitutionalism and civil society, would it not leave the rest of Ukraine solidly in the Russian sphere of influence? Election results and opinion polls do not support such a hypothesis. Although three-quarters of present-day Ukrainian territories were part of the Russian Empire and the Soviet Union at least since the late eighteenth century, they do not vote as a bloc. The political landscape of these lands is both diverse and fluid. It is influenced by a variety of factors, such as ethnic composition, age profile, industrial development, trade patterns, and tourist routes. A changing economy, combined with generational differences, influences political choices. For example, the Communist Party, which was a formidable political force in eastern and central Ukraine in the mid- to late 1990s, with its emphasis on stronger ties with Russia, has become marginalized. If, in the 1990s, central Ukraine tended to vote with the east against the west, in the 2000s the center has voted increasingly often with the west against the east.

If this is so, how can one explain the apparent popular support for separatism in the Crimea and, to a lesser degree, in the Donbas? The answer is to be found in the fusion of Soviet nostalgia with Russian cultural identity. Both regions had an established local identity that was associated with Soviet history: the Donbas as the industrial region of proud miners and steelworkers "providing" for the rest of the country, and the Crimea as the headquarters of the Black Sea Fleet and the site of historic battles, as well as a popular resort welcoming tourists from the Soviet Russian republic. In both cases, pride in the region's Soviet past went hand in hand with the predominance of Russian culture. In the Crimea, the percentage of Russian speakers is considerably higher than the share of ethnic Russians in the population (60.4 percent). In the two Donbas provinces, the percentage of ethnic Ukrainians in 2001 stood at 58 percent and 56.9 percent, correspondingly, but only 30 percent and 24.1 percent of the population claimed Ukrainian as their mother tongue. In the last decade, the powerful Party of Regions played on the linked issues of Soviet nostalgia and the Russian language in order to maintain its electoral base in eastern Ukraine, and in the Donbas in particular. Thus a transitional, fluid cultural identity became mobilized for political ends, making political identification with Putin's Russia possible.

How large is the Ukrainian diaspora, and what role does it play in North American politics?

Mass emigration from the Ukrainian lands started in the late nineteenth century in connection with rural overpopulation and the lack of opportunity at home. Beginning in the 1870s, Ukrainians from the Austro-Hungarian Empire, who at first were predominantly young men intending to return home after earning some money, went to the northeastern United States as coal miners and industrial laborers. In the long run, however, many were joined by their families, and vibrant Ukrainian communities developed in such American cities as Pittsburgh, Philadelphia, and Chicago. Beginning in the 1890s, another stream of Ukrainian immigrants began arriving in the New World from the Austro-Hungarian Empire: peasants who were willing to resettle permanently with their families if they could obtain arable land. Their original destinations were Brazil and Argentina, but Canada soon emerged as the most popular choice. Seeking to colonize the prairie provinces and secure a workforce for the construction of the Canadian Pacific Railroad, the Canadian authorities welcomed Ukrainian peasant immigrants. By the time of World War I, an estimated 500,000 Ukrainians had left for the New World.

As Ukrainian peasants from the Austro-Hungarian Empire crossed the ocean in search of a better life, about two million of their brethren in the Russian Empire migrated eastward to western Siberia and Central Asia, where vacant land was still available. Very few ethnic Ukrainian immigrants came to North America from the tsarist state, but by the late nineteenth century the majority of Jewish immigrants arriving in North American cities hailed from the Russian Empire. Usually self-identifying as "Russian Jews" or "Polish Jews," they were more often than not from the territories that today constitute Ukraine. Jewish immigrants from Ukraine were fleeing the legal and economic discrimination they suffered under the tsars, as well as the violent pogroms of 1881 and 1903–1905.

The next large immigration wave from Ukraine came at the end of World War II and consisted of refugees from the Stalin regime, as well as some slave laborers in Nazi Germany, who preferred to resettle in the West. Numerically much smaller than the earlier wave of economic immigrants, with only some 80,000 coming to the United States and 30,000 to Canada, this well-educated generation of "displaced persons" soon took over Ukrainian community organizations in North America, establishing the anti-communist political profile of the Ukrainian diaspora. For the first time, postwar immigrants established notable Ukrainian communities in Great Britain and Australia, with an estimated 20,000 settlers each.

Whereas these earlier immigration waves created and maintained Ukrainian churches and community organizations in the West, the new economic migrants of the post-communist period have rarely joined them. Most of the new arrivals since 1991 have been Soviet-educated economic migrants who found it difficult to identify with the nationalist and clerical agenda of most diasporic organizations. Young professionals leading a busy urban lifestyle also constitute a significant portion of the new Ukrainian immigration. It was really only during the Orange Revolution of 2004–2005 and again during the crisis of 2013–2014 that the new immigrants came out in large numbers to organize, together with the established Ukrainian community organizations, public rallies and vigils in major Western cities.

Recent censuses counted 1,209,000 people of full or partial Ukrainian descent in Canada and 961,000 in the United States. Such major North American cities as New York, Chicago, Philadelphia, Toronto, Edmonton, and Winnipeg have visible Ukrainian neighborhoods or a strong Ukrainian cultural presence. Voters of Ukrainian background exercise some political influence in Canada's prairie provinces, where they constitute a significant share of the population, as well as in Toronto. Ray Hnatyshyn, a Ukrainian Canadian, served in 1990–1995 as the twenty-fourth governor general of Canada; the provinces of Alberta, Manitoba, and Saskatchewan have all had Ukrainian-Canadian premiers. Ukrainian-American and Ukrainian-Canadian community organizations have consistently supported democratic change in Ukraine.

3

THE MAKING
OF MODERN UKRAINE

Was Ukraine always part of Russia?

This popular misconception is based on a recent and relatively brief period in Ukrainian history—1945 to 1991—when the entire territory of the present-day Ukrainian state (then constituted as the Ukrainian Soviet Socialist Republic) was part of the Soviet Union. The Ukrainian SSR and the Russian Socialist Federative Soviet Republic were just two of 15 theoretically equal republics in the federation, although in practice the Russian language and culture predominated. Historically, however, relations between these two peoples were more complex. One could argue, as do Ukrainian patriotic historians, that originally Russia was part of Ukraine and not the other way around. They refer to the fact that the first East Slavic state, Kyivan Rus, was centered in what is now the Ukrainian city of Kyiv, while the present-day Russian heartland, including the Moscow region, was colonized somewhat later.[1]

After the disintegration of Kyivan Rus, the Ukrainian lands west of the Dnipro River became part of the Grand Duchy of Lithuania and, subsequently, the Polish-Lithuanian Commonwealth. The Kingdom of Hungary and the Romanian principality of Moldavia (itself a vassal of the Ottoman Empire) also incorporated some present-day Ukrainian territories. For centuries, these lands had very limited contacts with the realm of the Muscovite tsars. Instead, they experienced the influence of European legal and corporatist concepts. Unlike Muscovy, the Grand Duchy of Lithuania had an elaborate legal code that was composed in Old Slavonic, the bookish language of Kyivan Rus. The Polish-Lithuanian Commonwealth, which at its peak included roughly half of present-day Ukraine, instituted municipal self-government under Magdeburg Law and the notion of an elected monarch responsible to the elites. Also unlike Muscovy, Poland professed religious tolerance and allowed a significant Jewish population to reside within its borders. Ukraine's historical relations with Poland and other Western neighbors had a profound and lasting impact. There is little that is "Russian" about the architecture and multinational historical heritage of such western Ukrainian cities as Lviv or Chernivtsi. Most Ukrainians in the three western provinces constituting the historical region of Galicia belong to the Ukrainian Catholic Church, which differs from the Orthodox churches in that it recognizes the pope.

Russia came to control most of what is now Ukraine as a result of imperialist expansion. The signing of an ambiguously worded treaty with the Ukrainian Cossacks in 1654 inaugurated the gradual incorporation of Ukrainian lands east of the Dnipro, but the Russian Empire annexed much larger swaths of territory west of this river during the partitions of Poland in the late eighteenth century. Additional territories in the southern steppes were gained in conquest from the Ottoman Empire at around the same time. Meanwhile, Galicia and other smaller historical regions in the west became part of a different expanding empire, Austria (later Austria-Hungary). While the Romanovs refused to acknowledge the existence of Ukrainian culture and eventually banned it, the Habsburgs allowed publishing and education in Ukrainian. As a result, in the late nineteenth century the center of Ukrainian cultural life shifted temporarily to Galicia. Ukrainians also received their first experience of modern political participation and civic organization in the Habsburg Empire.

After the Romanov and Habsburg empires collapsed in 1917–1918, Ukrainian republics were proclaimed on both sides of the border, but they were ultimately unable to survive in the military turmoil engulfing the region. However, the Bolsheviks constituted the Ukrainian territories they had inherited from the Russian Empire as a separate Ukrainian Soviet republic within the Soviet Union, rather than incorporating them into the Russian SFSR. The Ukrainian regions previously held by the Austro-Hungarian Empire were divided among Poland, Romania, and Czechoslovakia. Ethnic

Ukrainians had very mixed experiences in these new states during the interwar period, but their experiences certainly differed from those of Ukrainians in the Soviet Union who endured Stalinist "socialist construction." When the Soviet Union annexed the remaining Ukrainian regions from its western neighbors in 1939–1945, these lands underwent extensive and painful "Sovietization." However, in no sense did they become part of Russia. Rather, their incorporation contributed to Soviet Ukraine, which acquired a more defined Ukrainian ethnic character.

When the Soviet Union collapsed in 1991, its 15 constituent republics became independent states. As the two most populous republics of the USSR, Russia and Ukraine legally seceded from the Soviet federation, which ceased to exist as a result. The popular perception of Ukraine's relatively recent separation from a common whole does exist among Russians and some Ukrainians, but it has more to do with belated acknowledgment of a separate Ukrainian ethnic identity.

What was the medieval state of Kyivan Rus, and was it a Russian or Ukrainian polity?

In existence from the ninth through the thirteenth centuries, Kyivan Rus was the first East Slavic polity; today it is claimed by Ukrainians, Belarusians, and Russians as the foundation of their respective state traditions. The irony in this contest for historical primacy is that the mighty medieval state in question was actually created by the Varangian or Norman invaders, who came to rule over autochthonous East Slavs by advancing from the shores of the Baltic Sea down the Dnipro River sometime in the mid-ninth century. For a century or so, the rulers preserved Scandinavian names and close contacts with their homeland, but they eventually assimilated into the local Slavic culture. Kyivan Rus prospered thanks to its location on the trade routes from Northern Europe to the Byzantine Empire; it was from the latter, the major power of the time, that the young state adopted its religion, as well as its political and cultural models.

Around 988, Prince Volodymyr the Saint (or Vladimir in modern Russian, a popular East Slavic first name ever since, including Lenin's and Putin's) accepted the Byzantine version of Christianity as a state religion. In addition to fostering the state's consolidation, the new religion meant the promotion of literacy in Old Church Slavonic, a bookish language based on the Cyrillic alphabet, which the Byzantine missionaries Cyril and Methodius had devised for the Slavs. Accepting Christianity in the form of the Eastern-rite Orthodox Church soon proved to be a momentous cultural choice, when the rift between Catholicism and Orthodoxy became formalized in the eleventh century. However, Kyivan Rus was never isolated from Central and Western Europe, either before or after the religious schism. Kyivan princes concluded alliances with and declared wars on their European neighbors, and Volodymyr's son Yaroslav married off his daughters to the kings of France, Hungary, and Norway.

The East Slavic population of Kyivan Rus did not possess a modern ethnic identity. Ordinary people thought of themselves as locals and Christians, while surviving literary sources also feature the concept of the "Rus land" as an object of premodern patriotism. Territorially, Kyivan Rus was centered in what is now Ukraine, but it also included significant parts of Belarus and European Russia; the present-day Moscow region was a frontier in the process of colonization. Moscow, which is first mentioned in the chronicles under the year 1147, was then no more than a village with a wooden stockade. The bookish language of the time, Old Church Slavonic, cannot be used as a marker of ethnic identity either, because it is genetically as close to modern Serbian and Bulgarian as it is to Ukrainian or Russian. Ordinary people likely spoke East Slavic dialects that in the south would be related to modern Ukrainian and, in other parts of the very large Rus state, to modern Belarusian and Russian.

Europe's largest state in terms of territory, Kyivan Rus was a loose federation of principalities governed by the princely Riurikid family (from the name of its legendary Norman founder, Riurik). Once members of the family stopped moving from one princely seat to another in the order prescribed by the complicated seniority system, local dynasties became entrenched and political fragmentation ensued. By the late twelfth century, Kyiv had lost its importance as a national center. Less than a century later, the invading Mongol army easily overcame the princes one by one and incorporated the Rus principalities into the gigantic Mongol empire. In the northeast the rulers of Vladimir-Suzdal and eventually the princes of Moscow would rise to prominence as the most reliable tax collectors on behalf of the Mongols, before challenging their masters in the late four-teenth century. To the west, another ascending Eastern European power, the Grand Duchy of Lithuania, took control of the former lands of Kyivan Rus.

It was only with the advent of modern nationalism in the nine-teenth century that historians began claiming the Rus legacy for their ethnic groups. From the Russian point of view, there was an in-stitutional and dynastic continuity from Kyivan Rus to the modern Russian state. Ukrainian historians have countered that their people were the most direct descendants of the Rus population. For as long as Kyiv remained part of the Russian Empire and the Soviet Union, Russian historians could keep presenting the Rus heritage as either Russian or as a common historical legacy of the three fra-ternal East Slavic peoples. Ukraine's declaration of independence in 1991 presented a direct threat to Russian historical mythology. The ancient capital of the "Russian" state, its first monasteries, and the graves of legendary knights were now in Ukraine. Under Putin, Russia has tried to compensate for the "loss" of its Kyivan heritage by intensifying archaeological explorations in the northwestern re-gions of Novgorod and Ladoga, but Kyiv has not lost its special place in Russian historical memory.

Who were the Cossacks?

The name "Cossack" originated from the Turkish word *qazaq*, which means "freebooting warrior" or "ranger." The original Cossacks were runaway serfs who made their living in the underpopulated steppes on the southern frontier of Rus, where the nomadic Muslim Tatars roamed freely in search of captives to be sold into slavery. In this no man's land, the Cossacks survived by hunting, fishing, and beekeeping—and also by attacking and looting the Tatars. By the mid-sixteenth century, the Lithuanian governors of the frontier lands (the former Rus principalities) employed the Cossacks to de-fend the southern frontier. The authorities also created a register of Cossacks, granting those included on it the right to own land, a tax exemption, and a degree of self-government.

By the late 1500s, the international political and economic config-uration in the region had changed, creating the conditions in which the Cossacks would rise to prominence. The expanding Ottoman

Empire in the south threatened Eastern and Central Europe. The Crimean Tatars, who were the vassals of the sultan, regularly raided the former Rus lands. In 1569 the dynastically linked kingdoms of Poland and Lithuania forged a closer constitutional union as the Polish-Lithuanian Commonwealth. The former Rus lands west of the Dnipro fell under Polish rule. The local Orthodox Slavic nobles initially welcomed this change because in Poland the nobility enjoyed far-reaching privileges, but soon the Orthodox Church came under pressure from the Catholic Polish elites and was even banned for periods of time. In 1596 the Polish state supported the creation of the Uniate Church (known later as the Ukrainian Greek Catholic and today simply as the Ukrainian Catholic Church), which combined observance of the Eastern rite with subordination to the pope.

At the same time, the expanding Polish state developed into a major exporter of grain to Western Europe, including England. This led to the increased demand for arable land, especially in what is now Ukraine, and the establishment of a manorial landholding system. In order to secure labor for the noble estates, beginning in the 1570s, Polish kings decreed the enserfment of the peasantry. Within a generation or two an explosive social situation developed: discontented East Slavic Orthodox peasants were forced to toil on land belonging to their Polish Catholic noble owners (often recent converts from Orthodox Christianity). To make matters worse, absentee landlords often engaged in tax farming by leasing their manors, breweries, and the right to collect duties to live-in managers, usually Jews. The social tensions thus ran along both economic and religious lines. What allowed the whole system to work was the protection from Tatar raids afforded by the Cossacks; at the same time, the most popular peasant resistance strategy was running away to join the Cossacks.

By the early 1600s, the Cossacks had grown into a formidable force, with the register reaching 20,000 in 1620. The "register" Cossacks were led by an elected general called "hetman" (a term borrowed in this meaning from Polish but originally related to the German *hauptmann*, or captain). Hetmans from that period, such as Petro Sahaidachny, also saw themselves as protectors of the Orthodox faith and their people. In 1620 he enrolled his entire army in Kyiv's Orthodox fraternity, thus forcing the Polish government's hand in recognizing the previously banned Orthodox Church. In addition to the registered Cossacks, a significant number of unregistered ones had amassed in the Cossack stronghold on the lower Dnipro, the so-called Zaporozhian Sich ("Fortress beyond the Rapids"). The size of the register became a contentious issue between the Polish authorities and the Cossacks, who increasingly developed a distinct group identity as defenders of the Orthodox people.

Following a series of unsuccessful Cossack uprisings, Hetman Bohdan Khmelnytsky's rebellion of 1648 developed into a peasant war and national revolution, resulting in the creation of an autonomous Cossack polity. This precedent of statehood served as an inspiration for future generations of Ukrainian patriots, even though the revolt ultimately resulted in an alliance with Russia and the eventual absorption of Cossack lands by the Russian state. The Cossack social estate, signifying a distinct class of crown peasants, survived in central Ukraine until the Bolshevik Revolution, but they did not play any significant historical role.

The Cossacks encountered in books and films set in the late tsarist empire—the ones seen cracking down on protest rallies and brutalizing civilians—have different historical origins. Just as the Polish governors of the 1500s began using the Cossacks to guard the steppe frontier, so did the Russian tsars in their borderlands, both in the south and during the conquest of Siberia. The main groups of Russian Cossacks were the Don Cossacks in the south and the Ural Cossacks in the east, as well as the Kuban Cossacks on the eastern shores of the Black Sea (the latter were originally Ukrainians who resettled there in the late 1700s). Late Imperial Russia provided Russian Cossacks with land and made them into an irregular police force, similar to a national guard. During the Revolution the conservative Don Cossacks in particular would prove to be the Bolsheviks' most powerful opponents.

Is it true that Ukraine was "reunited" with Russia in 1654?

The "reunification" of Ukraine with Russia was the official term for the 1654 Pereiaslav Treaty; the term was prescribed for obligatory use in Soviet historical works and public discourse by the Communist Party's Central Committee in 1954. The concept of the treaty as a "restoration" of a single nation's ancient unity resonates to this day with Russians in particular, and for good reason. When Soviet ideologists gave it their stamp of approval in 1954 for the treaty's tercentenary, they were actually resurrecting the axiom of pre-revolutionary Russian official discourse that Ukrainians lacked a separate national identity.[2] Before the Central Committee's authoritative pronouncement, Soviet historians of the prewar period had spoken less approvingly of Ukraine's "incorporation" into the Russian state and even of the ensuing colonial exploitation of Ukraine and persecution of Ukrainian culture. Reverting to the language used in the Russian Empire removed any sense of guilt for tsarist policies and also muted the notion of Ukraine's separate identity. "Reunification" was thus an ideologically loaded label, one implying inordinate closeness between Ukrainians and Russians. This was the historical narrative that the last generations to grow up in the Soviet Union learned in school.

What really happened in 1654, however? In 1648 the disaffected Cossack officer Bohdan Khmelnytsky launched a rebellion against Polish rule, which, unlike earlier such uprisings, developed into a full-scale war with armies fighting each other in the field. The conflict had features of a peasant war, with villagers rising en masse against the economic order, but it was also a religious war of the Orthodox against the Catholics and Jews. A contemporary Jewish chronicler described the Cossack slaughter as an "abyss of despair," and indeed, scholars estimate that the rebels killed as many as 18,000 to 20,000 of the 40,000 Jews in the land.[3] The same fate awaited Catholic Poles and Uniate Ukrainians, who did not manage to escape before the advancing Cossack army. Assisted by the Crimean Tatars (always interested in booty), early in the war the Cossacks inflicted a series of defeats on the Polish army. The 1649 Treaty of Zboriv resulted in the transfer of three Polish provinces to the Cossack administration headed by Hetman Khmelnytsky and an increase in the number of registered Cossacks to 40,000. Thus an autonomous Ukrainian Cossack polity known as the Hetmanate came into existence.

By the early 1650s, however, military setbacks forced Khmelnytsky to search for allies other than the unreliable Tatars. Orthodox Muscovy appeared to be a natural choice, not only because of shared religion, but also because it was Poland's long-standing rival in the region. Yet Tsar Alexei was hesitant to lend support to the Cossacks precisely because this would mean another exhaustive war with Poland. Only the very real danger of Khmelnytsky accepting the suzerainty of the Ottoman Empire prompted the Russians to act. After protracted negotiations, Russian envoys arrived in January 1654 to the Ukrainian town of Pereiaslav (just south of Kyiv) to finalize the agreement. The final text of the treaty has been lost, and historians have been arguing for centuries whether the signatories had in mind a temporary political and military alliance or an irreversible voluntary incorporation. One thing is certain: the signing ceremony itself revealed deep-seated differences between the two countries' political models. After the Cossack officers took an oath of allegiance to the tsar, they expected the Muscovite envoys to reciprocate with an oath in the tsar's name to observe the rights of the Cossacks. Yet the Russians refused, because for them the tsar was an absolute monarch not accountable to his subjects.

Following the signing of this treaty, the Cossack lands that correspond approximately to present-day central Ukraine became a protectorate of the Russian tsars, who from then on referred to themselves as rulers of Great and Little Russia (i.e., Russia proper and Ukraine). The Cossack polity preserved full autonomy in internal affairs and the right to conduct foreign policy independently, except in interactions with Poland and the Ottomans, which theoretically required Moscow's approval, but in practice the Cossack leaders ignored this provision. Following a protracted war with Poland and Khmelnytsky's death in 1657, however, the Muscovite government began increasingly limiting the Hetmanate's sovereignty, which caused discontent among the Ukrainian Cossacks.

Who was Ivan Mazepa, and why is he considered a "traitor" in Russia?

The tsars, as well as later Soviet and Russian ideologists, presented the Treaty of Pereiaslav as the restoration of primordial historical ties rather than the Cossack elite's pragmatic decision. Any subsequent attempt to break away from the Russian state was therefore viewed as more than high treason; it was also an assault on the Russian identity itself. There were a few such attempts in the decades after Pereiaslav, but the one launched by Hetman Ivan Mazepa in 1708–1709 was by far the most famous (or infamous, from the Russian point of view).

During the late seventeenth century, the Ukrainian territories along the Dnipro River, with the exception of Kyiv, were split between Poland and Russia. Although back then the city stood on the western bank, it remained part of the Cossack polity. (Today the sprawling metropolis of Kyiv straddles both banks of the Dnipro.) The territory of present-day southern Ukraine remained under the Ottomans' control, enforced by their Tatar vassals. All of these masters also appointed their own hetmans in Ukraine. Historians commonly refer to this period as the "Ruin," in reference to the constant warfare and devastation that characterized it. A modicum of political stability on the Russian side of the border only ensued during the long tenure of Hetman Ivan Mazepa (1687–1709), who enjoyed good relations with his sovereign, Peter I, the reform-minded Russian tsar.

Mazepa had long-term political ambitions, and his goal was to consolidate the Cossack officer class and incorporate the Ukrainian lands west of the Dnipro into the Hetmanate. The timing was not right, however. Social tensions in the Hetmanate were on the rise, because Cossack officers were turning into landowners needing agricultural labor, and because Peter I used the Cossacks mercilessly as manpower in his protracted Northern War with Sweden and on his grand construction projects. The tsar also gradually dismantled the Cossacks' autonomy and officer privileges. The latter factor in particular led Mazepa and a group of Cossack officers to conspire against the tsar. In 1708 Mazepa switched sides in the war by allying himself with King Charles XII of Sweden. However, not all the Cossacks followed him, and Peter I had another hetman elected in Mazepa's place. In 1709 Peter I and the loyalist Cossacks solidly defeated Charles XII and Mazepa in the Battle of Poltava (in central Ukraine). Mazepa soon died in exile, but not before being formally excommunicated and anathematized by the Russian Orthodox Church. The anathema against Mazepa was read in churches for centuries and, in fact, has not been lifted to this day.

Although Mazepa was no modern ethnic nationalist, in the late Russian Empire his name became a term of abuse for Ukrainian patriots, who were called "Mazepists" (*mazepintsy*). One can still encounter this derogatory moniker in the Russian public discourse. Because of this Russian and Soviet stigma, much of Mazepa's legacy is only now becoming public knowledge in independent Ukraine, in particular his patronage of architecture and the arts. Mazepa's own striking life, which included, besides political turnarounds, alleged romantic misadventures as a young page at the Polish royal court and a marriage late in life to his goddaughter, also made for a great story. Byron and Pushkin wrote romantic poems about him, and Tchaikovsky made him the subject of an opera.

What were Russia's imperial policies in Ukraine?

After the disastrous Battle of Poltava, the Russian authorities secured the Hetmanate as part of their state, which Peter I formally proclaimed an empire (thus claiming a great-power status) in 1721, although in reality it had been a multinational empire since at least the mid-sixteenth century. The tsars never developed a consistent policy toward their national minorities. In the Ukrainian case, however, the fact that they were never considered to be a minority population in the first place was itself a source of oppression.

In the early modern period, the ethnicity of the empire's new subjects was not yet an issue for imperial bureaucrats. The "Little Russians" were Orthodox and took an oath of loyalty to the tsar, which was all that mattered. The language they spoke differed from Russian, but with some effort interlocutors could understand the gist of what was being said. Of course, it was the Ukrainians who were expected to learn Russian and not the other way around. Over time, the empire slowly eliminated Ukrainian political and social institutions. The right to conduct autonomous relations with foreign states and to collect taxes was rescinded in 1666, although these measures were initially difficult to enforce. From 1686 the Orthodox Church in the Hetmanate was de facto subordinated to the patriarch of Moscow. After Mazepa's defection, Peter I strictly limited the power of his immediate successor and in 1722 forbade the election of the next hetman. Instead, the tsar created a bureaucratic institution for running the Cossack polity, the Little Russian Collegium, which was staffed with non-Ukrainians. Empress Elizabeth then restored the office of the hetman briefly for her lover's brother, Kyrylo Rozumovsky (1750–1764), but he was more of an eighteenth-century courtier than a Cossack leader. As part of Empress Catherine II's centralizing reforms, the regimental territorial structure of the Hetmanate was replaced by three large provinces in 1782, and Cossack officers were accepted into the Russian nobility, although securing the required paperwork was a long and arduous process. Shortly before that, the Russian army razed the old Cossack stronghold, the Zaporozhian Host fortress on the lower Dnipro. The Hetmanate was now officially abolished, its lands incorporated directly into the Russian Empire.

At approximately the same time, Catherine acquired the Ukrainian lands west of the Dnipro as her share of the recently partitioned Polish state (but not Galicia and two other small adjacent historical regions in the west, which went to the Austrian Habsburgs instead). In the new provinces west of the Dnipro, she began liquidating the Uniate Church, a process that her grandson Nicholas I would complete in 1839. But other than that, assimilating the local Ukrainians was not among the imperial government's concerns. Rather, it was preoccupied with the very substantial Jewish population in these provinces, because historically the Russian Empire had not allowed Jews on its territory. Catherine's solution was to create the "Pale of Settlement" in this region, an area in which Jews could settle but not own land and from which they were barred from leaving, with a few exceptions. Similarly, when Catherine's generals defeated the Ottoman Empire in the 1770s, thereby opening up for settlement the territory of what is now southern Ukraine, she did not pursue resettlement policies favoring Russians. In fact, Italians, Greeks, Bulgarians, German-speaking Mennonites, and other foreigners took the lead in developing the region and its main port, Odesa. Eventually, Ukrainian peasant settlers followed them.

Ethnicity appeared belatedly on the Russian authorities' radar in the 1830s, when Polish nobles rebelled in the provinces west of the Dnipro (as they did in all of the former Polish lands). Suddenly it became important for the tsarist government to demonstrate that this region was "Russian," meaning Little Russian. In a paradoxical turnabout, the learned societies and educational institutions that were established by the imperial authorities produced patriotic Ukrainian intellectuals. The development of modern Ukrainian literature was spearheaded by a former serf who would become the national bard, Taras Shevchenko (1814–1861). By the time of the second Polish rebellion in 1863, the alarmed tsarist officials thought it prudent to adopt measures against the Ukrainian movement as well. They banned educational and religious books in Ukrainian because these could reach the peasants, and in 1876 all publications in Ukrainian were banned. The power of modern nationalism as a mobilizing force was lost on tsarist officials. Instead of teaching Ukrainian peasants (or, indeed, Russian peasants) that they belonged to the Russian ethnic nation, the government preferred to suppress patriotic intellectuals' efforts to enlighten the people.

Ukrainian cultural organizations and the press existed legally in the Russian Empire only for a brief period between the 1905 Revolution and the start of World War I. That was just enough time for the educated Ukrainians to reach out to the people, but too short a time to spread the sense of a modern civic Ukrainian identity and link it to the concept of democratic freedoms.

Did the Austrian Empire govern its Ukrainian lands differently?

The dominant ethnic group in the Habsburg Empire, Austrian Germans, constituted only a small minority of its population and could not hope to assimilate the rest. Their preferred nationality policy was exploiting the tensions among the major ethnic groups. This approach was particularly evident in the empire's Ukrainian lands. The Habsburg emperors acquired Galicia in 1772, during the partitions of Poland; two years later they annexed the Bukovyna region from the Principality of Moldavia, an Ottoman vassal.

Neither region was ethnically homogenous. Ukrainian (or "Ruthenian" in the parlance of the time) peasants constituted an overwhelming majority of the population in eastern Galicia, whereas in the western part of this region, the Polish population predominated. Today these two halves of Galicia are divided by the Polish-Ukrainian border; western Galicia, whose main city is Cracow, is Polish, and eastern Galicia, with its center in Lviv, is Ukrainian. However, under Habsburg rule the political elites in all of Galicia were predominantly Polish, because the native Rus nobility had been assimilated long ago. The Habsburg balancing act, therefore, required giving some political voice to Ruthenians as well, in order to undermine Polish political domination in the region. The only educated class among the Ruthenians was the Ukrainian Catholic clergy, which adhered to Eastern Christian rites and thus (except for monks and bishops) could marry and have children. The political leadership of the Ukrainian movement in the Austrian Empire thus fell by default to the clergy, supplemented in the next generation by lawyers and teachers, who often hailed from clerical families.

When the Galician Poles rebelled during the Revolution of 1848, the Austrian governor encouraged the loyal Ruthenian bishops to create, as a counterweight, their own representative body, the Supreme Ruthenian Council. Thus began the history of Ukrainian political and cultural organizations in the Habsburg Empire. Unlike in Russia at the time, they could exist legally. The Ruthenians also acquired experience in electoral politics during periodic elections to the national parliament and local legislatures. During the second half of the nineteenth century, a Ukrainian press and a network of reading rooms developed in the countryside. A full spectrum of Ukrainian political parties came into existence in the 1890s, when the Ruthenian activists also accepted the ethnic designation "Ukrainians" for their people. By that time the Austrian authorities, apprehensive of the possibility that the Ruthenians could become a fifth column in a likely conflict with Russia, actively discouraged a pro-Russian cultural orientation among the Ruthenian intelligentsia. They also made sure that the language used in school instruction in eastern Galicia was modern Ukrainian and not some antiquated church vernacular closer to Russian. By the 1900s, patriotic activists in Galicia made great advances in mobilizing the peasantry for the national cause, but their main demands, such as a separate Ukrainian crown land or a Ukrainian university, remained unfulfilled by the imperial government.

Developments in neighboring Bukovyna just to the south paralleled those in Galicia, with one important distinction. Instead of the Catholic Poles, the ruling class there was Romanian, and it had little influence in Vienna. Because Romanians were also Orthodox Christians, the Uniate church did not take hold in Bukovyna, where the Ukrainian peasants remained Orthodox. However, like Galicia, this historical region was ethnically divided. Ukrainian peasants predominated in northern Bukovyna (part of present-day Ukraine) and Romanian ones in its southern part (part of present-day Romania). The third ethnic Ukrainian historical region that came under Habsburg rule, Transcarpathia, which is southwest from Galicia across the Carpathian Mountains, had been under Hungarian rule since the twelfth century and part of the Habsburg Empire since the sixteenth. There, the ruling stratum was Hungarian, and the Ukrainian national movement (led by Uniate priests) did not make much headway until 1867, when the Austrian

Empire officially became Austro-Hungarian after the 1867 constitutional compromise empowering the Hungarian nobility. After that, the Hungarian authorities closed down Ukrainian organizations and promoted creeping assimilation of the local peasantry.

When the European empires went to war in 1914, Ukrainians in Austrian Galicia in particular identified with the conflict as a means to liberate their brethren in Russia from the oppressive tsarist regime. They established a Ukrainian volunteer unit in the Austro-Hungarian army. Approximately 28,000 men volunteered, but only 2,000 were accepted by the Austrian authorities. As the war dragged on, however, Ukrainian patriots on both sides of the Eastern Front understood that what would benefit them most would be the defeat of each of their respective imperial masters.

What happened in the Ukrainian lands during the revolutionary turmoil of 1917–1920?

When the multinational empires in Eastern and Central Europe collapsed at the end of World War I, the leaders of their constituent nationalities attempted to reorganize the postwar political space according to the principle of national self-determination, which the victorious Allies endorsed. In practice, Ukrainians became a major exception to this principle, as the Allies resolved to incorporate the Ukrainian lands of the former Austro-Hungarian Empire into several new Eastern European states that were to serve as a *cordon sanitaire* against the Bolshevik menace. The Bolsheviks, in turn, sought to keep as much of the former Russian imperial territory as they could, while also realizing the need for federalization, or at least its appearance.

The unexpected collapse of the Russian monarchy in the spring of 1917 allowed the Ukrainian national movement to come out in the open, quickly capturing the sympathies of the peasant and soldier masses. Prolonged negotiations took place between the Ukrainian revolutionary parliament, the Central Rada, and the Russian Provisional Government concerning the provinces that should come under the authority of the newly proclaimed Ukrainian People's Republic and what the extent of this authority should be. Meanwhile, by the year's end, the Bolsheviks took power in the imperial capital and promptly initiated peace talks with the Central

Powers. The Bolsheviks also proclaimed their own Ukrainian Soviet Republic and brought its representatives to the negotiation table, just as their troops were marching on Kyiv.

However, the Germans and the Austrians preferred to settle separately with Soviet Russia and the independent Ukrainian People's Republic, which they hoped to use as a breadbasket for their starving populations. The Brest-Litovsk Peace, signed in early 1918, forced the Bolsheviks to recognize the former Russian Ukraine as an independent state in its ethnographic borders (without the Crimea and the Ukrainian lands of the Austro-Hungarian Empire). A large German and Austrian occupation force marched into the Ukrainian People's Republic to ensure the collection of foodstuffs, which was spelled out in a secret protocol. The Germans soon replaced the left-leaning Ukrainian republican government with the more congenial conservative, monarchist regime of General Pavlo Skoropadsky, who was proclaimed "hetman." However, in the fall of 1918, the Central Powers lost the war and had to evacuate Ukraine, taking their puppet monarch with them.

The defeat of the Central Powers also meant the disintegration of Austria-Hungary, allowing the Ukrainian activists to proclaim the Western Ukrainian People's Republic in eastern Galicia. However, the newly reconstituted Polish state also laid claim to eastern Galicia. A Ukrainian-Polish war broke out there, in which the Ukrainians eventually suffered defeat when fresh Polish forces marched in (the Allies had originally trained and equipped them for use against the Central Powers). Still, the Western Ukrainian People's Republic lasted long enough to solemnly declare its union with the Ukrainian People's Republic, by then restored in the east.

In 1919 the Ukrainian lands of the former Russian Empire became a bloody battlefield in the Russian civil war between the Bolshevik Reds and the anti-Bolshevik Whites, with the Ukrainian republican troops fighting against both by turns. It was a Ukrainian civil war as well, because ethnic Ukrainians fought in all of these armies for their respective visions of "Ukraine," which many of them still saw as inseparably linked to Russia. This period also saw the collapse of civic order, marked by the free reign of peasant bands in the countryside that sometimes grew into real armies. For example, the anarchist leader in southern Ukraine, Nestor Makhno, commanded a force of 40,000 and fought alternately with or against the Bolsheviks.

The collapse of authority in the countryside also led to bloody pogroms against Jews in the provinces west of the Dnipro, claiming an estimated 50,000 lives. All the armies marching through the land committed them, but peasant gang leaders loosely affiliated with the Ukrainian republican government were apparently responsible for the largest share, even though the helpless Ukrainian leaders issued appeals against the pogroms.[4] In the Ukrainian south, Mennonites also became victims of violent pogroms.

In 1920 the Bolsheviks finally defeated the Whites in mainland Ukraine, although the latter still held out in the Crimean Peninsula until the fall, and pushed the Ukrainian army into Polish-controlled territory in the west. The Bolshevik leader Vladimir Lenin saw the main cause of the Ukrainian national movement's growth in the failure of successive Russian governments to economically placate the peasantry, which he construed as petty landowners susceptible to nationalist agitation. In order to disarm the peasantry's suspicions, the Bolsheviks organized a massive distribution of the land and also declared that Ukraine would remain a separate republic in feder-ation with Soviet Russia. After the brief Soviet-Polish war in 1920 ended in an impasse, the Bolsheviks squeezed the Whites out of the Crimea. The period of revolutionary wars in the former Russian Empire ended.

Agreement was also reached about the former Austro- Hungarian territories. Frightened by the Bolshevik threat in the east, the Allies sacrificed the principle of national self-determination in favor of se-curity. They assigned eastern Galicia to Poland, northern Bukovyna to Romania, and Transcarpathia to the new state of Czechoslovakia. The Ukrainian population in the former Austro-Hungarian lands ac-tually became the largest national minority in interwar Europe.

Why did the Bolsheviks create a Ukrainian republic within the Soviet Union, and how did they determine its borders?

The Bolsheviks came to power in the age of imperial collapse, when the principle of national self-determination was being increasingly established as the foundation of a new world order. Lenin and Stalin saw nationalism as a transitory phenomenon, characteristic of late capitalist society. Yet they could not ignore the popular slogan of self-determination, especially in the conditions of the multinational

Russian Empire. In their theoretical writings both before and during the Revolution, the Bolshevik leaders accepted the right of national minorities to self-determination up to and including the creation of nation-states, but with a crucial stipulation. They inserted the hypocritical addendum that the party would be guided by the "interests of the working class" in deciding whether to support the separation of nations from empires. Ideally, the Bolsheviks would have preferred to transform the Russian Empire into a strong unitary state that they would govern in the name of the proletariat. In practice, however, they were forced to accept the separation of Poland, Finland, and the Baltic states, and to adopt a federative structure for what remained of the empire.

In the Ukrainian case, the Bolshevik policies were reactive from the outset. After the Ukrainian revolutionary parliament, the Central Rada, proclaimed the Ukrainian People's Republic in Kyiv in November 1917, the Bolsheviks responded with the creation of the Ukrainian People's Republic of Soviets in the eastern city of Kharkiv in December 1917. Its existence was soon forgotten amidst the chaos of the civil war, which was followed by the founding in 1919 of the Ukrainian Socialist Soviet Republic (the word order later changed to "Soviet Socialist" in accordance with the Constitution of 1936)—theoretically an independent state in military alliance with Soviet Russia but, in reality, a part of a united Bolshevik political space. Regardless of the lack of real sovereignty, it is significant that the Bolsheviks felt the need to create and maintain such a polity. In 1922 Soviet Ukraine became one of the four founding (theoretically equal) republics of the Soviet Union.

The non-communist Ukrainian People's Republic also established a territorial precedent that later determined the borders of its Soviet equivalent. In its negotiations with the Russian Provisional Government, the Ukrainian Central Rada had laid claim to nine provinces of the former Russian Empire where ethnic Ukrainians constituted a majority, while agreeing to exclude the ethnically non-Ukrainian Crimean Peninsula from the southernmost Taurida province. This geographic definition of Ukraine was used when the Central Powers signed the Treaty of Brest-Litovsk establishing peace between Soviet Russia and the Ukrainian People's Republic in 1918. In defining its borders, the Ukrainian SSR also used the old administrative borders and ethnicity of the population's majority within these units.

In the mid-1920s, the old provinces were divided into a larger number of districts, and the Bolshevik authorities took this opportunity to adjust the borders among the various Soviet republics. They tried to factor in populations' ethnic makeup as well as economic rationality, but in the end they made only minor adjustments, as opposed to a complete border makeover. The most notable change involved transferring the important port city of Taganrog (the birthplace of playwright Anton Chekhov) from Soviet Ukraine to Soviet Russia. There were significant pockets of ethnic Ukrainian population left within the Russian republic and small enclaves of Russians settled compactly in Ukraine.

Beginning in the mid-1920s, the Bolshevik party introduced measures to bridge the gap between its primarily Russian and Jewish urbanite membership and the Ukrainian peasant masses. These measures were part of the larger policy of indigenization, which the party officially adopted in 1923. Stalin had originally developed the theory of indigenization as a means of defusing national sentiment and making the Soviet Union attractive to colonized nations abroad. According to this policy, the state promoted local cultures and education in the language of indigenous nationalities in the republics, while pursuing an affirmative-action program to increase indigenous participation in Soviet republican administrations. In its application to Ukraine, the policy of indigenization was known as "Ukrainization." It had a twofold aim of making Soviet power less alien to the Ukrainian peasantry and presenting Soviet Ukraine as a cultural beacon for the "oppressed" Ukrainians in Poland and other Eastern European countries. By the early 1930s, education and publishing in Ukrainian were flourishing, and the proportion of ethnic Ukrainians in the ranks of the Communist Party in Ukraine increased from 23 percent in 1922 to 60 percent in 1933.[5]

The Ukrainization policy made the Ukrainian SSR more than a nominally Ukrainian polity, even if the Bolshevik leadership in Moscow held the ultimate authority. The decade of Ukrainization also made Soviet Ukraine look attractive to Ukrainians abroad. Many political émigrés, including the former head of the Central Rada, the historian Mykhailo Hrushevsky, returned to Soviet Ukraine. At the same time, however, Stalin was growing concerned about the potential for Ukrainization to promote political nationalism in the republic instead of disarming it. What spurred him into taking action was peasant resistance to the forced collectivization of agriculture in Ukraine.

What was the Holodomor (the Ukrainian Famine of 1932–1933), and was it genocide?

As one of the Soviet Union's main grain-producing areas, the Ukrainian SSR suffered particularly badly during the forced collectivization campaign of 1929–1932. The Soviet state was determined to extract from the republic the maximum amount of grain for sale abroad, in order to fund the Kremlin's mammoth industrial projects. Ukrainian peasants resisted collectivization by concealing grain, slaughtering draft animals rather than surrendering them to collective farms, and sometimes rebelling openly. Soviet policies in the Ukrainian countryside were also distinguished by their unusual harshness. Famine in some parts of Ukraine, southern Russia, and Kazakhstan had begun already in 1931, yet the Soviet leadership refused to reduce grain-requisition targets.

The situation escalated during 1932, when the party's high expectations clashed with a much poorer harvest. Ukrainian officials requested that the quota be lowered considerably, but Stalin and his emissaries instead blamed the Ukrainian peasants for allegedly hoarding the grain out of hatred for the Soviet power as well as local officials for abetting them. As villages descended into mass starvation in the fall of 1932, army units and gangs of party activists searched rural households, confiscating every scrap of food. Early in 1933 armed guards were posted at the Ukrainian-Russian border to prevent Ukrainian peasants from crossing it in search of food. Entire villages and districts died out in the winter of 1932–1933; numerous cases of cannibalism were recorded. All the while the Soviet government officially denied the existence of the famine. Only in February 1933 did Moscow finally allow the release of seeding stock in Ukraine for limited famine relief, targeting the children and families of Red Army servicemen.

The government did not maintain official data on famine-related mortalities in Ukraine or Union-wide; moreover, it suppressed the results of the 1937 census and had its organizers executed as "enemies." Today Ukrainian historians estimate direct population losses in the republic at between 3 and 3.5 million famine deaths; an overall population loss as calculated by demographers (with the unborn children) was higher still, up to 4.8 million.[6] Overall famine deaths in the Soviet Union are estimated at up to 7 million people.

The famine broke the peasantry's back, resulting in the establishment of Stalinist order in the countryside. It also inflicted irreparable damage on the Ukrainian people, who remember it as their greatest national catastrophe. The famine was felt in all of the Soviet Union's grain-producing areas, but it particularly ravaged Ukraine and the southern Russian region of Kuban, which had a majority Ukrainian population. An American historian has shown how, by 1932, Stalin connected peasant resistance to an alleged nationalist conspiracy in Ukraine and linked both to the Ukrainization campaign. The Soviet dictator ordered the harshest measures against the Ukrainian farmers at the same time as he was decreeing the scaling back of Ukrainization and plotting the purging of the Communist Party ranks in Ukraine.[7]

Seeing the man-made famine as part of a broader attack against the Ukrainian nation, in the 2000s the Ukrainian authorities initiated an international campaign to have the Holodomor (the Ukrainian term meaning "extermination through starvation") recognized as genocide. A number of countries passed legislative acts to this effect, including Canada and the United States, while Russia protested against such a definition. It did so not only as the legal successor of the Soviet Union, potentially liable to answer for this crime against humanity, but also because the Russian authorities saw defining the Holodomor as genocide as a move to distance modern Ukraine from its Soviet past—and from historical ties with Russia.

Although not presenting a clear-cut case for ethnic genocide of Ukrainians, the Holodomor was definitely an intentional murder of the peasant population in the Ukrainian SSR—overwhelmingly Ukrainian, but also including among its victims Russians, Poles, Germans, and Jews living in the countryside. As such, it was definitely aimed at undermining the Ukrainian nation, a point reinforced by the simultaneous campaign of political terror against the Ukrainian political and cultural elites conducted during and immediately after the famine.

Is it true that all the Ukrainian lands were united in a single polity for the first time under Stalin?

Ukraine in its current borders is indeed largely the product of Stalinist conquests during 1939–1945, but it would be wrong to attribute to the Soviet dictator the "invention" of Ukraine. He merely used modern nationalism's concept of the right of ethnic groups to self-determination as a cover for the Soviet Union's expansionism in Eastern Europe.

Long before Stalin "reunited" western Ukraine with the Ukrainian SSR, all these regions had been part of Kyivan Rus. In the mid-1600s, Hetman Bohdan Khmelnytsky spoke of including the western regions under his rule, as they were also populated by the "Rus people." Beginning in the nineteenth century, Ukrainian patriotic intellectuals established the concept of Ukrainian ethnic territories and the ideal that one day a united Ukrainian polity would bring them all together. The two short-lived Ukrainian republics that emerged in the east and west when the multinational empires in the region began disintegrating in 1917–1918 from the very beginning saw themselves as two parts of a whole and indeed proclaimed their union in January 1919. Moreover, the concept of Ukrainian ethnic territories was by then receiving some international recognition. In 1920, when the Allies tried to stop the Red Army's advance on Poland, British Foreign Secretary Lord Curzon proposed the so-called Curzon Line as an ethnographic border between Poland and Soviet Ukraine, with eastern Galicia assigned to the latter, although both belligerents rejected it, and the war's outcome was much more favorable for Poland.

The Ukrainian SSR inherited this implicit claim to eastern Galicia, northern Bukovyna, and Transcarpathia, regions that were part of Poland, Romania, and Czechoslovakia, respectively, during the interwar period. Such territorial claims dovetailed with the strategic aims of Soviet territorial expansion in Europe. In addition to following up on the principle of self-determination, the Bolsheviks could claim that "reuniting" Ukrainians would help save them from capitalist exploitation and national oppression. When the Soviet-Nazi Pact of 1939 divided Eastern Europe into spheres of influence, Stalin took the opportunity to claim the western Ukrainian lands. On September 17, 1939, soon after the German attack on Poland on

September 1 and the start of World War II, the Red Army marched into eastern Galicia without declaring war on Poland, ostensibly to protect the local Ukrainian population. In reality, it was annexation. Stalinist functionaries promptly organized sham elections, and the resulting People's Assembly asked for the region's admission to the Soviet Union.

A similar script was followed in the other two historical regions. In 1940 the Soviet Union issued an ultimatum to Romania to "return" the territories that had previously belonged to the Russian Empire, including northern Bukovyna. Facing an imminent invasion, Romania accepted and withdrew from these regions, and northern Bukovyna was incorporated into the Ukrainian SSR. By the end of World War II, as the Red Army occupied most of Eastern Europe, Stalin's appetite for expanding the Soviet Union proper grew. The dictator's Ukrainian viceroy, Nikita Khrushchev (an ethnic Russian who grew up in the Donbas and served as the Communist Party boss in the Ukrainian SSR from 1938 to 1949), also enthusiastically promoted the expansion of "his" republic. As soon as the Red Army took Transcarpathia under its control in 1944, he organized the collection of petitions for joining Soviet Ukraine. The region was then transferred from Czechoslovakia to the Soviet Union according to a 1945 bilateral agreement between the two countries and constituted as the Transcarpathian province of the Ukrainian SSR.

Khrushchev even pushed for the annexation of additional ethnic Ukrainian lands from Poland, which lay beyond the Curzon Line.[8] He organized similar petitioning campaigns there, but the effort was aborted after the Allies agreed to use the Curzon Line as the border between the Soviet Union and Poland. However, Stalin got to keep all the territories he had annexed according to the Nazi-Soviet Pact of 1939, most notably eastern Galicia. Thus the Ukrainian SSR came to include nearly all the territories where ethnic Ukrainians constituted the majority of residents. Both voluntary and forcible mass population exchanges with Poland right after World War II made this ethnic border even more pronounced.

As for the newly reunited regions of the Ukrainian SSR, they underwent Sovietization in accelerated form. In mere years, as opposed to decades, the Soviet state eliminated in the new regions its political opponents, Ukrainized cultural life, pursued forced collectivization, and started encouraging closer ties with the "elder Russian brother."

However, the long history of the Ukrainian national movement in eastern Galicia under Habsburg and Polish rule could not be undone. Even unto its final days, the Soviet Union's leaders remained suspicious of the three Galician provinces, viewing them as the bulwark of Ukrainian nationalism.

What is Babi Yar, and how did the Holocaust unfold in Ukraine?

Babi Yar or, more properly in Ukrainian, Babyn Yar, was a ravine on the outskirts of Kyiv that the Nazis turned into a killing field and burial ground for the city's Jews. In just two days in late September 1941, German machine-gunners killed 33,771 Jews there. The name Babi Yar became a symbol of the "Holocaust by bullets" on the Eastern Front, where most Jews were killed by firing squads close to their homes, rather than being transported to extermination camps. After the initial slaughter of the city's Jews, the Nazis continued using the ravine as a killing field for thousands of Red Army POWs and other categories of undesirables, including Ukrainian nationalists. Estimates of the total number of bodies buried there range from 100,000 to 150,000. Today the site is a park filled with a variety of memorials, ranging from a large Soviet-era monument to all civilians and POWs killed there to more specific monuments to Jews and other groups, which were erected later.

On the eve of the Nazi invasion in June 1941, some three million Jews, or a fifth of the world's Jewish population, lived in the Ukrainian SSR. The traditional areas of Jewish settlement in Ukraine included the provinces west of the Dnipro, the birthplace of Hasidism, and also eastern Galicia, the latter having been annexed from Poland in 1939. These were also the first areas that the German army occupied after invading the Soviet Union. In the first days of the occupation of Galicia, the Germans incited the locals to organize Jewish pogroms, which they filmed for documentaries to be shown in Germany. Soon, however, a difference emerged between the extermination policies in Galicia (and other former Polish lands) and the rest of the Nazi-occupied Ukrainian SSR. In Galicia, which the Nazis included in the same administrative unit along with parts of Poland, Jews were herded into ghettos, which the Nazis subsequently emptied in waves of deportations to death camps and shootings carried out on location. In the Ukrainian lands further east, mobile SS execution groups usually shot the Jews immediately. In Babi Yar, as elsewhere, local auxiliary police assisted in herding the victims to the execution pit.

Hiding or assisting Jews in any way carried the punishment of death, yet as of 2015, Israel has recognized 2,515 Ukrainians with the honorary title of Righteous Among The Nations for saving Jews. This is the fourth greatest number of such heroes after Poland, France, and the Netherlands.[9]

The total number of Ukrainian Jews killed during the Holocaust is estimated at 900,000 to a million people. A significant number of Ukrainian Jews survived by retreating with the Soviets; many also fought in the ranks of the Red Army. Nevertheless, after the war Jews never again constituted such a notable share of Ukraine's population, and they also left in large numbers when legal immigration to Israel and the West became possible.

Nazi occupation policies toward ethnic Ukrainians and other Slavs did not call for their immediate extermination, unless they could also be identified as communists or homosexuals. However, Hitler planned to turn Ukraine into an area of German agricultural colonization, which in the long run meant decimating the local Slavs and turning the survivors into a slave labor force. With this aim in mind, the German authorities abolished schooling beyond the fourth grade and denied medical care to Ukrainians. They blockaded the delivery of food supplies to major cities, causing famine in Kyiv. The Nazis also treated Red Army POWs inhumanely, with over half of them dying of malnutrition and disease. Scholars estimate the total losses of Ukraine's civilian population in World War II (including the victims of the Holocaust) at 5 million, with a further 1.5 million of the republic's residents killed in action while serving in the Red Army.

Who was Stepan Bandera, and what was the Ukrainian Insurgent Army?

Much in the same way as the tsarist government in its day branded all patriotic Ukrainians as "Mazepists" after Hetman Ivan Mazepa, the Russian state-controlled media have labeled EuroMaidan activists as "Banderites" after the twentieth- century nationalist leader Stepan Bandera (1909–1959). This stigmatization is unjust because radical nationalists constituted only a small minority among EuroMaidan revolutionaries, and their political parties performed poorly in the parliamentary elections that followed the revolution. Yet, it was a clever propaganda trick to associate a separate Ukrainian national identity exclusively with the most radical branch of Ukrainian nationalism. To most Russians and many Russian-speakers in eastern Ukraine, the term "Banderite" still carries negative historical connotations, established in Stalin's time. After World War II ended, the Soviet press denounced the Bandera-led insurgents, who resisted the Sovietization of eastern Galicia.

Radical Ukrainian nationalism originated in Galicia under Polish rule in the 1920s. Disaffected veterans of the Ukrainian Revolution, who refused to accept Polish domination of their land following the Polish-Ukrainian war, formed the Ukrainian Military Organization (1923) and then the Organization of Ukrainian Nationalists (1929). Soon they were joined by radical students, who were antagonized by the Polish administration's oppressive policies. Stepan Bandera belonged to the latter group. The son of a Ukrainian Catholic priest from Galicia, he studied agronomy at Lviv Polytechnical University, but chose the career of an underground fighter against Polish rule. In the 1930s, he organized protest campaigns and assassinations of Polish officials. In 1938, when Bandera was serving a life sentence in a Polish prison, the Organization of Ukrainian Nationalists split into the more radical Banderite branch and a more moderate Melnikite branch (led from abroad by Andrii Melnyk).

Bandera was freed from prison following the outbreak of war in 1939, and at first his followers sought to use the Nazi invasion as an opportunity to restore a Ukrainian state in the form of a German satellite. After the German army took Lviv in June 1941, the Banderites (in Bandera's absence) solemnly proclaimed the creation of the Ukrainian state. The Nazis were angered by this unauthorized declaration, because their plans for Ukraine involved only unfettered economic exploitation, not cooperation with local leaders. After they refused to rescind the declaration, Bandera and many prominent Banderites were arrested and spent most of the war in German concentration camps. Bandera was released from the Sachsenhausen camp only in the fall of 1944; two of his brothers perished in Auschwitz.

While Bandera was languishing in Sachsenhausen, popular dissatisfaction with the brutality of Nazi rule grew in Ukraine. By 1943 the Banderites had formed a small guerrilla force calling itself the Ukrainian Insurgent Army (UPA) and began fashioning it into a mass partisan movement of over 40,000 fighters. At first, this army fought against the Germans, but by 1944 the Germans and the UPA largely observed neutrality in the face of an approaching common enemy, the Red Army. Bandera's insurgents did not serve in the volunteer SS Galicia Division as some historical accounts would claim; the Division was in fact a project of the rival Melnyk faction. However, this is not to absolve the Banderites of war crimes. Like all sides in the messy guerrilla warfare that engulfed much of western Ukraine, they engaged in the killing of civilians. The ideologically motivated mass extermination of Polish civilians in the region of Volhynia during 1943–1944 was essentially an ethnic cleansing aimed at making Volhynia a "Ukrainian" land. The victims numbered in the tens of thousands, perhaps 50,000.[10]

The Soviets managed to destroy larger UPA detachments by 1947, but smaller cells continued armed resistance to Soviet power in western Ukraine until the early 1950s. It was during the first postwar decade that Stalinist culture propagated the image of brutal Banderites shooting Soviet soldiers in the back and slaughtering female schoolteachers sent in from Russia. This myth has outlived Bandera, who was killed by a Soviet agent in Munich in 1959, as well as the Banderite political organization, which never developed any significant following in post-communist Ukraine.

In 2010 the outgoing Ukrainian President Viktor Yushchenko, his approval rating having dropped by then to single digits, awarded Bandera a posthumous Hero of Ukraine medal in an act calculated to infuriate Russia and salvage Yushchenko's popularity in western Ukraine. Yet the ensuing scandal only highlighted the changing meaning of Bandera as a political symbol. The ideology of radical Ukrainian nationalism with its cult of a strong leader and subjugation of individual will to the interests of an ethnic nation belongs to the past. In present-day Ukrainian mass culture, Bandera functions more as a recognizable symbol of anti-Russian resistance, a vague protest statement not unlike the image of Che Guevara on a T-shirt.

In the first years of independence, nationalist-dominated municipal councils in the westernmost regions created a Bandera cult complete with Lenin-like statues of the leader, but the modern, European-oriented urban society developing there is outgrowing it already. The conflict with Russia may have delayed this process, but in the long run it is impossible to remake Bandera into a symbol of a new, European Ukraine, if only because the closest European neighbor, Poland, opposes his glorification as well.

What were the Soviet policies in Ukraine during the postwar period?

As one of the major battlefields of World War II, Ukraine suffered the nearly complete destruction of its industries and major cities. Postwar reconstruction focused on heavy industry and mining, but by the 1960s the Soviet authorities finally began paying some attention to the consumer needs of the modern, urban society Ukraine had become. State industries increased their production of television sets and refrigerators; a car factory in the city of Zaporizhia began producing the first Soviet subcompact automobile in 1960. In the absence of market mechanisms in the socialist planned economy, however, most Soviet products were substandard. Like other Soviet citizens, Ukrainians craved fashionable and high-quality Western goods, but could get hold of them only rarely. A sense of inequality simmered among the masses. For all the communist rhetoric of equality, only functionaries enjoyed access to luxury apartments, well-supplied stores, and resorts that were closed to ordinary citizens.

Party decrees during the postwar period never referred to Ukrainization; rather, ideologists organized periodic campaigns against vaguely defined manifestations of Ukrainian nationalism in culture. The party line called for the glorification of Russian-Ukrainian friendship and unity. The number of Ukrainian books, newspapers, and schools decreased gradually and were replaced by Russian ones. The authorities never formally decreed assimilation into Russian culture, but their policies clearly promoted it. By the end of the Soviet period, most cities in eastern and central Ukraine became Russophone again, thus undoing the bilingualism achieved during prewar Ukrainization. Industrial areas in the east, although Ukrainian in ethnic composition, never really became Ukrainian-speaking, because the Soviet policies did not give modern Ukrainian culture a chance to take root there. As was the case under the tsars, peasants coming to work in the Donbas assimilated into the dominant Russian culture. The Ukrainian language held its ground in western Ukraine and in villages of the central region. In the 1950s and 1960s it was also the official language of the Ukrainian SSR, the language of party speeches and government decrees. Beginning in the 1970s, however, the party and state apparatus in the republic expanded the use of Russian in official capacities.

Official Soviet ideology saw Ukrainians as junior partners of the Russians in running the Soviet Union. Individual Ukrainians could make outstanding careers in the party and the government anywhere in the Soviet Union, but the state impinged upon their group rights as a nation. Party bureaucracy promoted assimilation into Russian culture, and the Ukrainian SSR's sovereignty was nothing but a formality, with all important decisions dictated from the Kremlin.

Who were the dissidents, and how did they contribute to the collapse of communism?

Ukrainian history textbooks today lionize the dissidents of the 1960s and 1970s who picked up the torch of resistance to communist rule and helped bring down the Soviet system. However, the seemingly obvious historical continuities could be deceiving. The last nationalist insurgents fought in the forests of western Ukraine until the early 1950s, and the first dissident intellectuals appeared in the republic's cities by the decade's end, but there was little connecting them to the UPA's radical nationalist ideology and violent methods.

Soviet Ukrainian dissidents of the 1960s were products of the Soviet system. Usually first-generation college students of working-class background, they viewed the Soviet regime as corrupting "true Leninism," in particular by promoting the assimilation of Ukrainians into Russian culture. The dissidents also insisted on operating legally and forcing the state to fulfill its constitutional obligations. They signed petitions, organized non-violent protests, and distributed self-published (*samvydav*) underground literature. The Ukrainian dissidents also saw themselves as part of a wider movement for democracy and human rights in the Soviet Union. They cooperated closely with Russian dissidents, especially with their leader, the famous physicist and peace advocate, Andrei Sakharov.

In 1966 the Ukrainian literary critic born and educated in the Donbas, Ivan Dziuba, wrote a book-length dissident manifesto entitled *Internationalism or Russification?* Quoting from Lenin extensively, if selectively, he argued for the return to the Ukrainization policies of the 1920s. In a revealing move, he even sent the manuscript to the Ukrainian party bosses, as if hoping that they would come to their senses. The state responded with firings and arrests of dissident intellectuals. Some, like Dziuba, were forced to repent and recant; others ended up in the Gulag.

After the Soviet Union signed the Helsinki Accords in 1975, promising to observe human rights, the dissidents established the Ukrainian Helsinki Group in 1976 to monitor the Soviet government's compliance. The group included Jewish and other minority activists and worked closely with its counterpart in Moscow. The group's protest actions and petitions had largely symbolic significance, but its *samvydav* publications reached a much wider Ukrainian audience when they were read on Western shortwave radio stations broadcasting in Ukrainian, like the Voice of America and Radio Liberty.

Still, by the early 1980s the KGB managed to crush the organized dissident movement in Ukraine, as elsewhere. Its leaders were exiled abroad or imprisoned in the Gulag. The authorities incarcerated 24 of the group's 39 members, who eventually served a total of 170 years.[11] Four died in the Gulag.

The Ukrainian dissidents did not cause Soviet communism to collapse; rather, it disintegrated during the attempt to implement radical reforms of a political and economic model that appears "unreformable" in hindsight. However, they kept alive the notion of national rights during the bleakest days of the late Soviet period, affirming the intrinsic value of civil resistance. Many former dissidents returned to politics when this became possible in the heady days of the Soviet collapse, but neither they nor the political organizations they created played a significant role in Ukraine's post-communist transformation.

Why did the Chernobyl accident happen, and what was its impact on Ukraine?

The worst nuclear accident in history took place on April 26, 1986, at the Chernobyl nuclear power station, located about 70 miles north of Kyiv. The faulty design of Soviet nuclear reactors, in combination with human error, caused a powerful steam explosion in the station's Reactor No. 4. The reactor did not explode in a chain reaction like a nuclear bomb would, but its heavy lid was blown off, releasing into the atmosphere an enormous amount of radioactive contamination—90 times that emitted during the nuclear bombing of Hiroshima.

The Soviet authorities delayed the announcement of the catastrophe to their own citizens until the radioactive fallout reached Northern Europe and caused an international scandal. Soviet engineers managed to encase the damaged reactor in a concrete sarcophagus, but for the disaffected population in Ukraine and elsewhere, Chernobyl (or Chornobyl, according to Ukrainian spelling) was the proverbial last straw. The catastrophe happened just as the new Soviet leader Mikhail Gorbachev announced his new policy of *glasnost*, supposedly promoting greater official transparency and accountability. The official handling of the accident was decidedly "old-style," however, and now the people could speak more freely about the regime's criminal negligence.

Widespread popular discontent after Chernobyl forced Gorbachev to give society more of a voice. Ecological concerns following the Chernobyl disaster gave rise to the first Ukrainian mass civic organization independent from the state, the ecological association Green World (1987). It was followed in 1989 by the Taras Shevchenko Ukrainian Language Society and a mass popular front in support of democratic reforms, Rukh (Movement). Gradually, a modern political sphere came into being, although no political parties other than the ruling Communist Party could be registered until 1990. The assertion of popular sovereignty during the Soviet Union's last years took the form of vesting political power in the 15 union republics, including Ukraine, where a growing number of citizens held the federal center responsible for both the Soviet legacy of Stalinist terror and Chernobyl, a new and potent symbol of everything that was wrong with Soviet communism.

Thirty-one people, most of them responding firefighters, died of radiation sickness immediately after the Chernobyl disaster. Tens of thousands were exposed to high radiation levels during the hectic cleanup effort. Over 200,000 people in Ukraine and neighboring Belarus had to be permanently resettled away from the contaminated exclusion zone. Long-term health and ecological effects of the Chernobyl catastrophe are difficult to estimate, in part because the Ukrainian state had neither the resources nor the political will to prioritize post-Chernobyl rehabilitation programs in the decades immediately following the accident. Even urgent maintenance work on the concrete-and-steel sarcophagus was funded by the West.

4

UKRAINE AFTER COMMUNISM

*Did the Ukrainians have to fight the Russians in order to secede
from the Soviet Union?*

In the last years of the Soviet Union, Mikhail Gorbachev's incon-
sistent attempts to democratize political life resulted in the devo-
lution of power from the centralized party apparatus to the 15
union republics. This process did not result from any constitutional
changes; rather, with the decline of the Communist Party's power,
the republics began claiming the authority that had technically always been vested in them by the Soviet constitution. The Ukrainian
Soviet Socialist Republic and the Russian Soviet Federative Socialist
Republic (SFSR) soon came to see themselves as allies against the declining Soviet center. In the last year of the Soviet Union's existence,
the elected leader of the Russian SFSR, Boris Yeltsin, often clashed
with Gorbachev in defense of the republic's rights. Yeltsin, a speaker
of the Russian legislature, was elected president of the Russian SFSR
in 1990, which resulted in two sitting presidents claiming authority
in Moscow, the Soviet one resident in the Kremlin and the Russian
one with his offices in the republic's parliament across the river.

Yeltsin and his young team of pro-Western reformers positioned
themselves as defenders of democracy against the imperial center,
which was prone to conservative backlash. In reclaiming their constitutional rights, other Soviet republics drew inspiration from
Yeltsin's contest with Gorbachev. Democratic activists in Ukraine
envied the reformist momentum of the Yeltsin administration in
Russia, as old-style communist functionaries still controlled the

legislature in their own republic. They did not see Yeltsin's fledgling democratic Russia as an enemy, but as a beacon in the joint struggle against the Soviet center and communism. Those Ukrainian party functionaries who cautiously embraced the notion of republican sovereignty also regarded the Russian president as a natural ally.

The tumultuous events of August 1991 afforded Yeltsin an opportunity to assert democratic Russia's authority against the weakening Soviet state. When conservative party apparatchiks tried to organize a coup against Gorbachev, it was Yeltsin who led popular resistance in Moscow. In contrast, the speaker of the Ukrainian parliament, Leonid Kravchuk, took a cautious stand in Kyiv, not coming out openly on either side. The all-Union governing structures and institutions essentially disintegrated with the collapse of the coup, and the republics filled the power vacuum by formally declaring independence. Any remaining hopes to salvage the former Soviet polity in the form of a loose confederation were laid to rest on December 1, 1991, when Ukraine held a national referendum to confirm its declaration of independence. Their hopes buoyed by optimistic projections of economic prosperity that was to follow liberation from Soviet imperial fetters, the overwhelming majority of the republic's citizens voted in favor of independence: 92.3 percent nationally, including a majority in each province, and 54.2 percent even in the Crimea with its ethnic Russian majority.[1] On the same day, Ukrainian voters also elected Kravchuk as the country's first president.

At the time, this historic choice was not seen as a parting of ways with Russia, but as a farewell to the oppressive communist empire. Gorbachev, the discredited Soviet president, was the only prominent politician advocating the "no" vote in the Ukrainian referendum, while Yeltsin's Russia appeared to be a valuable ally in constructing the new democratic future. Later in December the Soviet Union was officially dissolved.

What is the Commonwealth of Independent States?

Following the Ukrainian referendum, on December 8, 1991, the leaders of the three Slavic republics of the Soviet Union— Russia, Ukraine, and Belarus—proclaimed the creation of the

Commonwealth of Independent States (CIS) as a regional coordinating organization for the Soviet successor states. All the other republics, except Latvia, Lithuania, and Estonia, eventually signed the relevant protocol to become member states. The leaders' aim was twofold. On the one hand, they needed to invent a quasi-legal procedure that would present the Soviet Union's dissolution as a collective decision. On the other, they wanted to reassure the population that the Soviet collapse would not mean the severance of economic and cultural ties among the republics. Apparently the organization's founders did not intend to create a more structured political union.

Tensions among the member states soon developed. As Yeltsin's economic and democratic reforms faltered, his administration increasingly adopted the rhetoric of Russian great-power chauvinism. Other former republics, Ukraine in particular, also responded to the economic collapse of the early 1990s by blaming everything on Russia's past and present imperial ambitions. Within the CIS, Russia soon found itself promoting closer cooperation, whereas Ukraine resisted any such efforts, especially in the fields of joint security and legislative coordination. In 1993 Ukraine refused to ratify the organization's charter, thus officially becoming a "participant state" rather than a "member state." It was, however, interested in remaining part of the de facto free-trade zone existing within CIS, which was formalized in 1994 and again in 1999.

Since the mid-1990s, Russia has worked to create a closer economic and political union within the CIS. Its first incarnation was the 1996 Customs Union of Russia, Belarus, and Kazakhstan. In 2000 Kyrgyzstan and Tajikistan joined these three states to create the grander-sounding Eurasian Economic Community. In January 2015 this entity was transformed into the Eurasian Economic Union with six post-Soviet states as members. Although the CIS continues to exist, Russia has increasingly focused its energies on developing this Eurasian Union, which Ukraine has never joined. Under governments of various political stripes, both those seen as pro-Russian and pro-Western, Ukraine's policy toward the CIS and its derivative projects remained remarkably consistent. Ukraine participated in CIS free-trade agreements, ratifying the most recent of them in 2011, but refrained from taking part in most other policy-coordinating projects.

The post-Soviet states have not viewed membership or participation in the CIS as an obstacle to cooperation and closer ties with the European Union. In 2009 six members and participants of the CIS, including Ukraine and Belarus, joined the EU's Eastern Partnership program. Nevertheless, some CIS institutions have been used to promote Russia's regional interests at the expense of other member states. Relations between Ukraine and the CIS worsened briefly in 2005, for example, when the CIS election-monitoring mission, in deference to Russian objections, initially refused to endorse the repeat runoff elections in Ukraine that brought President Viktor Yushchenko to power.

However, the most recent conflict between Ukraine and Russia emerged not in relation to the CIS but, rather, resulted from Russia's attempt to strong-arm the Ukrainian government into joining the Eurasian Economic Union. In November 2013 the Yanukovych administration yielded to Russian pressure by abandoning its plan to sign an Association Agreement with the European Union. This about-face proved to be the last straw for many Ukrainians, who launched a popular revolution. Following Russia's annexation of the Crimea and involvement in the Donbas war, in December 2014 Ukrainian MPs tabled a bill that would formalize the country's withdrawal from the CIS.

When and why did Ukraine give up its nuclear arsenal?

After the Soviet Union disintegrated, so many of its nuclear armaments were left on Ukrainian territory that Ukraine was briefly the world's third largest nuclear power. It found itself in possession of 176 intercontinental ballistic missiles armed with 1,240 nuclear warheads, as well as 42 nuclear bombers with hundreds of nuclear cruise missiles and bombs stockpiled for them, and some 3,000 tactical nuclear weapons. Although the list sounded impressive, the Ukrainian military really only had physical custody of the former Soviet nuclear arms, not access to the so-called permission action links (launching and retargeting codes). Operational control of the weapons remained in Moscow's hands.

The Ukrainian governments of the early 1990s pursued an ambivalent course on the nuclear arms issue. On the one hand, Ukraine's possession of nuclear weapons could serve as a deterrent against increasingly assertive Russian foreign policy moves toward Ukraine. On the other, the economic collapse of the early 1990s left the young state in no position to maintain the aging Soviet nuclear arsenal. The United States saw the ambiguous Ukrainian position as jeopardizing international nuclear non-proliferation and threatening the implementation of the 1991 Strategic Arms Reduction Treaty, which reduced the American and Soviet nuclear arsenals by 80 percent. In order to force Ukraine into compliance, the US administration employed both diplomatic pressure and the threat of economic sanctions, while promising economic assistance.

In 1992 all tactical nuclear weapons were removed from Ukrainian territory to be disassembled in Russia. However, the Ukrainian authorities felt that they had been unfairly denied their share of the generous American financial compensation paid to Russia in exchange for weapons-grade uranium obtained from the discarded weapons. Diplomatic relations between Ukraine and Russia also continued to deteriorate, with some Russian politicians voicing territorial claims on Ukraine. As a result, the Ukrainian government delayed both the transfer to Russia of its strategic nuclear warheads and accession to the Nuclear Non-Proliferation Treaty, while bargaining with the United States for compensation and security guarantees.

A resolution was finally reached in 1994. First, the United States, Russia, and Ukraine signed a memorandum in Moscow, requiring the transfer of the remaining Ukrainian strategic warheads to Russia in exchange for Russian-made fuel for Ukrainian nuclear power stations, with the United States compensating Russia in cash. Then, on December 5, 1994, the United States, Russia, and Britain signed the Budapest Memorandum on Security Assurances, which France and China also endorsed in separate official statements. In recognition of Ukraine's voluntary surrender of its nuclear weapons, the five major nuclear powers promised to "respect Ukraine's independence and sovereignty and the existing borders of Ukraine."[2] On the same day, Ukraine acceded to the Nuclear Non-Proliferation Treaty.

All remaining nuclear weapons were removed from Ukraine by 1996, and by the end of the decade, missiles and silos were also destroyed as part of a separate US-funded program.

In 2014 Russia's annexation of the Crimea and its involvement in the Donbas war prompted public debates in Ukraine on the wisdom of giving up nuclear weapons in exchange for vague security guarantees. Nevertheless, Ukraine's President Petro Poroshenko stated that his country would not seek to regain the status of a nuclear state. The United States and other Western countries condemned Russia's actions in Ukraine as a breach of international law, specifically Russia's obligations under the Budapest Memorandum.

What were Ukraine's relations with the West and Russia in the first decade after independence?

The US government's treatment of Ukraine on the issue of nuclear non-proliferation encapsulated the policies that the administration of George H. W. Bush pursued toward the post-Soviet states. The American authorities saw the region as a potential tinderbox and supported Russia as the regional power capable of maintaining peace and democracy there. Yet Yeltsin's Russia was moving quickly in a direction away from peace and democracy. After his economic reforms faltered and living standards collapsed in the early 1990s, Yeltsin found himself facing an opposition-dominated parliament, which he ordered his tanks to shell in 1993. After a brief ban, the Communist Party came back with a vengeance, its candidate coming a close second to Yeltsin in the first round of the 1996 presidential elections. Beginning in 1994, the inefficient Russian army became bogged down in the rebellious Muslim region of Chechnya. Amid all this turmoil, the Yeltsin administration increasingly embraced Russian nationalist rhetoric. The Russian position was also becoming openly anti-Western, which became clear by the time of the Kosovo crisis in 1998–1999.

Starting in Bill Clinton's first term in the mid-1990s, US foreign policy gradually shifted from reliance on Russia to building strong relations with Ukraine as the key element in the new Eastern European security architecture. The conservative commentator Zbigniew Brzezinski succinctly summed up this new vision of Ukraine's strategic importance by saying that "without Ukraine, Russia ceases to be an empire."[3] In the late 1990s, Ukraine became the third-largest recipient of American financial aid, surpassed only by Israel and Egypt. President Clinton made two official visits to Ukraine, and the Ukrainian president Leonid Kuchma reciprocated with two official visits to the United States. It was also during

Kuchma's first term (1994–1999) that Ukraine became the first CIS country to sign a cooperation agreement with NATO as part of the Partnership for Peace program (1995) and announced its desire to join the European Union (1996).

Improved relations with the West brought a number of benefits to the Ukrainian elites, not least of which was additional leverage in their difficult negotiations with Russia. In the early 1990s, many Russian politicians questioned Ukrainian territorial integrity, especially its control over the Crimean Peninsula, which had been transferred from the Russian SFSR in 1954. In 1993 the Russian parliament (which was about to be dissolved and shelled by Yeltsin for unrelated reasons) voted to reclaim the Crimean naval base of Sevastopol as Russian territory. Talks between Russia and Ukraine over the question of control of the former Soviet Black Sea Fleet based there dragged on for years. Finally, in 1997, Kuchma skillfully exploited Russian anxieties about Ukraine's developing contacts with NATO to normalize Ukrainian-Russian relations. Shortly after the first joint NATO-Ukrainian military exercises in the Crimea, Ukraine and Russia signed a comprehensive treaty of friendship and cooperation. This June 1997 agreement repeated Russian recognition of Ukraine's territorial integrity and also divided the Black Sea Fleet between the two countries.

As Kuchma's second term began in 1999, it seemed that Ukraine had succeeded in playing Russia and the West against each other in order to gain maximum benefits for the Ukrainian state and its elites. Ukraine's foreign trade, too, diversified successfully. Trading almost exclusively with other former Soviet republics in 1991, Ukraine arrived at a nearly equal division of its foreign-trade balance by the early 2000s: approximately one-third representing trade with Russia and other CIS states, another third with the European Union, and the final third with the rest of the world. However, Ukraine's continued reliance on imported Russian energy remained a glaring imbalance, which left it vulnerable to Russia's manipulation of the energy market for political purposes.

Did the presidents of independent Ukraine promote a united national identity?

Ukraine's first president, Leonid Kravchuk (term of office 1991–1994) was uniquely qualified to promote a Ukrainian national identity because he had spent decades destroying and controlling it in his previous career as a Communist Party ideologist. A long-serving functionary of the Communist Party of Ukraine, he headed the Propaganda and Agitation Department before his elevation in the late 1980s to secretary for ideological questions. After decades of fighting against any and all suspected manifestations of Ukrainian nationalism, he knew better than any other apparatchik what it took to build a new nation-state. He was also well aware of just how well the party's assimilationist agenda had been implemented during the late Soviet period, because he had overseen the party's inculcation of a supranational Soviet identity and the promotion of "eternal" Russo-Ukrainian friendship, in addition to the creeping promotion of the Russian language in Ukraine.

When the Soviet Union collapsed in 1991, the political elites in Ukraine and other republics changed their colors quickly. By then, the more dynamic functionaries, like Kravchuk, were well on their way toward abandoning communist ideology and the notion of historical Russian guidance. What they embraced instead defies easy explanation; suffice it to say that it was *not* an exclusive Ukrainian ethnic nationalism claiming Ukraine for Ukrainians. The foundational documents of the new Ukrainian state embraced an inclusive, civic concept of the Ukrainian nation and named the "people of Ukraine," rather than ethnic Ukrainians, as the source of sovereignty. At the same time, some concepts reflective of ethnic nationalism received wide circulation, in particular that of independent Ukraine as the completion of the Ukrainian nation's long struggle for independence. Accordingly, it followed that the state "owed" it to ethnic Ukrainians to elevate the Ukrainian language and culture to "official" status, much like French language and culture in France, for example.

The new state's old elites also found cultural Ukrainization politically expedient. It secured for them the support of the national-democratic political parties, which saw the state as an instrument for the ethnic nation's "awakening" and commanded electoral support in the westernmost regions. More generally, however, the turncoat functionaries truly wanted their own nation-state, simply because ruling it outright seemed vastly preferable to governing at the Kremlin's pleasure. Affirming Ukraine's cultural identity as separate from Russia's thus also served their pragmatic interests. For the majority of ordinary citizens, most of whom were bilingual to some degree, Ukrainization meant simply a change in language usage patterns, with the language previously reserved for home and cultural festivities now becoming the state language. After all, 72.7 percent of the population identified as ethnic Ukrainians during the census of 1989, and 64.7 percent claimed Ukrainian as their mother tongue. In other words, for them it was a heritage reaffirmed rather than a foreign identity imposed. However, the language question quickly became politicized.

President Kravchuk introduced Ukrainian as the language of administration, strengthening it as the language of instruction in schools and as the language of the national media. These policies went hand in hand with his other state-building measures and the assertion of Ukrainian sovereignty. In the early 1990s, Ukraine also distanced itself from the Russian-dominated CIS and created its own full-fledged ministries and embassies abroad. The Kravchuk administration promoted public use of the blue-and-yellow flag, the "trident" state emblem, and the anthem "Ukraine Has Not Yet Perished"—all long used by Ukrainian nationalists and now causing a backlash among those nostalgic for the red flags and the Russo-centric culture of the Soviet past. Because he had neglected painful economic reforms, however, Kravchuk's political opponents succeeded in linking his emphasis on building the nation-state with economic crisis and rampant corruption. In 1994 Kravchuk was defeated by his former prime minister, Leonid Kuchma, who promised economic reforms and the promotion of Russian as a state language. Yet, Kuchma never attempted this latter task because he, too, realized that his power was vested in the existence of an independent Ukrainian state. Instead, he continued Kravchuk's policies of cultural and administrative Ukrainization, particularly during the mid- to late 1990s. Kuchma realized the dangers of getting too close to Russia both culturally and politically. He even published a book entitled *Ukraine Is Not Russia* (2003).

For all this, Kuchma's electoral victory in 1994 and the parliamentary elections held earlier that year—both of which clearly showed the political division of the country into western and southeastern "halves"—confirmed the language issue as the new rallying cry of Ukrainian politics. West of the Dnipro River, the Ukrainian language became shorthand for both Ukrainian nation building and Western-style democracy, whereas east and south of it, the defense

of the Russian language became associated with nostalgia for a paternalistic Soviet state, now retrospectively remembered as more
"Russian" that it had really been. Politicians on both sides found it
much easier to exploit this divide than to pursue painful reforms or
nurture a unifying national identity. The voting boundary gradually moved eastward in subsequent years, as more regions switched
to the "pro-Ukrainian" side in 2004, for example, but the divide
remained in place.[4]

What religions came to prominence in Ukraine after the Soviet collapse?

Present-day political fault lines do not correspond neatly to any historical religious divides in Ukraine. Still, membership in any of the
three main Christian churches in the country involves a national-
identity choice as well, because of their different historical relationship to the Russian Orthodox Church, which functions as the de
facto state church in Russia.

Kyivan Rus adopted Eastern-rite Christianity in the tenth century
from the Byzantine Empire. After the Mongol conquest in the thirteenth century, the metropolitan (archbishop) of Kyiv escaped to the
northeast, eventually moving the metropolitan see to Moscow. In
1589 Tsar Boris Godunov forced the head of the mother church, the
patriarch of Constantinople, to acknowledge the ecclesiastical independence of the Russian Orthodox Church. From that point, its head
also wielded the title of patriarch. However, the ecclesiastical territory of the patriarch of Moscow did not include the Ukrainian lands.
There, under Polish rule, a separate Orthodox church existed, and
it was still under the authority of the patriarch of Constantinople.
After Muscovy's absorption of the Ukrainian Cossack polity, the
Muscovite government arranged with the Ottomans in 1686 to
pressure the patriarch of Constantinople into transferring these
lands to Moscow's canonical jurisdiction.

Even before that, in 1596, a new Christian church was established in the Ukrainian lands under Polish rule, the Ukrainian
Greek Catholic Church (the word "Greek" referring to the Byzantine
rite; historically, this church was also known as the Uniate Church
and is now referred to simply as the Ukrainian Catholic Church).
Most Orthodox bishops in the Polish-Lithuanian Commonwealth

accepted the ecclesiastical authority of the pope, while preserving the Eastern Christian rite and the ordination of married men to the priesthood. Relations between the Uniates and the Orthodox were violent, at first; Cossacks slaughtered Uniates during the Khmelnytsky Uprising in the 1640s. Since the late eighteenth century, however, the Ukrainian Greek Catholic Church has served as a national church for Ukrainians in Galicia, the region of the Habsburg Empire that became the center of the Ukrainian national movement.

After the Russian Empire's collapse in 1917, the independent Ukrainian Autocephalous Orthodox Church was established, and it competed with the Russian Orthodox Church for parishioners in the Ukrainian SSR, until the Stalinist authorities suppressed it in 1930. Following the Soviet annexation of Galicia during World War II, the Ukrainian Catholic Church was dissolved, its parishes transferred to the Russian Orthodox Church. Many Ukrainian Catholics continued practicing their religion underground.

The Soviet leader Mikhail Gorbachev lifted the ban against the Ukrainian Greek Catholic Church in 1989, on the eve of his historic visit to the Vatican. Since then, the church quickly reclaimed most of its parishes and its dominant position in Galicia, as well as in the smaller western Ukrainian region of Transcarpathia, but it has only a token presence elsewhere in the country. It now has over 4,000 parishes and an estimated 4 million faithful in Ukraine, as well as a considerable following in the Ukrainian diaspora.

The Ukrainian Autocephalous Orthodox Church (UAOC), which had survived in the diaspora as well, was also re-established in Ukraine shortly before the fall of the Soviet Union in 1990. Initially, there was considerable interest in an indigenous Orthodox church free from Moscow's control, but the UAOC was disadvantaged by the lack of recognition from canonical Orthodox churches, dating back to its establishment in 1921 in a ceremony that was marked by the absence of bishops. Also, a powerful new competitor soon emerged for the role of a Ukrainian alternative to Russian Orthodoxy.

Following the emergence of independent Ukraine in 1991, the leader of the Russian Orthodox Church in Ukraine, the metropolitan of Kyiv, Filaret, embraced the idea of a separate Ukrainian Orthodox Church (UOC). This plan, which President Kravchuk supported as part of his nation-building efforts, led to a new schism in what had been the country's dominant religion. A significant number of bishops and parishes followed Filaret into the UOC (Kyiv Patriarchate), which they created by merging temporarily with the UAOC. However, the majority remained with the Russian Orthodox Church, which excommunicated Filaret and elected a new metropolitan of Kyiv, Volodymyr, in his place. In 1995 Filaret became patriarch of the UOC (Kyiv Patriarchate).

After the split, the Russian Orthodox Church in Ukraine (which is also technically called the Ukrainian Orthodox Church, but often with the explanatory designation "of the Moscow Patriarchate") retained its position as the country's most influential religion. It boasts over 11,000 parishes and claims up to 75 percent of Ukraine's population as members. Most Ukrainians are not regular churchgoers, however, and many identify themselves to pollsters simply as "Orthodox," without specifying the church they belong to, if any. In recent years and especially after the EuroMaidan Revolution, however, the Ukrainian Orthodox Church (Moscow Patriarchate) was forced to scale down, at least publicly, its dependence on Moscow and involvement in Ukrainian politics. In contrast, the Ukrainian Orthodox Church (Kyiv Patriarchate) has increased its visibility and has tried to position itself as a Ukrainian national Orthodox church, although it still lacks international canonical recognition. By the mid-2010s the Kyiv Patriarchate had some 4,300 parishes, and the UAOC approximately 1,200; together they claimed some 7 million faithful.

In addition to the traditional Eastern Christian churches, Protestants of various denominations have been proselytizing actively in independent Ukraine, with their share of the faithful now estimated at between 1 and 3 percent of the population. Over 450,000 Ukrainian citizens are Muslims, but most of them are Crimean Tatars residing in the Crimean Peninsula, now under Russian control.

The Orthodox churches in particular have felt the impact of recent political events. During the EuroMaidan Revolution, the St. Michael's Golden-Domed Cathedral in central Kyiv, which belongs to the Kyiv Patriarchate, served as a refuge and field hospital for injured protestors pursued by riot police. After the Russian takeover of the Crimea and the start of the Donbas war, 30 parishes reportedly switched their affiliations from the Moscow Patriarchate to the Kyiv Patriarchate.[5] The Ukrainian Orthodox Church (Moscow Patriarchate) has found itself in a difficult position following the deterioration of Russo-Ukrainian relations. The administration of President Poroshenko promoted the creation of a united Orthodox Church that would be under the jurisdiction of the Ecumenical Patriarch of Constantinople. In December 2018, a unification council took place in Kyiv, proclaiming the creation of the Orthodox Church of Ukraine (OCU), but it was constituted primarily through the merger of the Kyiv Patriarchate and the UAOC with only two bishops crossing over from the Moscow Patriarchate. There was initially a significant transfer of individual parishes from the Moscow Patriarchate to the new church, but it slowed down after Poroshenko's electoral defeat in 2019. The OCU also became weakened by the conflict between its head, the young and energetic Metropolitan Epiphanius, and his former mentor and head of the Kyiv Patriarchate, Metropolitan Filaret. Opinion polls show that the OCU has more public support in Ukraine than the pro-Moscow church, but it is unclear whether the OCU really has the 7,000 parishes it claims. The division of the Ukrainian Orthodox Christians into the "all-Russian" and "Ukrainian" orientations continues.

How did independent Ukraine become an inefficient economy and a paragon of crony capitalism?

From its Soviet predecessor Ukraine inherited an economy dominated by heavy industry, much of it simply incapable of being reformed. Large, inefficient factories produced military hardware for the Soviet army and in turn depended on dirt-cheap fuel from elsewhere in the Soviet Union. Huge, obsolete mines were kept running, in part to keep alive the Stalinist myth of model Soviet proletarians, the Donbas miners. In the 1990s the economic ties among the former Soviet republics loosened, leaving much of the Ukrainian-made machinery idle. The reorientation toward the production of consumer goods proved slow and painful.

The Kravchuk administration demonstrated little interest in economic reform, mostly because of its anticipated social and political costs. Instead, the government preferred to subsidize unprofitable state enterprises in order to prevent mass unemployment. In 1993 the government's free printing of currency led to annual hyperinflation of over 10,000 percent. Their savings wiped out and their salaries not keeping up with prices, three-quarters of Ukrainians lived below the poverty level. For many urban residents, having relatives in a village or owning a small garden plot in the countryside, where they could grow their own food, became the key to survival. At the same time, well-connected traders made instant fortunes by importing cheap indispensable goods.

During his first presidential term (1994–1999), Leonid Kuchma managed to introduce strict monetary controls and, eventually, a relatively stable new currency, the *hryvnia* (1996). His larger project, however, was the privatization of state enterprises, which originally succeeded only in relation to smaller, consumer-oriented businesses. Influential managers of large factories and mines, most of them former Soviet "Red directors" like Kuchma, initially resisted privatization because they thrived by exploiting state subsidies. It took some years for them and for more dynamic younger entrepreneurs to discover the benefits of embracing capitalism. Privatization took off in Ukraine in the late 1990s, concurrently with an industrial revival led by the export-oriented metallurgical industry. But this privatization was anything but transparent.

What emerged in Ukraine in the 2000s was crony capitalism at its worst. The new rich usually owed their instant wealth to their government connections, if not their own political appointments, but some of them also came from gangster backgrounds. Organized crime merged with big business and the political class to create an impenetrable ruling elite concerned only with its own enrichment. Its ostentatious display of wealth brought to Kyiv and other big cities brand-name boutiques and luxury cars, but social tensions were simmering in residential neighborhoods. The gap between rich and poor grew rapidly, exacerbating popular resentment against rampant corruption and political manipulation.

Who are the oligarchs?

Business tycoons in the former Soviet republics who had acquired immense riches and influence during the transition from a communist to a capitalist economy came to be known as oligarchs (*oligarkhi* in Russian, *oliharkhy* in Ukrainian). The choice of this ancient Greek political term is highly appropriate here. Oligarchy, or rule by a small group, is the opposite of democracy, and business oligarchs are the best symbol of crony capitalism, in which both economic opportunities and political decisions are reserved for a small group of elites. Unlike in the established Western democracies, big politics and big business have merged openly in Eastern Europe. Oligarchs in independent Ukraine have bankrolled and controlled political parties, have bought parliamentary seats for themselves to ensure immunity from prosecution, and have served as cabinet ministers. Indeed, President Poroshenko was also a major oligarch, worth an estimated US$1 billion as of 2013 and US$1.4 billion as of 2020.

The oligarchs came from various backgrounds. Many had previous experience in industry or trade as Red directors or were dynamic, younger communist functionaries, while others started from scratch by opening casinos or serving as bankers to the mafia. Yet, all of them had two things in common. At some point, all had managed to establish close links with the state apparatus, which allowed them to benefit from insider deals. Also, all of them to some degree took advantage of the fire sale of state assets in the late 1990s, when they acquired major enterprises for symbolic sums, usually paid for with state-issued privatization certificates, obtained for a pittance from workers who did not understand their value.

For as long as Russia was selling gas to Ukraine at a highly discounted price, the most lucrative business in Ukraine was reselling it in Europe at world prices, a trick that brought instant riches but required the connivance of both Russian and Ukrainian government figures. From the late 1990s, the export of metals and minerals (produced cheaply in Ukraine at Soviet-built factories) became another attractive option.[6] In the 2000s, the oligarchs diversified their assets by acquiring regional power-distribution companies and creating rival media and communications empires. Corruption and insider deals by no means disappeared, as demonstrated by the popularity in the 2010s of fraudulent VAT returns on nonexistent products allegedly exported from Ukraine or imported from abroad. State procurements also involved enormous kickbacks and the outright embezzlement of billions, never more so than in the last year of the Yanukovych regime, when state companies were exempt from open tender.

Ukrainian oligarchs have tended to get involved in politics very closely, if sometimes covertly. The country's richest person, Rinat

Akhmetov (worth an estimated US$15 billion as of 2013) started out in coal trading and banking in the Donbas before expanding nationally and internationally into metallurgy, machine building, and communications, among other things. However, for years he retained close links with the Donbas political machine and especially with Viktor Yanukovych, the former governor from this region, who went on to serve as prime minister and president. Akhmetov also reportedly bankrolled Yanukovych's Party of the Regions, which cultivated its electoral base in southeastern Ukraine. Still, after the disintegration of the Yanukovych regime and the start of the Donbas war, Akhmetov came out forcefully on the side of Ukraine's territorial integrity.

So, too, did Ihor Kolomoisky, reputedly the third-richest person in Ukraine, with a fortune of US$3 billion (as of 2013) made in the banking, steel, chemical, and airline industries. Following the EuroMaidan Revolution, Kolomoisky agreed to serve as the governor of Dnipropetrovsk province, which borders on the troublesome region near the Russian border. He also funded volunteer Ukrainian battalions fighting in the Donbas. In contrast, the second-richest Ukrainian, Viktor Pinchuk, who started out in pipe production and is now worth an estimated US$4.6 billion, kept a low profile throughout the conflict. Indeed, ever since the 2004 Orange Revolution against the regime of his father-in-law, President Leonid Kuchma, he has stayed out of big politics, preferring to make a name for himself as a philanthropist and patron of the arts.

The war in the Donbas and the loss of the Crimea undermined Ukraine's economic growth and resulted in a decrease in the estimated fortunes of Ukrainian oligarchs. In May 2020 *Forbes* ranked the three richest persons in Ukraine in the following order: Akhmetov (US$2.8 billion), Pinchuk (US$1.4 billion), and Poroshenko (US$1.4 billion).

What are the roots of corruption in Ukraine and how have the changing Ukrainian governments been addressing it?

The widespread corruption in Ukraine can be traced back to the country's Soviet past, but it does not represent a direct continuation of the Soviet tradition. The transfer of corrupt practices was more complex.

Because the Soviet "command economy" rejected free-market mechanisms of regulating the supply and quality of goods, Soviet citizens employed their own little strategies to obtain desired items. By far the most common of these involved finding a connection to somebody in the lower or middle ranks of the state's distribution chain. People cultivated such connections by returning favors or offering small gifts—something the state declared unacceptable, but in reality tolerated. Aware of its inability to satisfy consumer demand, the state actually maintained separate distribution networks for the elites, who also participated, from a much better position, in the informal "economy of favors."

Yet large-scale economic corruption, which became the plague of post-Soviet Ukraine, could not have existed under communist rule. With all enterprises under state ownership, a large unlawful property transfer simply could not take place. On several occasions in the postwar Soviet Union, the state made a point of sentencing to long prison terms or executing the organizers of larger informal networks, especially when these involved diverting the production of state factories through private channels.

It was rather a different kind of Soviet legacy that crippled Ukraine as well as Russia and some other post-Soviet states: the Communist Party's flagrant disregard for the rule of law and the absence of checks and balances. Its arbitrary exercise of power formed a widespread understanding that the political leaders could do anything they wanted, including in the economy, because they were the real owners of the country, its economy, and the people. In the absence of independent business elites or functioning trade unions, which in Soviet times existed mostly on paper, high state officials in post-communist Ukraine have found themselves the unchallenged masters of the land, natural resources, and the economy in general. They also realized that they could profit from the reallocation of this wealth and that neither the citizens nor the compliant Soviet-style justice system would hold them accountable. State-sanctioned corruption on a grand scale thus became possible.

The mismanaged transition from command economy to market mechanisms during the early 1990s produced widespread shortages of even basic necessities. This strengthened the pre-existing "economy of favors," which in the long run also became monetized to the extent that the price tags for essential services were announced openly, without much fear of the state. If underpaid Soviet doctors could expect from their grateful patients a box of chocolates or some return favor, many of their post-Soviet colleagues boldly named the amounts in US dollars, all the while as medicine remained theoretically state funded. So, too, did state officials, college admission specialists, vehicle-safety inspectors, and judges. Corruption thus became ubiquitous in its reach and was accepted by society as normal.

It took the Ukrainian state until 1995 to enact a rather basic law, "On the Struggle against Corruption," which served to assuage the country's new allies and financial supporters in the West, just as the large-scale industry privatization under President Kuchma was about to produce stunning examples of large-scale corruption, collusion, extortion, and embezzlement involving the highest officials of the state. As experts have argued, the system constructed in Ukraine during the late 1990s was not just corrupt—it ran on corruption.[7] The missions of the International Monetary Fund, now a major supporter of Ukraine's elusive reforms, and the embassies of the leading Western powers, found themselves pushing on behalf of Ukrainian society for the implementation of real anti-corruption measures. The Kuchma administration had no problem approving a national Program against Corruption in 1997, and the following year it approved the Principles of Fighting against Corruption for 1998–2005. These were mostly declarative, however, and the various coordinating committees they established often merely pursued the business rivals of the tycoons associated with the government.

Ukrainian civil society's rebellion against the system during the Orange Revolution of 2004–2005 created the first real opportunity to destroy the corrupt symbiosis of the state and the oligarchs. President Viktor Yushchenko clearly intended to use this momentum. During his term in office, Ukraine signed the UN's and the Council of Europe's conventions against corruption and invited international monitoring of Ukraine's national anti-corruption measures, primarily through the Council of Europe's Group of States against Corruption. Armed with the recommendations of international experts, the Ukrainian authorities prepared a package of new laws and amendments, which would tighten up the existing legislative loopholes. Yet Yushchenko's continued infighting with his prime minister, fellow reformist Yulia Tymoshenko, delayed the passage of this legislation until 2009.

The next president, Viktor Yanukovych, representing the defenders of the old regime, inherited the so-called Anti-Corruption Package together with the promises made to Ukraine's Western partners, but his party disliked the proposed tighter controls over the role of state officials in economic decisions. The strategy they chose consisted of delaying the package's implementation and pressuring the Constitutional Court to declare that some parts of the package allegedly contradicted the Constitution. This allowed the Yanukovych government to abrogate the package in 2011 and, after leaving the country for several months with no anti-corruption legislation in place, it finally enacted a new law that was more acceptable to party leaders and their cronies.[8] To keep up appearances, Yanukovych also created the National Anti-Corruption Committee and promulgated the National Strategy for Combatting Corruption for 2011–2015.

Nevertheless, in 2012 Ukraine remained in the bottom part of the Transparency International corruption-perception index, ranking 144th of the 174 states surveyed. That same year, the global audit firm Ernst & Young ranked Ukraine, Colombia, and Brazil as the three most corrupt countries in the world, based on the perception of international businesses.[9] In 2013, the unchecked systemic corruption in Ukraine would become one of the main causes of the Euromaidan Revolution.

Is Ukraine dependent on Russian gas supplies?

Ukraine is indeed dependent on Russian gas and other energy supplies, although to a much lesser degree now than during the "gas war," which lasted from 2005 to 2009. Ukraine produces only about a third of the oil and gas it consumes, with the rest before 2014 imported from Russia. Russian oil is not as crucial for the country's economy as natural gas, and it is the latter that has generated tensions between the two countries. Ukraine produces enough of its own coal and electricity; it even used to export both, although the fuel for Soviet-built nuclear power plants comes from Russia.

Much of Ukraine's energy dependence is a legacy of the Soviet past. Back then, planners had little concern for the energy efficiency of industrial enterprises in Ukraine because they had at their disposal the immense natural gas deposits of the entire Soviet Union. Ukraine itself used to be a major gas-producing region, supplying other parts of the Soviet Union and even its Eastern European allies, until the deposits started showing signs of exhaustion in the mid-1970s. Since then, the indigenous production of gas has decreased threefold. At the same time, Ukraine became an important gas transportation hub, as new Soviet pipelines to Europe crossed the republic's territory.

For about a decade after the Soviet Union's disintegration, the price that Russia charged Ukraine for natural gas increased gradually but still remained well below world prices. There were some political strings attached, which became clear particularly during Kuchma's second term. As well, a number of corrupt officials in both countries benefited from the resale of subsidized Russian gas to Europe at world prices. The oligarchs, too, enjoyed making hefty profits from the sale of metals produced using heavily subsidized gas.[10]

This corrupt symbiosis came to an end with the 2004 Orange Revolution, when the new Ukrainian government attempted to remove gas trade intermediaries, shut down other fraudulent economic schemes, and reverse the most notorious cases of insider privatization in metallurgy. The first dispute over the price of gas and its transit flared up in 2005 and resulted in Russia briefly cutting the supply in January 2006. As the Russian state monopoly Gazprom kept increasing the price of gas for Ukraine, further disputes developed over the exact amount of the Ukrainian gas debt and accusations that Ukraine had been siphoning off gas intended for Europe. In January 2009 Russia again halted all gas deliveries to and via Ukraine, this time for 12 days, which caused supply disruptions in several European countries. Ukraine was thus forced into signing a disadvantageous gas agreement with Russia, which later served as the pretext for imprisoning then Prime Minister Yulia Tymoshenko.

Following these developments, Ukrainian industry began seriously reducing its dependence on the now expensive Russian gas by replacing it with Ukrainian coal. The import share of Ukraine's overall gas consumption decreased from the high point of 90 percent before the "gas wars" to something like 70 percent in 2013.

Yet, until the winter of 2014, the government achieved little progress in reforming the other Soviet legacy in gas consumption: the inefficient residential-heating system. The Soviet state held the municipal authorities, rather than residents, responsible for supplying heat and hot water in urban areas. The system used centralized water heating in district stations, with hot water then transported to apartment buildings by underground pipes. In independent Ukraine, the authorities had no choice but to keep this economically unsustainable model running, yet they also did not increase residential rates to keep up with the price of gas because they feared the consequences at the ballot box. Only during the difficult winter of 2014 did the new authorities, in Kyiv in particular, call on urban residents to install boilers where practicable because of the impending rate increases and possible supply disruptions. The complete rebuilding of the urban heating infrastructure is probably not feasible in the near future.

In 2014 the new Ukrainian government began looking for other ways to reduce its dependence on Russian gas, such as increasing domestic production and reversing supply from Europe. However, the country's energy dilemma has only worsened following the outbreak of war in the Donbas. As some 40 percent of the country's energy is produced by coal power plants, disruptions in the production and transportation of coal from the troubled region has had a negative impact on industrial enterprises and residential power supply. In the winter of 2014, scheduled power outages took place throughout the country for two hours a day in cities and for up to eight hours in rural areas. The Ukrainian authorities had to resort to buying coal from Russia, thus increasing the country's energy dependence on its worrisome neighbor. In subsequent years, Ukraine explored purchasing coal from South Africa and even the United States before settling on its indirect purchase from the occupied Donbas.

Ironically, the economic contraction caused by the war helped Ukraine by making it less dependent on Russian gas. In order to avoid dealing with Russia directly, Ukraine switched to buying Russian gas from European intermediaries. In December 2019, the two countries finally signed a five-year contract for the transit of Russian gas through the territory of Ukraine and its purchase by Ukraine. The experts saw this agreement as a compromise acceptable to both sides.

5

THE ORANGE REVOLUTION AND THE EUROMAIDAN

What did the two recent revolutions in Ukraine (2004 and 2013–2014) have in common?

Both the Orange Revolution and the EuroMaidan were massive popular revolts that used Kyiv's main square, the Maidan, as their central political stage. Both involved long standoffs with the authorities lasting through the cold winter months, an indication of the revolutionaries' determination and their popular support in the capital. Both targeted the political order represented by Viktor Yanukovych: in 2004 he was the prime minister, trying to reach the presidency through rigged elections; in 2013, he was the president, who personified a corrupt and inefficient regime and was increasingly subservient to dictatorial Russia. The leaders of both revolutions called for Western-style democracy and transparency; in both cases, the West supported them and Russia denounced them as illegitimate.

Placed in the broader historical context of Ukraine's Soviet past, such parallels reveal a deeper connection between the two movements. Ukraine did not experience the Soviet collapse as a social revolution complete with the removal of the old elites. Manipulative and corrupt former Soviet bureaucrats and Red directors continued running the state for the first decade after independence. By the first decade of the 2000s, they tried to transfer their power to the next generation of politicians representing the interests of the oligarchs. The latter not only accumulated their wealth by looting state assets during insider privatizations, but also represented regional economic clans that, at least in some cases, developed from the organized-crime structures of the early 1990s. Yanukovych's own criminal record symbolized the nature of the system that could select him as a candidate for the highest office.

Yet, Ukrainian society changed much in the decades following independence. A new, primarily urban middle class developed, with attendant expectations of economic opportunity for small businesses and decent pay for professionals. A new generation of Ukrainian urbanites vacationed abroad, and their children studied in the West. It was increasingly difficult for them to tolerate a kleptocratic regime employing familiar Soviet methods of political manipulation. The transfer of power from the old Soviet elites to the new, "criminal" ones was what prompted many urban professionals, small business owners, and students to rebel. Both revolutions generated impressive grassroots support in central and western Ukraine, but not in the southeastern regions, where the Communist Party and the Party of Regions cultivated the governance style familiar from the Soviet past. Scholars have noted the prominent role of civil society and grassroots initiative in the Euromaidan Revolution.[1] Both revolts reflected a clash between civil society and a paternalistic state, as well as between Western-style democracy and Soviet-style authoritarianism, the latter being the mark of Putin's regime in today's Russia. In other words, it was a conflict of political models masquerading as ethnic strife.

Although the revolt in both cases was caused by domestic factors, the revolutionaries defined their vision of Ukraine in geopolitical terms by necessity. They opposed the crooked Ukrainian regime associated with the Soviet past and buttressed by present-day Russian support. Such Russian complicity made the West appear attractive as a democratic model and potential counterweight against Ukraine's backward-looking eastern neighbor. The "West" was a metaphor, of course: an idealized "Europe" of prosperity and democracy rather than the reality of the bureaucratized and economically troubled European Union. In any case, neither revolution was waged merely for the privilege of moving from one geopolitical sphere of influence to another but, rather, to build a new Ukraine for the benefit of its people.

It is also telling in this respect that, whereas in 2004 it was the parliamentary opposition that issued a call for mass protests, in

2013 the spontaneous mass rally in the capital caught the opposition parties unprepared. This change testified to both the deep-seated popular discontent that fueled the revolutions and distrust of politicians in general. The leaders of the Orange Revolution ended up playing only a minor role in the EuroMaidan Revolution. New parties came to prominence, and other political figures moved into leadership positions.

Why did mass protests against President Kuchma develop in the early 2000s, and who led them?

Kuchma narrowly won his second term as president in 1999, largely thanks to his control of the media and his willingness to engage in every kind of political manipulation, up to and including ballot stuffing. In order to accomplish this ignoble feat, he had to rely even more heavily on the support of the oligarchs. The following year, his administration employed electoral fraud freely in a constitutional referendum aimed at weakening the parliament, although any constitutional changes required approval by two-thirds of the parliament, so the regime's fraudulent victory at the polls was ultimately in vain. However, it took a much more shocking revelation to propel the Kuchma regime on its downward spiral.

In September 2000 the investigative journalist Georgii Gongadze, who specialized in documenting government abuses, suddenly disappeared; his headless body was eventually discovered in fields near Kyiv. In November, the leader of the Socialist Party, Oleksandr Moroz, made a stunning accusation against Kuchma in parliament, claiming that the president himself had ordered the journalist's disappearance, as confirmed by recordings made secretly in the presidential office. As it turned out, a member of Kuchma's security detail, Major Mykola Melnychenko, provided Moroz with some 300 hours of conversations that he claimed to have recorded with a simple digital recorder left under a couch. Some people heard speaking on the "Melnychenko tapes" confirmed their authenticity, while others claimed that the content had been doctored. The blow to Kuchma's reputation was nonetheless enormous.

The tapes revealed the president repeatedly asking his minister for internal affairs and security service chief to "take care" of

Gongadze, even suggesting a possible scenario for the journalist's disappearance; other revelations were no less shocking.[2] The recordings seemed to indicate the highest Ukrainian leadership's direct involvement in large-scale electoral fraud, money laundering, insider privatization, and the illegal arms trade. On top of that, Kuchma's speech on the tapes was full of obscenities and replete with anti-Semitic and misogynistic slurs.

Early in 2001 a broad opposition movement sprang up in Ukraine and, for the first time since independence, the Communist and Socialist parties did not lead the way. Adopting the name "Ukraine without Kuchma," this large democratic coalition focused on the removal of the rotten political regime. The new Ukrainian middle class resented the rampant corruption and the lack of equal opportunity, but the opposition slogans resonated even further, especially their populist message of reining in the oligarchs. The leaders of the opposition also seemed to represent a new breed of politician, as exemplified by Viktor Yushchenko, a patriotic Ukrainian banker who had served as prime minister without acquiring a reputation for being corrupt—a nearly impossible feat under Kuchma. His dynamic political partner, the charismatic Yulia Tymoshenko, was a master of fiery, populist rhetoric and was also well informed about government corruption in the energy sector by virtue of her own business background in that area.

In preparation for the 2002 parliamentary elections, the new center-right opposition reconstituted itself as the electoral bloc "Our Ukraine," led by Yushchenko. His skillfully run campaign focused on economic reform and clean government. Kuchma's coalition of small, oligarch-backed parties managed to win the elections by employing the usual fraudulent tactics, but Our Ukraine formed the second-largest faction in the parliament. It also acquired its own oligarch supporters, most notably the "chocolate king," Petro Poroshenko. The opposition and the West protested the stolen elections, but the Kuchma administration was able to carry on business as usual, at least temporarily.

In fact, by then Kuchma had become a pariah on the international scene. Shunned by Western leaders after the Gongadze scandal and the many instances of electoral fraud, he also incurred the ire of the United States after revelations of illicit arms deals with Saddam Hussein's Iraq emerged. Washington was particularly outraged in

2003, when it became known that the Ukrainian authorities had either sold or planned to sell to Iraq the Soviet-made Kolchuga radar system, capable of detecting stealth bombers. Kuchma was unable to salvage his reputation by sending 1,650 Ukrainian troops to Iraq as part of the US-led multinational contingent. Trapped in semi-isolation from the West, the Kuchma regime was drifting against its better judgment closer to Putin's Russia, which wanted to swallow Ukraine economically and politically.

What sparked the Orange Revolution in 2004?

The mass protests that became the Orange Revolution occurred in the wake of revelations of the government's massive attempted fraud in the 2004 presidential election. As Kuchma's second term was nearing its end, the powerful Donetsk economic clan pressured him into supporting as successor the clan's political face, Viktor Yanukovych. Formerly the governor of Donetsk province, Yanukovych served as Kuchma's last prime minister from 2002 to 2004. A poor public speaker lacking charisma, Yanukovych had been twice convicted for theft and assault in his youth, making him an unusual candidate for the highest political office. It is telling that a person like him could rise during the late Kuchma period, when loyalty to the clan and the trust of the oligarchs mattered more than political aptitude or suitable background. In cultivating his support base (primarily in the eastern and southern regions), Yanukovych relied on the political machine he created under the auspices of the Party of Regions.

Predictably, his main opponent was Viktor Yushchenko, supported by his Our Ukraine bloc. It was the first presidential election since 1991 in which the candidate of the party of power was not challenged by a scary-sounding orthodox communist. Instead, a cultured and charismatic proponent of free-market capitalism and Western democracy took on the unpolished functionary with a criminal past whose campaign focused on developing closer ties with Russia. However, Yanukovych was buoyed by generous funding from friendly oligarchs, the power of the state apparatus, and open support from Russian state-controlled television (then still a major news source, especially in the eastern regions of Ukraine).

There were 24 candidates on the ballot in the first round, but Yanukovych and Yushchenko squared off in the second round on November 21, 2004. A serious disparity appeared between the preliminary results released by the Central Electoral Commission and the exit polls. While the former gave victory to the official candidate, the latter indicated that the challenger had won. As it turned out, the Yanukovych team had gained access to the Central Electoral Commission's server and was modifying the numbers as they were coming in. The opposition had prepared for such a scenario, however, by bugging the phones in the Party of Regions headquarters to secure evidence of blatant electoral fraud (inadmissible in court, however), in addition to the usual ballot stuffing in the provinces.

The opposition then called for a mass rally on the Maidan. Spreading the word through text messaging and social media websites, Our Ukraine managed to gather some 200,000 people in the city center by November 22. Thousands more, especially from the western regions, made their way to the capital by bus or train. They occupied the Maidan and much of Khreshchatyk Boulevard by putting up large tents decorated with orange flags. Orange, the campaign color of Our Ukraine, held no particular symbolic significance until then; Yushchenko's campaign made a wise choice to avoid the red and black flag of radical Ukrainian nationalists and generally to focus on clean government rather than the promotion of the Ukrainian language.

As the West condemned the fraudulent elections, pro- opposition Orange rallies spread across the country, especially in central and western Ukraine, and a political standoff ensued. The government did not have the nerve to crack down on the Maidan, where 500,000 or more people gathered for regular rallies and concerts, while tens of thousands were present on the plaza at any given time. The radical student group *Pora* (It's Time!) put additional pressure on the authorities by blockading government buildings. Most important, the Supreme Court agreed to review the opposition's appeal, which meant postponing the official confirmation of Yanukovych as the winner.

The opposition needed continued mass support in order to keep up the pressure on the disoriented authorities, and the public delivered it emphatically, thus making the Orange Revolution a true popular revolution. The few pro-Yanukovych rallies in the eastern provinces were organized by the local authorities and, as a result, featured less than enthusiastic civil servants and paid protesters-for-hire. In contrast, large and numerous Orange rallies had a wide appeal and relied on a huge network of enthusiastic volunteers. By standing guard on the Maidan on chilly winter nights, the revolutionaries kept alive the hope of a new Ukraine.

Was Yushchenko poisoned, and were the culprits ever prosecuted?

For many in the West, the disfigured face of a poisoned presidential candidate remains one of the most memorable images from Ukraine's Orange Revolution. The scandal surrounding Viktor Yushchenko's poisoning before the elections played some role in sparking the revolution. For years the issue remained highly politicized in Ukraine, with accusations flying back and forth, but the truth of the matter remains elusive.

On the evening of September 5, 2004, Yushchenko arrived at a villa outside Kyiv for a secret meeting with Victor Smishko, the head of the Ukrainian Security Services (SBU), and his deputy, Volodymyr Satsiuk. Yushchenko was accompanied by a prominent businessman supporter, David Zhvaniia, who also served as head of the parliamentary subcommittee on organized crime and police corruption. In all likelihood, the two of them wanted to establish connections with the security service in order to help prevent provocations during the elections. The four wined and dined (the main dish that fateful evening was sushi), but the next morning Yushchenko became violently ill with abdominal pain and nausea.

To Ukrainian doctors, the symptoms seemed to indicate food poisoning or stomach flu, but Yushchenko's oligarch supporters had him airlifted to a private clinic in Austria for treatment. After Yushchenko's face became covered with lesions and half-paralyzed, more specific tests showed that the level of dioxin in his blood was some 50,000 times higher than normal.[3] The swelling of his abdominal organs indicated that the opposition candidate had unwittingly consumed dioxin with food or drink. The kind of dioxin used, TCDD, was widely known as a poisonous component of Agent Orange, the controversial herbicide sprayed by the US Army during the Vietnam War and which was later linked to multiple health problems. It was not immediately lethal, but it would certainly have incapacitated Yushchenko had it been left untreated.

However, Austrian and later Swiss doctors managed to stabilize him, and he returned to the campaign trail after a week, with an IV catheter in his back. He was required to return to Europe a few times for follow-up treatment. Yushchenko gave a speech in parliament accusing the powers that be of poisoning him. In light of the suspiciously timed flight of the deputy security service head and villa owner, Volodymyr Satsiuk, to Russia, Yushchenko's speech rallied supporters of the opposition. The poisoning also grabbed the attention of the international media, serving as further proof of the outgoing regime's criminal nature.

However, Yushchenko's opponents immediately questioned his version of events, blaming his blisters and lesions on sushi poisoning or a Botox injection gone wrong. An initial parliamentary commission of inquiry suggested in 2004 that a herpes infection was the likely cause, while a second claimed in 2009 that the candidate's team had falsified his blood tests by adding dioxin. Significantly, a criminal investigation into the poisoning made little progress, even during Yushchenko's presidency (2005–2010), ostensibly because of Russia's refusal to extradite several key figures. In the meantime, Yushchenko's companion at the dinner, David Zhvaniia, had a falling out with him and also started speaking out against the poisoning theory.

Public interest in the investigation into the poisoning declined as disillusionment with the new Orange authorities set in, especially after Yushchenko ceased being a major political player in 2010.

How was a peaceful resolution reached in the winter of 2004–2005?

Disunity among the key figures in the governing clique was a major factor favoring a peaceful resolution. Outgoing President Kuchma, who still controlled the police and the military, refused to stand by Yanukovych, the troublesome successor that the Donetsk clan had imposed on him. Kuchma appeared more interested in securing from whoever was going to be the next president a promise that the new administration would not seek to prosecute him or his family. The West also applied pressure at a critical moment, forcing all sides to accept high-level international mediators: the presidents of Poland and Lithuania, the EU foreign policy commissioner, and the speaker of the Russian parliament. The mediators arrived on November 26, just four days after the start of mass protests. It was now too late to attempt a violent dispersal of protesters, something Putin had reportedly advised behind the scenes.[4]

In this atmosphere of uncertainty, members of the political and economic elite started defecting to the Orange side. On November 27 the parliament passed a resolution condemning the fraudulent elections. Sensing defeat, Yanukovych's advisors from the Party of Regions played their last card, the threat of separatism. A conference of provincial governors from eastern Ukraine demanded a referendum on the country's federalization, while the authorities in Donetsk province actually scheduled a referendum on autonomy, which then had to be called off. The separatist movement did not have enough time to build momentum. At the time, there seemed to be little popular support in the east for such steps, which would have had no binding legal consequences in any case.

On December 2, 2004, the Supreme Court declared the results of the runoff election invalid and scheduled a repeat runoff for December 26. In order to make such a rerun constitutional, Ukrainian parliamentarians scrambled to put together a package satisfying all sides, at least in part. In addition to promulgating a new elections law that contained a clause on repeat elections and mandated personnel changes at the discredited Central Electoral Commission, the deal included constitutional reform transferring some powers from the president to the parliament. The repeat runoff on December 26 became the most monitored election in Ukrainian history, with 12,000 foreign observers and 300,000 Ukrainian ones. Yushchenko won, with 51.99 percent against Yanukovych's 44.19 percent, and was inaugurated as president in late January 2005.

The elections of 2004 demonstrated a change in Ukraine's electoral geography. Yushchenko won by carrying the central region in addition to the west, which at the time seemed to indicate an emerging civic national identity based on Ukrainian culture and democratic values, rather than the historical tradition of Ukrainian nationalism.[5] However, the southeast still voted for Yanukovych in the fair election, signaling the growth of a separate Ukrainian political identity based on cultural identification with Russia and the rejection of "Western" values, sentiments that the Party of Regions both inculcated and exploited.

Did the victors of the Orange Revolution manage to create a new Ukraine?

Splits in the Orange camp appeared almost immediately. Yushchenko had promised the prime minister's position to his valuable revolutionary ally, Yulia Tymoshenko, who was herself a powerful political player with her own party machine, the Yulia Tymoshenko Bloc (BYuT). Yet, the new president was quickly growing uncomfortable with Tymoshenko's independence and popularity. His own team in Our Ukraine detested the need to share power with the BYuT people, and one of Yushchenko's oligarch supporters, Petro Poroshenko, also had prime ministerial ambitions. Instead of implementing a consistent reform package, the leaders of the Orange side struggled to undermine each other and to score points with voters in advance of the 2006 parliamentary elections. Their power struggles led to popular disillusionment and allowed the Party of Regions to reconstitute its support base.

Tymoshenko's first term as prime minister turned out to be short-lived and controversial. She spent much of it fighting with Poroshenko, who was appointed head of the National Security and Defense Council, an organization with an ill-defined portfolio that he tried to build into an alternative cabinet. In the economic sphere, Tymoshenko showed a propensity for radical measures with a populist bent. Reversing insider privatizations of the late Kuchma period had been at the top of her economic agenda, and she managed to undo the biggest of them all, the 2004 sale of the country's largest steel mill, Kryvorizhstal, to the former president's son-in-law and another friendly oligarch (Viktor Pinchuk and Rinat Akhmetov, respectively) for US$800 million. At an open tender in 2005, the international giant Mittal Steel bought the same enterprise for US$4.8 billion. However, the government quietly shelved plans for additional re-privatizations after Western investors expressed concern over the instability that such a massive campaign would entail. Tymoshenko's populist side emerged in her attempts to micromanage the consumer basket, most memorably in her promises to control the rising prices of pork and gasoline. She also increased public sector wages and some social benefits, thereby creating mounting inflationary pressures. In the fall of 2005 the power struggle between Poroshenko and Tymoshenko escalated into open and mutual accusations of corruption. As a result, Poroshenko resigned his position and Tymoshenko was dismissed by the president.

The new cabinet, headed by Yuri Yekhanurov, a bureaucrat whom Yushchenko did not see as a threat, could not focus on any serious reforms either because the government was soon preoccupied by a "gas war" with Russia. As punishment for the Orange Revolution, the Russian monopoly Gazprom increased the price of gas for Ukraine from US$50 to US$230 for 1,000 cubic meters. With no deal reached by the year's end, on January 1, 2006, Russia cut gas deliveries to Ukraine, which then started diverting some of the gas being sent to Europe over Ukrainian territory. An international heating crisis in the middle of a cold winter forced all sides back to the negotiating table, but the new price of US$95 undermined the Ukrainian economy. It also became clear that in the future Russia would keep increasing it to the levels it charged other European countries.

Indeed, as far as the Russian leadership was concerned, there was no longer any reason to extend special treatment to Ukraine. Foreign policy came within Yushchenko's purview as president, and he pursued a policy of attempting to distance Ukraine from Russian influence. He established a separate ministry for "European integration," which proved unable to make much headway with the EU bureaucracy. As counterweights to the Russian-led CIS, Yushchenko attempted to develop such regional organizations as GUAM (Georgia, Ukraine, Azerbaijan, Moldova) and later, together with the Georgian president Mikheil Saakishvili, the Community of Democratic Choice, which included nine post-Soviet and post-communist Eastern European countries. During his triumphant visit to the United States as a victor of the Orange Revolution, Yushchenko self-assuredly discussed with President George W. Bush how Ukraine and the United States could work together to "support the advance of freedom" in Cuba and Belarus.[6] Putin's administration was no less offended by Yushchenko's cultural policies, which involved decreasing somewhat the previously dominant share of

Russian channels on Ukrainian television and mandating Ukrainian subtitles for Russian films.

How did Viktor Yanukovych return to power, first as prime minister and later as president?

President Yushchenko's popularity began sliding rapidly during his first year in office. The constitutional compromise of 2004 included the transfer of some powers from president to parliament, to take effect in 2006. Ukrainians expected Yushchenko to initiate radical reforms during this period, but he could not even contain the infighting inside his own camp. The president was fast acquiring a reputation for arriving late at all appointments, giving long-winded speeches, and general aloofness. Scandals involving some of his ministers and family members demonstrated that the Orange Revolution had not wiped out the culture of corruption and special deals among the Ukrainian elites. In dismissing Yulia Tymoshenko, the president also created a powerful political opposition, which claimed to uphold the revolution's ideals.

The parliamentary elections of 2006 resulted in the Party of Regions scoring 32 percent of the vote, BYuT coming second with 22.3, and Yushchenko's Our Ukraine third with 14 percent. An Orange parliamentary majority could only be formed if Yushchenko and Tymoshenko joined forces again and also secured the support of the Socialist Party with its 5.7 percent. But Yushchenko hated the prospect of having his erstwhile ally as prime minister again. The logic of political infighting made it easier for him to invite his old political nemesis, Yanukovych, to form the government. After a long summer of bargaining, the Party of Regions, the socialists, and the communists formed a coalition with the president's Our Ukraine, and parliament approved Yanukovych as the new prime minister in August 2006. After a brief period of revolutionary idealism, Ukrainian politics reverted to the old system of unstable, pragmatic coalitions, and powerful oligarchs dictating policies behind the scenes.

Yanukovych served as prime minister from August 2006 to December 2007. It was a chaotic, three-way power struggle between himself, president Yushchenko, and opposition leader Tymoshenko.

Meanwhile, the Party of Regions engaged in bribing or blackmailing MPs elected on other party lists to cross the floor and join it. In response, an outraged President Yushchenko dissolved parliament in April 2007, apparently an unconstitutional decision, and then began illegally dismissing the Constitutional Court judges to prevent the court from overturning his decrees. After a lengthy standoff and the resignation of 150 deputies from the Orange parties, new elections were finally held in September 2007. The positions of the three main parties did not change, although the Tymoshenko Bloc increased its popularity at the expense of the presidential party and the socialists. The Party of Regions received 34.4 percent of the vote, followed by BYuT with 30.7 and Our Ukraine with 14.2.

Yulia Tymoshenko became prime minister by forming a coalition with Our Ukraine and the Communist Party, but vicious infighting with the president consumed her second term. In September 2008 she ended up voting, together with Yanukovych and the communists, for a bill further limiting the president's powers and facilitating his impeachment. In response, Yushchenko dissolved parliament again and called snap elections. However, parliament refused to fund the elections, and Tymoshenko challenged the president's decision in a regional administrative court, which the president then dissolved. As the Ukrainian leaders engaged in these vindictive political games, the country was being drawn into the whirlwind of the 2008 global financial crisis. A new gas war with Russia only aggravated the economic slowdown.

The 2010 presidential elections were held amidst the economic crisis and widespread popular disillusionment with the Orange politicians. Yushchenko came in fifth in the initial round, with an embarrassing 5.45 percent of the vote. The once-disgraced Yanukovych then defeated his rival Tymoshenko in the subsequent runoff, capturing 48.95 percent of the vote to her 45.47. Voters apparently associated Tymoshenko's premiership with the economic downturn, while Yanukovych's more distant one was remembered as a time of relative prosperity. Still, it was a close election and, like most Ukrainian elections after independence, it demonstrated a political divide between the vote-rich southeast and the west. The center was a deal-breaker, as usual: Tymoshenko won a majority there, but only a small one.

Why was Yulia Tymoshenko imprisoned?

After losing to Yanukovych in February 2010, Tymoshenko fully expected the new authorities to go after her and her team by leveling various criminal charges against them, in keeping with the well-established custom in Ukrainian politics. But she did not leave without a fight. First, she tried to challenge the election results in court, in connection with the ballot rigging in Crimea in particular, and then refused to resign as prime minister. In March 2010 her cabinet was finally brought down by a parliamentary vote of non-confidence.

By the year's end, the new prosecutor general opened or reopened several investigations targeting Tymoshenko, including a case of alleged bribery of Supreme Court judges back in 2004 and an alleged misuse of the funds that Ukraine had received under the Kyoto Protocol for having reduced industrial emissions. The authorities also detained some of her ministers, including the former Minister of the Interior Yuri Lutsenko, charging them with abuse of office and misuse of funds. The Yanukovych team initially thought its best chance to convict Tymoshenko lay in the missing Kyoto funds, which she had allegedly spent on pensions instead of environmental projects. In December she was officially charged and ordered not to leave Kyiv without the prosecutor's permission. There was just one problem: even if it could be proven that she had misappropriated funds to pay for pensions that directly benefited Ukrainian seniors, such a move would almost certainly have been viewed positively by voters.

In May 2011 the prosecutor general charged Tymoshenko in another case, this one calculated to present her in a negative light for a domestic audience, but at the same time bound to be seen in the West as political misuse of the justice system. She was accused of abuse of power in connection with the 2009 Ukrainian-Russian gas deal.

This particularly nasty installment of the ongoing energy dispute with Russia was still fresh in popular memory in 2011, reinforced as it was by higher heating bills. Since the previous gas contract was set to expire at the end of 2008, the Russian and Ukrainian state gas companies engaged in their usual standoff over prices and the exact amount of the previous Ukrainian debt to Gazprom. As was also the case in 2006, the two countries began the new year without a deal. On January 1, Russia cut off gas supplies to Ukraine, which then started diverting some of the gas in transit to Europe. Russia then completely halted the flow of gas through Ukraine, leading to a notable decrease in gas deliveries to parts of southeastern Europe. Factories had to be stopped in Bulgaria, and Slovenia even declared a state of emergency.

The European Union stepped in to mediate, but it was still up to the Ukrainian government to reach a deal with Russia, and the former did not have many more cards to play. Tymoshenko and Putin (who was prime minister at the time and thus her counterpart) finally reached an agreement on January 18, with the flow of gas restored on January 20, 2010. The 10-year deal was not advantageous for Ukraine because it only received a 20-percent discount for one year, thereafter committing to pay at world market prices. The "discounted" price, US$360 per one thousand cubic meters, already represented a record high for Ukraine. The only thing Tymoshenko could be proud of was the elimination of intermediaries, who had been skimming billions under previous gas deals. Under the new agreement, Gazprom dealt directly with its Ukrainian equivalent, Naftohaz.

Soon after winning the presidency, Yanukovych signed a new gas deal with Russia. In exchange for extending the Russian navy's lease on its Black Sea base in Sevastopol, Crimea, from its previous expiry date of 2016 to 2042, Ukraine secured a multi-year 30-percent discount on Russian gas. Within a year, the prosecutor general laid charges against Tymoshenko, who had allegedly overstepped her authority in concluding the unfavorable 2009 deal. In October 2011 an obedient city-district court in Kyiv sentenced her to seven years in prison, with the additional stipulation that she be barred from holding public office after her release. The West condemned her sentencing as a clear case of politically motivated selective justice. In a similar high-profile case, former Minister of the Interior Yuri Lutsenko received a four-year sentence for abuse of office.

Tymoshenko began serving her term in a correctional facility in the city of Kharkiv, where she developed health issues (later diagnosed as spinal disc herniation) and twice went on a hunger strike. She was eventually moved to a prison hospital. With the victory of the EuroMaidan in 2014, parliament voted to remove from Ukrainian legislation the problematic clause under which

Tymoshenko was imprisoned. She returned to Ukrainian politics but was unable to reclaim her old popularity and influence, at least in the short term.

What caused the new popular revolt in late 2013?

Mass protests on the Maidan, prompted by the Yanukovych administration's last-minute refusal to sign an Association Agreement with the European Union, began in November 2014. But it would be wrong to see this spectacular political volte-face as the primary cause of the revolution. Popular dissatisfaction with the corrupt regime had been mounting for years, and the sudden diplomatic turn from Europe to Russia was simply the last straw. Very few protesters knew the details of the proposed Association Agreement, but "Europe" served as a popular shorthand slogan implying democracy, rule of law, and economic opportunity— all the things ordinary citizens found lacking in Yanukovych's Ukraine.

When Yanukovych became president in 2010, he and his clan sought to restore Kuchma's model of an oligarchic state. Its components included controlling the national media, helping the oligarchs to loot the country's economy, and maintaining a political balance between Russia and the West without getting too close to either—all with the ultimate aim of enriching the ruling group's families and allies. Ultimately, Yanukovych and his friends perfected Kuchma's scheme—too much so—by pushing Ukraine practically into bankruptcy. State procurements became the preferred method of instant enrichment for all sides involved, because of massive kickbacks, inflated costs, and outright embezzlement. The officials and oligarchs close to Yanukovych particularly liked mammoth construction projects generously funded by the state. In preparation for the 2012 European soccer cup, the state funded so many new airports, stadiums, roads, and high-speed trains that there was no way to patch the huge hole left in the budget. Nobody was even trying to find a solution, because the government was hoping for a bailout from either the West or Russia. The Yanukovych administration assumed that both these geopolitical rivals would be happy to spend US$15 billion and possibly more for the privilege of having Ukraine in their sphere of influence.

Carried away by the prospect of milking the country in perpetuity, the ruling elite misjudged the degree of popular discontent. Because their priority was exploitation of the system, the Yanukovych team did not initiate any economic reforms. The only political change came early in the new president's term, in 2010, when the Constitutional Court obediently struck down the 2004 political reform package that had transferred some presidential powers to the parliament. Having restored a strong presidency, albeit under questionable circumstances, Yanukovych proceeded to replace officials and governors across the country with party loyalists who were often Donbas natives. Yanukovych also consolidated his corrupt patronage network and used his own oligarchical group, composed of his sons and their friends and nicknamed the "Family," to move into the most lucrative sectors of the economy.

The president and his Party of Regions never followed up on their much-repeated promise to make Russian the second state language. Instead, parliament passed a more innocent-sounding law on regional languages in 2012, which gave regions with at least 10 percent of the population speaking a minority language the right to institute it as a second language of administration. The authorities were cautious when it came to fixing the elections, too, lest massive fraud incite another revolution. The 2012 parliamentary elections gave 34.4 percent of the vote to the Party of Regions and 30.7 percent to Yulia Tymoshenko's Fatherland Party, which took over from BYuT when electoral blocs were barred from participating. With the leader of the opposition in prison, Arsenii Yatseniuk led Fatherland's parliamentary faction. However, all opposition parties completely missed the start of popular protests in November 2013.

Everything was ready in November 2013 for the signing of Ukraine's Association Agreement with the European Union, which would provide Ukraine with free-trade status and significant funding for economic reforms. Only a few loose ends, such as the precise amount of the promised funding and an agreement allowing Tymoshenko to seek medical treatment in Europe, remained. But the Ukrainian authorities were also secretly talking to Russia, which threatened trade sanctions and in the end apparently promised the requested US$15 billion. On November 21, just a week before the scheduled signing ceremony, the Ukrainian

government suspended talks with the European Union and issued
a telling order to start aligning Ukrainian trade laws with those of
the Russian-led Customs Union. That evening Mustafa Nayem,
an influential, independent Ukrainian journalist of Afghani descent, posted an appeal on Facebook calling for a protest rally
on the Maidan.[7] Only about a thousand people showed up that
night, but in the following days tens and hundreds of thousands,
disaffected with their life under the Yanukovych regime, joined
the protests.

What role did the Ukrainian radical right play in the protests, and what symbols did they use?

Russian state-controlled media represented the EuroMaidan
Revolution as a coup by Ukrainian neo-Nazis bent on eradicating
Russian culture in Ukraine. In reality, the broad mass protest
movement that brought down Yanukovych was not ideological,
and its vague identification with "Europe" does not square with the
alleged neo-Nazi orientation. At the same time, the Ukrainian radical right did play a notable role in the revolution, which is worth
examining.

Prior to the Yanukovych presidency, radical Ukrainian nationalists
languished on the margins of politics. Unlike in most of Europe, in
Ukraine radical right parties were not represented in the parliament
and often functioned as mere front groups intended to take away
votes or credibility from the more mainstream opposition parties.
As disillusionment with the Orange governments set in, however,
the radical right Freedom party made an electoral breakthrough in
Galicia. During the 2009 and 2010 municipal elections there, it received roughly a third of the seats. Freedom was founded in the
early 1990s as the Social-National Party of Ukraine and used the
neo-Nazi Wolfsangel symbol. In the early 2000s it began moderating
its extremist image, changing the name to Freedom and discarding
the Wolfsangel, but some of its anti-Semitic and anti-Russian rhetoric remained.

The parliamentary elections of 2012 provided Freedom with an
opening into national politics. Amid growing dissatisfaction with
the kleptocratic Yanukovych regime, some voters began considering alternatives other than Tymoshenko. That year Freedom

harnessed a significant share of the protest vote in the western regions by promising to root out corruption, while styling themselves as the successors to such revered there nationalist figures as Stepan Bandera and his Organization of Ukrainian Nationalists (OUN). Freedom's total added up to 10.4 percent of the national vote, but it performed very poorly in east-central Ukraine, except for Kyiv. Another populist party managed to burst onto the national political stage with 14 percent of the total vote, but it was not a right-wing one. The aptly named UDAR (Ukrainian Democratic Alliance for Reform)—an acronym meaning "punch" that riffed on party leader Vitalii Klitschko's background as a heavyweight boxing champion—established itself as a credible opposition force in east-central Ukraine. This party grew into a major national force during the revolution, whereas Freedom lost much of its appeal with the fall of the Yanukovych regime. In 2014 it failed to clear the 5-percent threshold to receive the party allotment of parliamentary seats, although six of its members were elected in single-mandate districts in western Ukraine.

However, Freedom did play an important role during the revolution itself. Unlike the centrist opposition parties, it could supply militarized groups of radical youth for clashes with riot police. So, too, could the new entrant on the political scene, Right Sector. The latter was created in the spring of 2013 from a merger of several small right-wing nationalist groups, and it soon outdid Freedom in radicalism. Unlike the latter, Right Sector openly used as its official flag the OUN's red and black standard. During the phase of non-violent resistance on the Maidan, the radical right was less visible. In fact, field research by Ukrainian sociologists showed that only a small minority of protesters belonged to any political party at all: 3.9 percent in December 2013.[8] All that changed during the violent stage of the protests in January and February 2014. When the Yanukovych regime attempted a forceful crackdown on the Maidan, the radical right led the way in organizing an equally violent resistance. Right Sector and Freedom activists still constituted a small minority in the revolutionary crowd, but they were the best organized and the most visible.

It was at this critical juncture that some symbols and slogans of the radical right were introduced into the protest culture.

The nationalist greeting from the 1940s, "Slava Ukraini!" (Glory to Ukraine!), and its response, "Heroiam slava!" (Glory to the heroes!), acquired new meaning on the Maidan. When used by protesters, such slogans referred to a hoped-for democratic and pro-Western Ukraine and regarded as heroes those who had fallen in service to their cause. Tellingly, another nationalist slogan from the 1940s, "Slava natsii, smert voroham!" (Glory to the Nation, Death to Enemies), did not catch on. Thanks to Right Sector, but also Freedom, which used it unofficially, the red and black flag of the OUN became more acceptable to patriotic citizens outside western Ukraine. Images of Stepan Bandera, too, became widespread, although not everyone on the Maidan was comfortable with them, leading to the quiet replacement of a large, prominently displayed Bandera portrait with one of Taras Shevchenko, a nineteenth-century national bard and a much less divisive symbol of Ukrainian identity. Still, it can be argued that in the course of the EuroMaidan Revolution, the image of Bandera acquired new meaning as a symbol of resistance to the corrupt, Russian-sponsored regime, quite apart from the historical Bandera's role as a purveyor of exclusivist, ethno-nationalism.

Just as Freedom lost much of its popular support with the disappearance of its arch-nemesis Yanukovych, so did Right Sector. In the parliamentary elections of 2014, only 1.8 percent of voters nationwide supported Right Sector. During the presidential elections that took place the same year, its leader, Dmytro Yarosh, obtained just 0.7 percent of the vote, although Russian state television reported at one point on election night that he was allegedly ahead of all the other candidates.[9]

While the departure of Yanukovych reduced the radical right to a relatively small political niche, it gained disproportionate media exposure again, with the start of the Donbas war in the spring of 2014, largely because it served Russian interests to do so. However, radical right activists did help to form several volunteer battalions that took part in fighting alongside the Ukrainian army, and one of them, Azov Battalion, continues to use the Wolfsangel as its official emblem. Another battalion, which branched out from Azov, took the name "OUN," although the Ukrainian authorities refused to register it.

What led to the high number of casualties on the Maidan in 2013–2014, as opposed to 2004?

In 2004 the police and the military were still subordinated to outgoing President Kuchma, who was not prepared to authorize a brutal crackdown that would benefit his successor. In 2013, however, the Yanukovych administration was fully in control of law enforcement bodies and the armed forces. Unlike Kuchma in 2004, the new regime also had a lot to lose. After three years in power, the Party of Regions had installed its loyalists in key posts across the country and had established the most efficient schemes for milking the country's economy. Yanukovych and his cronies were also looking forward to securing a second presidential term. In addition, they had imprisoned Tymoshenko on dubious charges and fully expected to end up in prison themselves, should the revolution win. Putin apparently also urged toughness from behind the scenes.[10]

For all of these reasons, the authorities were determined not to give in to the mass protests. But they could not break them up either. On November 30, 2013, the regime's first attempt to remove the tent city and disperse the protesters caused their ranks to swell. As soon as social media spread the news, Kyivites started flocking to the Maidan in the tens of thousands, and supporters from other regions left for the capital, too. At least half a million attended a mass rally on the Maidan on December 1. To break the deadlock, on January 16, 2014, the government eventually imitated the Russian example by ramming through parliament draconian anti-protest legislation that limited freedom of speech and assembly, as well as NGO activity. Yet such a blatant restriction of democracy, together with subsequent attempts to break up the Maidan protests by force, met with an equally violent response.

Street fighting ensued in central Kyiv between January 19 and 25, with riot police using rubber bullets and water cannons, while the protesters armed themselves with cobblestones and Molotov cocktails. On January 22 the first three protesters were shot dead, allegedly by special-forces snipers. This event shocked the nation, as it represented the first time in over half a century that protesters were killed by the governing authorities in Ukraine. Amid calls for a general strike, EuroMaidan activists in the western regions began occupying government buildings.

The so-called *titushky* contributed greatly to the escalation of violence. They were young men from the provinces, often members of local athletic clubs, hired by the Party of Regions to pose as anti-Maidan protesters. The name refers to one Vadym Titushko, a paid thug from the city of Bila Tserkva, who had been convicted of physically assaulting journalists in 2013, before the EuroMaidan. Although they did not carry firearms, titushky freely employed violence and coordinated their actions with the police. During the winter of 2013–2014, they camped out in a park near the Ukrainian parliament, where several protesters died in clashes. *Titushky* also roamed the streets beating up protesters both in the capital and in other large cities, such as Kharkiv.

Several more deaths resulted from the skirmishes in Kyiv during the next month, but the violence reached its crescendo between February 18 and 20, 2014. The protesters' march on parliament led to clashes with the police, who responded by attempting to storm the barricaded tent city on the Maidan. Most of the deaths occurred on February 20, during fighting on the streets leading from the Maidan uphill to the government quarter. Whether or not government forces received an authorization to shoot, they definitely fired upon protesters, and in some cases the latter returned fire. It was not an all-out firefight, which would have caused casualties in the thousands. Shootings occurred covertly during the tensest moment of the showdown, in which the usual tactics were swarming, throwing rocks, and beatings with sticks. At one point, the protesters even constructed a catapult to throw various projectiles at the riot police. Still, the death toll was rising. By the end of the day on February 20, 67 protesters and 13 police officers were reported killed and hundreds wounded. Sixteen more protesters died later in hospital.

The bloodshed had immediate political consequences. Late on February 20, parliament condemned the use of deadly force against the protesters. At the same time, the three main opposition parties, including Freedom but not Right Sector, issued a statement distancing themselves from armed violence. That same day, the minister of the interior gave an order to distribute live ammunition to all police officers and authorized them to use it; then he slipped out of the capital. Meanwhile, the foreign ministers of France, Germany, and Poland arrived to mediate the negotiations between the two opposing sides. As word spread in the afternoon of February 21 that a deal had been reached between Yanukovych and the opposition, riot policemen who had been guarding government buildings unexpectedly began to desert their posts. They were not prepared to stand by the government in the event of an all-out armed assault and feared that the authorities would use them as scapegoats afterward. This move apparently came as a nasty surprise to Yanukovych, who saw from his office window how the units guarding the presidential administration building were leaving. He now had no option but to flee. Protesters organized into "Maidan Self-Defense" units took over government buildings, and the army either sided with them or remained neutral.

Where did Yanukovych seek asylum, and how was the transfer of power formalized?

The deal reached on February 21 included the restoration of the 2004 constitutional reform, early presidential elections no later than December, and an amnesty for protesters. The latter were to vacate all the occupied government buildings and surrender all illegally captured firearms. The authorities promised to refrain from using violence. The foreign ministers of the three EU countries signed the document as witnesses, but the Russian mediator refused to sign, probably in order to leave Putin the option of rejecting it as a concession extracted from Yanukovych under duress. As foreign mediators were leaving the building, however, they too beheld the puzzling sight of riot police deserting their posts. Neither they nor the opposition leaders realized that this signaled the immediate collapse of the Yanukovych regime.

That evening, political elites started defecting to the opposition. Parliament voted to restore the 2004 constitutional reform, suspend the minister of the interior, and return all troops to their barracks. Yanukovych escaped to his opulent residence in Mezhyhiria, just outside of Kyiv, where his staff began loading valuables into black, armored SUVs. Still not realizing what was happening, the leaders of the opposition went to the Maidan late at night to obtain symbolic approval of the deal. They were booed. Right Sector leader Dmytro Yarosh and the self-proclaimed "captains" of Maidan Self-Defense objected that the agreement did not go far enough. Supported by the crowds, they called for the arrest of the minister of the interior and the immediate resignation of Yanukovych.

On February 22 the president flew to the eastern city of Kharkiv, but failing to find much support there, he went underground. Most ministers and other politicians who were closely involved in the regime's corrupt schemes also escaped. Meanwhile, in Kyiv, many of Yanukovych's former political supporters voted together with the opposition to remove the president from power for abandoning his duties. They chose this clause, which is not in the Constitution, over a lengthy impeachment procedure that would have involved laying criminal charges and a review by the Constitutional Court. The parliament elected Oleksandr Turchynov of the Fatherland Party as the new speaker and acting president. It also scheduled presidential elections for May 25, 2014, and made legislative changes to annul Yulia Tymoshenko's conviction. The Party of Regions issued a statement distancing itself from the ousted president.

In the meantime, Yanukovych made his way secretly to the Crimea, where he apparently sought shelter at a Russian naval base and was subsequently taken to Russia. On February 27 the Russian government announced that it was granting asylum to Yanukovych, whom it still considered the legitimate president of Ukraine. In subsequent months Yanukovych gave several press conferences denouncing the "neo-Nazi coup" in the Russian city of Rostov-on-the-Don, just east of his traditional power base in the Donbas. Reportedly, he purchased a luxurious estate outside Moscow, which he now calls home. The new Ukrainian prosecutor general has charged Yanukovych in connection with the shootings of protesters, and in January 2015 Interpol placed the former president on its wanted list in connection with embezzlement charges.

Was either of the two Ukrainian revolutions the result of a Western conspiracy?

Conspiracy theories abound in regard to both the Orange and the EuroMaidan revolutions, in part because Russian state media and the Yanukovych camp persist in trying to present them as American plots not reflecting the will of the Ukrainian people.

The Orange Revolution had generic similarities to other so-called "color revolutions" of the first decade of the 2000s, in particular in Serbia in 2000 and in Georgia in 2003, which used nonviolent resistance to overthrow corrupt political regimes, often in the aftermath of rigged elections. Western agencies had indeed been involved with funding the training of political activists in democratic political practices, including tactics of grassroots political campaigning and nonviolent resistance. Notably, members of the Ukrainian organization *Pora* studied the experience of similar radical student groups, like *Otpor* in Serbia and *Kmara* in Georgia. However, the foreign agencies in question, including Freedom House and USAID, as well as the International Republican Institute and the National Democratic Institute for International Affairs, did not initiate these programs just before the revolts with the specific goal of removing an unfriendly regime from power. For many years such agencies have funded various projects in these countries with the general aim of promoting democratic governance and developing the public sphere. Moreover, during the period leading up to the Orange Revolution, the bulk of funding for building political networks and hiring foreign political consultants came from domestic sources, namely opposition-friendly oligarchs.

In any case, Russia has reportedly spent much larger sums that the West in funding Yanukovych's electoral campaign and the counterprotests during the Orange Revolution, contributing an estimated US$300 million versus an alleged US$65 million from Western countries.[11] Additionally, President Putin had campaigned openly on behalf of Yanukovych and had endorsed the latter's fraudulent electoral win.

If the Orange Revolution can be portrayed somewhat credibly as a political project that opposition parties brought slowly to fruition with some assistance from abroad, it still took spectacular electoral fraud on the part of the governing authorities to cause the rebellion. It is much more difficult to make a similar case for the EuroMaidan Revolution, which erupted spontaneously and caught the opposition parties and the West unprepared. Western and domestic opposition leaders often fell behind the rapid tempo of revolutionary events in the solutions they offered. Therefore, those seeking to present the EuroMaidan Revolution as a Western plot had to clutch at the most far-fetched conspiracy theories. The controversial American filmmaker Oliver Stone, for example, has advocated a theory emanating from the Yanukovych circle that "third-party" shooters were allegedly operating on the Maidan, killing both protesters and police in order to force a regime change. This theory insinuates that "CIA fingerprints" were all over the EuroMaidan.[12] An opposing conspiracy theory has also been advanced by some in Ukraine, namely that the mysterious snipers belonged to the Russian special forces, who were attempting to provoke a violent crackdown on the protests. In fact, bullets recovered from the bodies came from various types of firearms, mostly standard police or military issue.

What matters for the study of revolutions, however, is the big picture of a corrupt regime trying to restrict democracy and the willingness of disaffected citizens to engage in civil disobedience when faced with a particularly egregious subversion of the democratic process. It was beyond the power of any Western agency to bring hundreds of thousands of Ukrainians to the Maidan and make them risk their lives by standing up to the venal governing elites. It is equally beyond the power of any Western organization to complete the revolution by building a democratic and prosperous Ukraine.

6

RUSSIA'S ANNEXATION
OF THE CRIMEA AND THE WAR
IN THE DONBAS

What shared characteristics led the Crimean Peninsula and
the Donbas region to become conflict zones?

These two regions are not in immediate geographic proximity to one another. The Donbas, comprising Donetsk and Luhansk provinces, is Ukraine's easternmost region, bordering on Russia in the north and east. The Crimean Peninsula, which was constituted politically within Ukraine as the Autonomous Republic of the Crimea, was the country's southernmost tip extending into the Black Sea. The two regions are separated by Zaporizhia and Kherson provinces, which showed few signs of political separatism or pro-Russian sympathies. Historically, the Crimea was part of the Russian Soviet Federative Socialist Republic (SFSR) between 1920 and 1954, but the Donbas was not.

Moreover, the economic profiles of the two regions are diametrically opposed. The Crimea's economy is based primarily on tourism, with winemaking and servicing the naval bases the only notable industries prior to the exploration of offshore and onshore gas fields starting in the 2000s. The Donbas, in contrast, is an old industrial region, with coal mines and steel mills dominating its steppe landscape since the late nineteenth century. Many older mines and factories have become obsolete, but the Donbas's metallurgy and chemical industries have found their place in the global economy of the twenty-first century.

A look at the ethnic composition of the two regions does not reveal an obvious connection either. Whereas ethnic Russians have constituted a majority of the Crimean population ever since Stalin's deportation of the Crimean Tatars in 1944, ethnic Ukrainians have continued to outnumber them in the two Donbas provinces. As of the last census in 2001, the main ethnic groups in the Crimea were Russians (58.5 percent), Ukrainians (24.4 percent), and Crimean Tatars (12.1 percent). In the Donbas, ethnic Ukrainians constituted 56.9 percent in Donetsk province, where 38.2 percent claimed Russian ethnicity, and 58 percent in Luhansk province, which had 39.1 percent Russians. The proportion of ethnic Russians in the Donbas is thus the highest of any Ukrainian region except the Crimea, but they are not a majority there.

However, the same 2001 census put the Crimea and the Donbas in a category of their own as the only two Ukrainian regions where the majority of the population claimed Russian as their native language: 77 percent in the Crimea, 68.8 percent in Luhansk, and 74.9 percent in Donetsk province. This discrepancy between self-identified ethnicity and mother tongue is indicative of the cultural assimilation of Ukrainians during the late Soviet period. The resulting hybrid identity often correlated with an allegiance to the Soviet version of modernity and, after its disappearance, to the strong paternalistic regime in Russia.

In both regions, the local identity also has strong symbolic connections to the imperial past. Generations of Russian journalists and schoolteachers have perpetuated the image of Sevastopol as the "city of Russian naval glory," heroically defended both during the Crimean War and World War II. Soviet films, songs, and political pronouncements lionized the (always Russian-speaking) Donbas miners as model workers, shouldering their patriotic duty to provide the country with fuel. Such historical myth-making became ingrained in local identities. More important, however, it became encoded in Soviet great-power ideology, which Putin's Russia is trying to revive.

In the decades since Ukraine's independence, both regions initially served as the electoral base of the Communist Party; this residual allegiance made sense, as both regions cultivated identities linked to the Soviet past, in addition to being heavily Russian-speaking. In the 2000s, however, Yanukovych's Party of Regions gradually absorbed the Communist Party's constituency. The new political force promoted a Russophone regional identity that was also anchored to the belief in a strong state and extensive state services. When it was losing on the national political scene, the Yanukovych camp tried twice, in 2004 and 2014, to play the regional separatism card. As present-day events have shown, because of Russia's proximity and increasingly assertive policies, this was a dangerous game.

When mass protests began in 2014, the Yanukovych clique employed a familiar strategy of framing the unrest as an identity conflict, a war against Russian culture in Ukraine. Yet, they soon lost control over the genie they summoned when Putin's Russia marched in to "protect" its "compatriots." It mattered little whether the latter even wanted to be protected, for on the eve of the war, opinion polls in the Donbas showed that only about a third favored separating from Ukraine and joining Russia.[1] The conflict quickly shifted its focus from building a multicultural Ukraine to rebuilding a greater Russia.

What was "New Russia," and why did President Putin revive this concept?

Several years after the collapse of the Soviet Union, populist Russian politicians discovered that claiming the Crimea as a Russian territory was an easy way to score points with a nationalistic audience. They also spoke ominously about the need to protect Russians and Russian-speakers living in the other former Soviet republics, especially in the Baltic states, Ukraine, and Central Asia. Putin's administration inherited this populist rhetoric, but also framed it with explicit references to the empire of the tsars—and acted on it.

President Putin first reintroduced the tsarist concept of New Russia (Novorossiia) into modern Russian political discourse during his televised question-and-answer session on April 17, 2014. This town hall–style show was broadcast nationally more than a month after the Crimea's annexation, just as the first signs of "separatist insurgency" appeared in the Donbas. The timing was significant, as the Russian leader was trying to link the territory already seized to the regions where trouble was about to begin. He announced that the six provinces comprising all of southeastern Ukraine were "New Russia," which "had not been part of Ukraine in tsarist times" before the Soviet government transferred these lands to Ukraine in the 1920s, "God knows why."[2]

Putin's sweeping statement ignored the fact that the Russian Empire did not have an administrative unit named "Ukraine"; what is now the Ukrainian heartland was officially known as "Little Russia." In other words, if an imperial province was called "New Russia," it does not follow that it had been populated by Russians or that the Russian state today should have any special relation to it. In fact, there existed two "New Russias," but with different borders: one in 1764–1802 and another in 1822–1874, but neither included the major city of Kharkiv, which Putin included on his list. Created on the southern steppes recently reclaimed from the Ottomans, these provinces were sparsely populated at first. The tsarist government invited Italian, Greek, Bulgarian, Mennonite, and other foreign settlers to come there, but by the time of the 1897 census, Ukrainian peasants constituted a majority in every province that had been parceled out from the former New Russia, even in Taurida province, which at the time included the Crimea. "New Russia" was thus not really "Russian" from the get-go.

The pro-Russian militants in the Donbas took their cue from the Kremlin. They created a New Russia political party, an army of New Russia, and an official flag of New Russia; all this happened even before the self-proclaimed Donetsk People's Republic and Luhansk People's Republic formally established the union state of New Russia, into which they hoped to bring six more Ukrainian provinces. The changing terminology reveals an important ideological shift among local separatists and Russian volunteers in the Donbas. At first they operated within the old Soviet paradigm by creating the two "people's republics" and proclaiming the Union of People's Republics. But that sounded too much like a restoration of the Soviet Union. Putin offered them a different solution: thinking in terms of the Russian Empire.

It was also an important ideological transition for Putin's Russia. The protection of ethnic Russians had exhausted its potential as a political tool with the absorption of the Crimea. Ukraine's Russian-speaking population proved an elusive constituency lacking a common political identity. Kyiv residents remain mostly Russophone, for example, but they vote overwhelmingly for pro-Ukrainian parties. Soldiers and volunteers on the Ukrainian side speak mostly Russian, just as their opponents do. A political project harking back to the Russian Empire thus appeared as the next logical step for the Putin administration. But the resurrection of the imperial past also meant delegitimizing Ukrainian nationhood and increasing the likelihood of war.

Who are the Crimean Tatars?

The notion of the Crimea as a "Russian land" glosses over the peninsula's rich multicultural past before its conquest by the Russian Empire. It also conceals the inconvenient fact that ethnic Russians came to constitute a majority in the Crimea only after Stalin had all the Crimean Tatars deported on false charges of treason in 1944.

Beginning in the seventh century BC, Aegean Greek cities established trading outposts on the Crimean coast. These cities developed over time into thriving colonies. The Greeks traded with the nomads who controlled the rest of the peninsula and the lands beyond: at first, the Iranian-speaking Scythians, later the Sarmatians, and others. Some Germanic Goths apparently survived in the Crimea for a millennium after the Huns displaced them from what is now mainland Ukraine in the fourth century, incidentally prompting Hitler to consider the Crimea a historical "German land." During World War II, the Nazis conducted archaeological research on the Crimean Peninsula and renamed its capital of Simferopol as Gothenburg.

The masters of the Crimean coast changed over the centuries, and by the thirteenth century AD the Italian maritime republics of Venice and Genoa controlled trading emporiums on the Black Sea's northern coast. The Crimean hinterland also saw new nomadic, usually Turkic-speaking, peoples come and go, often assimilated by new arrivals. In the mid-thirteenth century the Mongols conquered the Crimea at the same time as they did the Rus principalities, but when their colossal empire began disintegrating two centuries later, the local Turkic elites invited a descendent of Genghis Khan to serve as the ruler of their own polity, the Crimean Khanate (1449–1774). However, the Khanate could not take the fortified Italian cities on the coast without the assistance of the ascendant great power across the Black Sea, the Ottoman Empire, and as a result it quickly became a vassal state of the Ottoman Sultans.

The Crimea's Turkic-speaking population gradually coalesced into the Crimean Tatar, or *Kirimli*, ethnic group that was ruled by khans of the Giray dynasty. Their palace and the minarets still standing in the city of Bakhchysarai serve as reminders of a rich Muslim Tatar cultural past in the Crimea. The Khanate generated much of its wealth from the slave trade, frequently raiding and taking captives from what is now Ukraine. It fell as a result of Russian imperial expansion southward in the late eighteenth century, after Catherine the Great's generals won a war against the Ottomans. In 1783 the tsarina incorporated the Khanate into her empire. Many Crimean Tatars took refuge in Turkey, and over half of the entire population was expelled by the Russian government or emigrated during several Russo-Turkish wars that were waged in the nineteenth century. Thousands escaped on Allied ships after the Crimean War.

Only since the 1860s, after the forced mass exodus of the Tatars, have Russian and Ukrainian settlers come to constitute any significant share of the Crimean population. The peninsula soon became a popular resort for the empire's upper and middle classes, as well as a major winemaking area. By 1897 the remaining Crimean Tatars still constituted the largest ethnic group, with 35.6 percent of the population. Mainly engaged in the service industry, the "European" settlers perceived the Tatars as second-class citizens, yet the small secular Tatar intelligentsia was already developing a modern national identity and a network of cultural organizations.

During the Revolution the Crimea became detached from the rest of Taurida province, which had a Ukrainian majority and had become part of Ukraine. The peninsula served as the last stronghold of the Russian Whites during the civil war, until the Reds stormed it in November 1920. By then the Russians had become a plurality in the Crimea, but the Bolsheviks recognized it as the historical homeland of the Crimean Tatars and briefly imagined it as a potential revolutionary bridgehead into the Islamic world. Ethnography and politics determined the Soviet authorities' decision to make the Crimea part of the Russian SFSR but constitute it as an autonomous republic, which meant recognizing the region's distinct ethnic character. During the "indigenization" of the 1920s, the Soviet state promoted the development of the Crimean Tatar culture.

The Crimea was under Nazi occupation for only about a year, in 1942–1943, but after its liberation Stalin perceived the Crimean Tatars as a nation of traitors. In fact, the degree of collaboration was not out of proportion to other occupied areas; only some 9,000

Tatars joined the German auxiliary Tatar Legion, and many more served in the Red Army. Still, in May 1944 the NKVD rounded up and deported to Central Asia the entire Crimean Tatar population of 239,000, with tens of thousands dying of starvation and disease in cattle cars along the way or in the place of exile, resulting in the death of some 100,000 people. The survivors' civil rights were restored in 1967, but the Soviet state allowed their mass return to the Crimea only in the late 1980s.

Why was the Crimea transferred from the Russian SFSR to the Ukrainian SSR in 1954?

Following the deportation of the Crimean Tatars, the Soviet authorities dissolved the autonomous republic, turning the Crimea into an ordinary province within the Russian SFSR. The share of ethnic Russians among the population, which stood at 49.6 percent in 1939, shot up to over 70 percent in the postwar years because of the Tatars' disappearance and a substantial migration from Russia proper. The only other significant ethnic group on the peninsula was now the Ukrainians, who formed just over 20 percent of the population during the first postwar decade.

Nevertheless, in February 1954, Stalin's successor, Nikita Khrushchev, initiated the transfer of the Crimea from the Soviet Russian to the Soviet Ukrainian republic. He was probably motivated by two considerations. First, the exact accommodation of ethnographic borders seemed far less important in the 1950s than it did immediately after the revolution. The Soviet leaders saw nationalism as having been largely disarmed and were convinced that the merging of ethnic identities into a single, all-union (read: Russian) one was close at hand. Efficient administration of more compact economic regions appeared far more important at the time. The Crimean Peninsula presented a reasonable case on these grounds because it had no land connection to Russia but was linked to Ukraine in the north by the narrow Perekop Isthmus, through which trains packed with vacationers and most goods arrived. The peninsula also received its electricity and fresh water from Ukraine.

Khrushchev's other motive likely involved pleasing the Ukrainian elites by enlarging their domain. An ethnic Russian whose working-class family moved to the Donbas when he was 14, Khrushchev began his party career in the Ukrainian SSR. After returning to Ukraine as its party boss, a post that he held between 1938 and 1949, Khrushchev considered the republic his power base, where he sought to keep the local functionaries happy and promoted many of them to important positions in Moscow.

Of course, the official pronouncements did not mention this second reason, emphasizing instead the symbolic occasion for the transfer: the tercentenary of the 1654 Treaty of Pereiaslav, which brought the Ukrainian Cossack polity under the tsar's protection. In the official interpretation, the transfer served as a token of eternal Russo-Ukrainian friendship. According to the Soviet Constitution, the procedure involved the executive organ of the Russian republic's parliament proposing the transfer, the executive of the Soviet parliament approving it, and the Ukrainian counterparts accepting it. However, after the Soviet collapse, some Russian politicians questioned the legality of a procedure that did not entail full parliamentary discussions, even though such a process would have been meaningless in Soviet times.

Furthermore, the decrees did not spell out that the city and naval base of Sevastopol was also included in the transfer. Sevastopol's situation was unclear because it had enjoyed special status as an "exempt" municipality since 1948, which meant that it was not subordinated to provincial authorities and received funding directly from Moscow. After 1954 the Soviet authorities used elections and various party structures to place the city more explicitly under Ukrainian administration but never really legalized the de facto transfer of its special economic-administrative status from Russia to Ukraine. This, too, seemed insignificant in Soviet times, but this lapse paved the way for Russian-Ukrainian discord after the collapse of the communist system.

Did the Crimea try to separate from Ukraine in the 1990s?

The last years of the Soviet Union and the first years after its collapse proved to be a confusing period in Crimean politics. The local communist functionaries at first managed to control the levers of power, but they faced a number of challenges: reaching an understanding with the new Ukrainian authorities in Kyiv, dealing with the return of the Crimean Tatars, and responding to the birth of popular politics on the Crimean Peninsula. Russia's forceful foreign policy soon complicated things even further, not least because the former Soviet Black Sea Fleet remained stationed in Sevastopol while Ukraine and Russia negotiated its fate.

The Soviet Union was still in existence in January 1991, when the Crimean leadership organized a successful referendum on restoring the autonomous republic. The plebiscite was largely a preemptive measure aimed against the Crimean Tatars, who might otherwise demand the restoration of "their" autonomous republic, a move potentially involving affirmative-action and land-restitution rights as the indigenous people. The result also afforded the Crimean authorities a stronger position in their negotiations with Kyiv. Indeed, a rapprochement of sorts was apparently reached, because the Ukrainian parliament did grant the peninsula the status of an autonomous republic, and in return the local bosses did not sabotage the December 1991 Ukrainian referendum on national independence. The "yes" vote reached 54.2 percent in the Crimea, albeit with the lowest voter turnout rate in the country at 60 percent.

By 1992, a year of economic collapse and escalating nationalist rhetoric in the post-Soviet states, Russian involvement had aggravated relations between Kyiv and the Crimean capital of Simferopol. The Russian parliament debated the legitimacy of the 1954 transfer, and the Russian vice president spoke openly in favor of reclaiming the Crimea. As Russian-Ukrainian tensions over the Black Sea Fleet heated up, pro-Russian populist political parties also increased their influence in the Crimea itself. In May 1992 the Crimean parliament declared the autonomous republic's independence and adopted a constitution; Kyiv immediately dismissed both acts as illegal. The Crimean authorities soon withdrew the declaration of independence after Kyiv agreed to grant them even more powers.

The Crimean functionaries of the old communist lineage soon lost control over the separatist movement that they had used as leverage against Kyiv. When the Crimean parliament created the position of republican president in 1994, the populist activist Yuri Meshkov from the "Russia" electoral bloc won the elections. A tug of war ensued between his administration and the Kyiv authorities, but the Russian position proved decisive. Using military means, President

Yeltsin of Russia had recently defeated his parliament and vice president, both of which represented a more extreme nationalistic position with respect to the Crimea. Accordingly, Yeltsin refused to meet with Meshkov and showed little enthusiasm for a major conflict with Ukraine. In 1995 the Ukrainian parliament annulled the "separatist" 1992 version of the Crimean Constitution, together with the president's position. Meshkov moved to Russia and communist functionaries returned to power in the Crimea. Beginning in the first decade of the 2000s, the Communist Party of the Crimea lost political influence, while the Party of Regions recruited into its ranks the more dynamic local establishment figures.

The rights of the Crimean Tatars continued to be neglected throughout this period. Since the late 1980s, some 250,000 of them returned to the peninsula without any assistance from either the Ukrainian or Crimean authorities. By the time of the 2001 census, the Tatars constituted 12.1 percent of the population, and their share has likely increased because of a higher birth rate and continued repatriation. However, they remain politically underrepresented. In 1991 the Crimean Tatars established their own representative organ, the Kurultai, and its executive arm, the Mejlis, which tended to side with Ukrainian democratic parties against the pro-Russian majority in the Crimea.

Was there a previous conflict between Russia and Ukraine over the Black Sea Fleet, and how was it resolved?

When the Soviet Union disintegrated, the successor states divided its armed forces according to the territorial principle. The formations stationed on Ukrainian territory were to become, together with all their property, part of the Ukrainian army. Officers had a choice as to whether to stay, and many returned to their home republics during the transition period. The men were conscripts from all over the Soviet Union; they also left after serving their two-year terms (or three years in the navy). The strategic (nuclear) forces were the only service excluded from this partitioning arrangement, theoretically subjecting the navy to division as well, but in reality most of the principal naval bases remained on Russian territory; few of the former Soviet republics would have had the resources to maintain the huge and aging Soviet fleet.

What set Russia and Ukraine at loggerheads over the navy was not the partition as such but the fact that the Black Sea Fleet's principal naval base in Sevastopol became part of Ukraine. There was simply no way to move the large navy to the eastern (Russian) shore of the Black Sea, where no convenient harbors existed. Just before the Soviet Union officially ceased to exist in December 1991, the central naval command transferred the only Soviet full-size aircraft carrier from the Black to the Northern Sea, so as to secure it for Russia, but hundreds of other ships remained. To complicate matters further, the city of Sevastopol occupied a nearly mythical place in Russian historical memory because of the city's heroic defense in both the Crimean War and World War II. Although in both cases it was defended by multinational troops, which including Ukrainians, these events became enshrined as "Russian" in imperial war mythology, a historical elision that persisted throughout the tsarist and Soviet eras and which continues to be perpetuated in Putin's Russia.

In 1992 the presidents of both Russia and Ukraine issued decrees claiming jurisdiction over the Black Sea Fleet before agreeing to operate it jointly for three years. In reality, this meant preserving the status quo: a de facto Russian navy on Ukrainian territory. At the same time, Ukraine started building its own small naval force in the port city of Odesa, which is not on the Crimean Peninsula. The Ukrainian-built frigate *Hetman Sahaidachny* (commissioned in 1993) became the flagship of the Ukrainian navy. Most other ships then constructed or repaired in Ukrainian docks were sold for scrap metal, often as a result of corrupt deals, with none more spectacular than that involving the unfinished aircraft carrier *Varyag*, which was acquired by a Hong Kong company for US$20 million as a floating casino, but was ultimately commissioned as China's first aircraft carrier, *Liaoning*.

By 1995 Russo-Ukrainian tensions over Crimea eased, and the two sides agreed in principle to divide the fleet, with both navies stationed in Sevastopol. This deal was formalized as part of the 1997 "Big Treaty" on friendship and cooperation that also included Russian recognition of Ukraine's territorial integrity, an implicit reference to the status of the Crimea. According to the 1997 agreement, Russia received 81.7 percent of the ships, and Ukraine 18.3 percent. Ukraine did not keep its share, selling some ships to Russia and scrapping some others. The coastal facilities had to be transferred to

Ukraine and then leased to Russia, with the lease amount reducing Ukraine's gas debt. The 20-year renewable lease was supposed to expire in 2017. As part of the deal, in addition to 388 ships, Russia was entitled to keep ground forces subordinated to the naval command in the Crimea; this provision would be used during Russia's absorption of the Crimea in 2014. These forces could number up to 25,000 in strength and included a fixed number of aircraft, artillery systems, and armored vehicles.

After 1997 the tiny Ukrainian navy shared the Sevastopol harbor with its much larger Russian counterpart and the two even conducted joint exercises and parades when interstate relations were good. At the same time, Ukrainian ships participated in international exercises and missions, including some NATO operations. Aside from a handful of model ships maintained in good order for such occasions, notably *Hetman Sahaidachny*, the Ukrainian authorities neglected their navy. Officer salaries were several times lower than in the Russian Black Sea Fleet across the harbor and the replacement of ships long overdue.

Realizing that its Black Sea Fleet was becoming obsolete as well, Russia began funding an ambitious new ship construction program during the first decade of the 2000s. However, it featured mostly updated Soviet designs, and none of the frigate-class ships was ready by 2015. During the Russo- Georgian War of 2008, Russian ships from Sevastopol took part in a battle with Georgian ships off the eastern shores of the Black Sea, the first naval engagement in the region since World War II. In 2010 Russia signed an agreement with the Yanukovych administration to extend its lease on the port facilities in Sevastopol to 2042 in exchange for a discounted gas price, an agreement that caused public protests in Ukraine. The Russian parliament terminated this document unilaterally after the annexation of the Crimea.

Why was Russia able to take over the Crimea so quickly and with so little resistance?

The Russian ethnic majority in the Crimea in and of itself did not translate into widespread separatist sentiments. Political mobilization around the slogan of "return" to Russia was the product of several interrelated factors. First, successive Ukrainian governments had little to offer the Crimeans, aside from intermittent attempts to increase the number of Ukrainian schools on the peninsula, hardly a popular measure. Kyiv was associated with corruption, inefficiency, and an overall low standard of living, not to mention the Ukrainian political parties' alliance with the Crimean Tatars, whom the Russian majority in the Crimea perceived as a threat. The Crimean political elites owed only superficial allegiance to the Yanukovych regime in Kyiv, even though both skillfully played the "Russian culture" card.

As a result, the peninsula's Russophone population, including many ethnic Ukrainians, developed an idealized image of Russia. Affluent Russian tourists helped Crimean seaside resorts to stay afloat, and the Russian navy also contributed to the economy in many ways. State-owned Russian television, a major news source for most Crimean residents, projected an image of Russia as a country with a high standard of living, headed by a strong president, who was reining in the oligarchs. This message resonated well with the post-Soviet nostalgia that had kept the Communist Party in power in the Crimea for a decade after the Soviet Union disintegrated. The Crimean elites also cultivated closer economic and cultural contacts with Russia in order to underscore their region's special status.

Nevertheless, in the years before the Russian annexation, public opinion polls in the Crimea remained inconclusive, indicating only minority support for joining Russia. Tellingly, a May 2013 Gallup poll showed unemployment and rising prices to be by far the greatest concerns for Crimeans. Only 23 percent of respondents wanted the Crimea to become part of Russia.[3] In another poll held just a month before the annexation, which featured a differently formulated question, only 41 percent of the Crimean population supported the idea that Ukraine and Russia should be part of the same state, a notion prevalent only among those 50 and older.[4] Those numbers cast a shadow over the subsequent referendum on joining Russia, which returned a nearly unanimous vote in favor. One should not discount the anticipatory conformism of citizens in post-Soviet Ukraine, where all referenda always return positive results and opinion polls on sensitive political issues can be skewed in favor of the current government.

As soon as Yanukovych fled from Kyiv in February 2014 and the Party of Regions began disintegrating, the Crimean elites seized their chance. They had much to lose. A revolutionary government in Kyiv could parachute in new functionaries, destroy their corrupt schemes (or reassign them to its own oligarchs), or side with the Crimean Tatars on the land claims issue. Of course, none of these concerns could be used as a pretext for armed resistance, so the propaganda war against the EuroMaidan Revolution focused instead on the "neo-Nazi coup" in Kyiv threatening the Crimea's Russian culture. The Russian media belabored the same themes. There was extensive television coverage of the 20,000-strong anti-Ukrainian rally in Sevastopol on February 23, but no cameras were rolling on the morning of February 27, when 60 armed men in unmarked uniforms captured the Crimean parliament building and hoisted the Russian flag. Functioning literally at gunpoint, the parliament passed a motion on secession from Ukraine and a referendum to confirm it. Parliamentary speaker Vladimir Konstantinov, who also doubled as the Crimean boss of the Party of Regions, stayed on and in due course joined Putin's United Russia Party. However, the parliament installed a new premier, Sergei Aksenov, from an openly pro-Russian party, which had only a few seats.

On the same day, commandos with no insignia captured Simferopol Airport and established checkpoints on the isthmus connecting the Crimea to mainland Ukraine. Beginning in early March, they took over government buildings and blockaded Ukrainian army units on their bases. Local volunteers and Russian "Cossacks" also took part in these operations, but regular Russian army units clearly constituted the majority, although President Putin denied their involvement until mid-April. Even afterward, the Russian authorities argued that Russian troops in the Crimea never exceeded the treaty allotment of 25,000, as if this somehow justified their complicity in severing the Crimea from Ukraine.

With the Crimean elites casting their bid with Russia and the lack of any strong pro-Ukrainian voice among the public, defending the Crimea was next to impossible. Not only had successive Ukrainian governments neglected the army, but they had also staffed most Crimean formations with local conscripts and officers, who chose to remain on the peninsula under Russian rule. An acting commander of the Ukrainian Black Sea Fleet and his immediate replacement both defected to Russia at this time. Some middle-ranking officers and their crews resisted, but were overwhelmed and deported to the mainland. Russian forces captured all local army installations and Ukrainian navy ships, only some of which were subsequently returned. The Ukrainian flagship, *Hetman Sahaidachny*, happened to be at sea at the time and dropped anchor at Odesa instead. Throughout the conflict the Ukrainian authorities never authorized the use of force against the attackers in the Crimea.

A hastily organized referendum on March 16, 2014, reportedly produced a 96.77 percent vote in favor of joining Russia. The following day, the Crimean parliament declared independence from Ukraine and asked to be admitted into the Russian Federation, which request was duly granted by the Accession Treaty signed in the Kremlin on March 18.

How is the Crimea being absorbed into Russia?

Administratively, the Russian Federation incorporated Crimea as two entities: the Republic of the Crimea and the Federal City of Sevastopol. In addition to its regular administrative units, the Russian state (unconstitutionally) divides its territory into larger "federal districts," headed by the president's special envoys, thus requiring the creation of a separate Crimean federal district—the ninth and the smallest in the country. However, it soon became apparent that the head of the federal district and the speaker of the parliament played relatively minor roles, whereas radical nationalist Premier Aksenov had Putin's ear. In October 2014 the Crimean parliament elected Aksenov as head of the republic while leaving him in the premier's position.

Local residents were to acquire Russian citizenship automatically, unless they refused it in writing. Very few people dared to do so, but some 20,000 left for Ukraine. For the majority that stayed, bureaucratic chaos accompanied the identification and registration paperwork changeovers, as well as the transition from private to state notaries and a different legal code. On the peninsula the Russian authorities soon established the same regime of controlling the media and suppressing dissent that was the hallmark of Putin's rule in Russia. A crackdown on Crimean Tatar organizations began almost immediately. The long-serving head of the Mejlis and member of the Ukrainian parliament, Mustafa Dzhemilev, was physically stopped at the border when he was returning from Kyiv and had his passport stamped with a ban preventing his entry into Russia (and thus the Crimea) for five years. The same was done to the man who succeeded him as the head of the Mejlis. Police conducted searches in the buildings of Crimean Tatar organizations and closed down some of them. The situation took an ominous turn when the authorities also announced that those Crimean Tatars who had been squatting on the choice coastland for decades since their return from exile would be relocated to another area inland. In subsequent years, the Russian authorities closed the Crimean Tatar television channel and started prosecuting Tatar activists by presenting them as Islamic fundamentalists.

Crimea had been a subsidized region in Ukraine; it became even more of a money drain for Russia, reportedly surpassing even the nation's greatest cash-guzzler, Chechnya, in its first year under Russian rule.[5] The railroad connection with mainland Ukraine had been cut, resulting in a disastrous tourist season in the summer of 2014. Russian ministries and state-owned corporations "organized" their employees for Crimean vacations, but the car and train route via ferry in the treacherous Strait of Kerch in the east involved long wait times. To add insult to injury, fortified Crimean wines did not even qualify as "wines" under Russian legislation and had to be marketed as "wine beverages." Thus, the two most profitable and most legendary Crimean industries suffered severe blows. Higher Russian salaries and pensions did materialize, but with them came higher prices. During the difficult winter of 2014–2015, the Ukrainian authorities made a point of extending to the Crimea nationwide electricity blackouts in order to emphasize the peninsula's reliance on power supplies from the mainland.

Foreign investors would not consider Crimean-based projects because of Western sanctions. Most major Western companies ceased their operations in the Crimea, and big Russian business arrived determined to play by its own rules. By far the grandest construction project to be funded from the national budget, the US$3.3 billion Kerch Bridge to connect Crimea to Russia, was handed without public tender to the company owned by Putin's childhood friend and judo partner, the billionaire Arkadii Rotenberg. The start of construction was delayed when the ruble fell and the Russian economy took a nosedive early in 2015. The bridge was finally opened under the new name of the Crimean Bridge for cars in 2018 and for railroad connection in 2019. However, Russia still relies on organized and subsidized vacation tours to fill Crimean resorts, and the supply of fresh water to the peninsula remains a problem. At least in the short run, Russia is not going to be able to deliver the hoped-for economic prosperity in the Crimea; the peninsula is bound to remain a heavily subsidized region.

Was the Donbas historically a Russian region?

The Donbas had been part of the Russian Empire, but this in itself is no argument for its "Russianness," as the empire also included present-day Finland and Uzbekistan, for example, not to mention Alaska. The region was always multinational, and in its complex past it probably never had a majority population of ethnic Russians. However, the post-Soviet Donbas is solidly Russian-speaking and votes for pro-Russian parties—a phenomenon requiring a political and cultural explanation, not an ethnic one.

The term itself—"Donbas" in Ukrainian or "Donbass" in Russian—is an abbreviation for "the Donets [River] Coal Basin" and refers to an economic or geographic region, rather than an administrative entity. In Soviet times, the Donbas was divided into Donetsk and Luhansk provinces, both named after their capital cities; this division persists in independent Ukraine.

The territory now constituting Donbas did not belong to the medieval East Slavic state of Kyivan Rus, and thus neither Ukraine nor Russia can possibly claim it as part of their ancient historical patrimony. Rus called these immense steppes to the east the "wild field," as it was controlled by powerful and frequently changing nomadic masters. Only in the seventeenth century did the Russian tsars feel strong enough to establish the first outposts staffed by Don Cossacks from the Russian frontier settlements immediately to the east. Serbs escaping from Ottoman rule became the first permanent settlers in the eighteenth century; then came the Greeks, who two centuries later still constitute the third largest ethnic group in Donetsk province (a very distant third behind Ukrainians and Russians at only 1.6 percent, or 77,500 people, in 2001) and are especially noticeable in the southern coastal districts. Yet, even from the earliest stages of the region's mass settlement in the 1790s, Ukrainian peasants predominated in the Donbas overall, except in the cities and in some pockets of Russian settlement in the east.

In this multinational imperial society, foreigners often showed leadership in developing new regions. An early British industrialist, Charles Gascoigne, is considered the founder of Luhansk because he opened an iron foundry there in 1795, when he was helping Empress Catherine II to arm the Russian navy with new guns—a treasonous undertaking in the eyes of the British. In 1869 the Welsh capitalist John Hughes laid the foundations of the largest city in the Donbas, Donetsk. At the time it was just a factory town that he named Yuzivka ("Hughesville") after himself. Sixty years later, Stalin would rename this major industrial center after himself: Stalino.

The Donbas as it is known today was truly born in the 1870s, when the industrial boom in the Russian Empire began. The rich coal fields of the Donbas were discovered in the 1720s, but only after a century and a half did the railroad connect them to iron ore deposits in Kryvyi Rih, located 300 kilometers west; new factories opening in the region provided demand. Significant foreign investment transformed the barren Donbas steppe into a landscape of mine-waste tailings and smokestacks. Factory settlements also sprang up all around. Factory managers, in a hurry to recruit large numbers of workers, often looked to older industrial regions, especially in Russia. In 1892, 80 percent of workers in Yuzivka were newcomers from Moscow province.[6] Mass migration of Russian workers made factory towns into enclaves of Russian culture, where even Ukrainian peasant trainees adopted the Russian language in order to fit in. The proportion of ethnic Russians in the Donbas also increased, although they were still a minority in the Donbas by the time of the revolution if one factors in the predominantly Ukrainian countryside.[7]

Is it true that a separate republic existed in the Donbas during the revolutionary era?

Local Bolsheviks proclaimed the Donetsk-Kryvyi Rih Soviet Republic in February 1918, just days after the Ukrainian People's Republic signed a peace treaty with the Central Powers. At the time, Soviet Russia was completing its own negotiations that would soon result in the Brest Peace in March 1918. It was already clear that the Kremlin would have to recognize the Ukrainian People's Republic in its ethnographic borders—including the Donbas—and accept the presence on its territory of German and Austro-Hungarian troops. Lenin's insistence on this controversial treaty sparked both figurative and real rebellion within the Soviet regime. Local Bolshevik cadres in the industrial centers of eastern Ukraine also opposed the treaty. They stood to lose power simply because the peasant majority in their provinces was Ukrainian, even though the political decisions were made in Russian-speaking cities and factory towns.

In creating a new republic, the local Donbas Bolsheviks hoped to exclude their territory from the provisions of both Brest peace treaties, the one already signed with Ukraine and the one anticipated with Soviet Russia. They went for the widest possible territorial claim, covering not just the Donbas, but also the entire industrial southeast of present-day Ukraine. Indeed, the major city of Kharkiv, which is not in the Donbas, became the republic's first capital. No matter how spontaneous and pragmatic the decision to proclaim a republic may have been, it relied on the local Bolsheviks' longstanding refusal to engage with or even acknowledge the Ukrainian national question. The central Soviet leadership apparently took its time forming an opinion on the matter. In principle, the Donbas initiative went against the notion of self-determination in ethnographic borders, which Lenin had to endorse, at least publicly. The recently proclaimed Ukrainian Soviet Republic was the official Bolshevik administration in Ukraine, and the emergence of the Donetsk-Kryvyi Rih Soviet Republic could have jeopardized, theoretically, the former's sovereignty. In practice, however, Lenin preferred to keep the industrial areas of eastern Ukraine out of the Germans' reach, no matter what it was called, in the hope that the Germans would stop before reaching the borders of the new ephemeral polity.

The Germans did not. Instead, they endorsed the ethnographic borders as claimed by the Ukrainian People's Republic: the nine provinces of the former tsarist empire without the Crimea. The institutions and the military of the Donetsk-Kryvyi Rih Republic folded as soon as German army formations started arriving. Without putting up a fight, the local Bolsheviks evacuated southward, where they were forced to make peace with a rival faction representing the Ukrainian Soviet Republic. The Kremlin merged both republics, now existing only on paper, into a single Ukrainian Soviet Republic, but the German army soon pushed its forces into Russia. When the

Bolsheviks reconquered Ukraine again in 1919 and finally in 1920, they did not revive a separate Donetsk-Kryvi Rih republic.

The antagonism between the two wings of the Communist Party of Ukraine survived into the 1920s. Functionaries from the Donbas and Kryvyi Rih spearheaded resistance to the Ukrainization policy that Moscow proposed and the Kyiv-Kharkiv group endorsed. Ukrainization was aimed at building local support for Soviet power and supplying literate workers for the new industrialization drive. Stalin had supported Ukrainization as an official party line in the 1920s, but presided over its dismantling in the 1930s, claiming that it was a breeding ground for Ukrainian nationalism. Curiously, some prominent members of Stalin's inner circle came from the revolutionary Donbas. His long-serving minister of defense and later Soviet president, Kliment Voroshilov, was a leading party organizer in the Donbas during the revolution, while the future Soviet leader Nikita Khrushchev started his party career there in 1918 with a junior appointment as a district party secretary.

Beginning in the late 1980s, the pro-Russian movement in the Donbas revived the much-embellished memory of the Donetsk-Kryvyi Rih Soviet Republic, but it truly came to the public's attention in March 2015, when the legislature of the self-proclaimed Donetsk People's Republic declared itself a legal successor of the revolution-era republic. The Luhansk People's Republic was reportedly to follow suit with a similar declaration. This surprising move was likely intended to revive the New Russia project in a different guise, but perhaps also to establish a historical predecessor dating back to the disintegration of the Russian Empire, when the modern Ukrainian state also acquired its present shape. It would legitimize Donbas irredentism if it could be presented as something accompanying modern Ukrainian statehood from its very beginnings.

Did the Donbas stand out among other Ukrainian regions during the late Soviet period and the post-communist transformation?

Major battles took place in the Donbas during World War II, as both Hitler and Stalin coveted the area's coal and steel. Postwar reconstruction soon re-established the Donbas as a major Soviet industrial region, complete with the attendant mythology of heroic miners who always answered the party's call to labor and defense of the Motherland. In other words, the Soviet authorities were rebuilding the Donbas as a model Soviet land at the very time when they were treating any manifestation of Ukrainian identity as suspect. The atmosphere was ripe for assimilation. Not all new workers in postwar Donbas were newcomers from Russia. Some came from solidly Ukrainian-speaking provinces, but the workplace culture gradually molded them into Russian speakers. It was in this respect that the Donbas stood out among the other Ukrainian regions: in postwar Soviet censuses it registered the highest proportion of ethnic Ukrainians who named Russian as their mother tongue: 17.8 percent in 1959 and a whopping 26.6 percent in 1970.[8] Postwar Donbas became the only region in the Ukrainian SSR that simultaneously had a majority ethnic Ukrainian population and a majority of Russian speakers.

Ukrainian culture did not entirely disappear from the Donbas, which produced a number of prominent Ukrainian writers and patriotic thinkers, including the leading political dissident of the 1960s, Ivan Dziuba. But the region's identity was above all Soviet; it was a densely populated industrial heartland not firmly grounded in any ethnic culture. Precisely because the Soviet authorities promoted the image of heroic miners, the latter developed the self-respect and solidarity that enabled them to go on strike repeatedly in 1989–1991, when the Soviet state could no longer deliver on its promises. Donbas miners could still force the state to listen during the early 1990s, already in independent Ukraine. Partly as a result of the miners' strike in 1993, the Ukrainian government of the day resorted to printing money with no controls, thus causing hyperinflation and providing few benefits to anyone but the mine managers.

By the mid-1990s, the old Soviet economy was largely destroyed and the mass workers' movement died with it. The remaining mines and large factories depended on their directors' ability to obtain state subsidies, whereas unemployed miners often resorted to eking out a living in unlicensed small mines "protected" by local criminal syndicates. New market capitalism also arrived in the region, and a wave of large-scale privatization began in the late 1990s. Some large enterprises, especially in export-oriented metallurgical and chemical industries, were modernized, but all independent worker organizations were discouraged.

Instead, in the twenty-first century, politics has increasingly provided additional income for the underemployed, who could now be hired to participate in mass rallies organized by the Party of Regions. The latter established its power base in the Donbas smoothly, with the support of both Red directors and the oligarchs.

In contrast to western Ukraine and Kyiv, in the Donbas the disintegration of Soviet ideological controls in the late 1980s did not result in the development of any strong democratic movement. Although the striking miners put forward some demands for democratization, they went largely ignored. Rukh, the Ukrainian popular front of the late Soviet period, never made much headway there. However, the International Movement of the Donbas, which was created in opposition to Rukh, and which the present-day pro-Russian separatists lionize as their predecessor, was also very marginal. As soon as the Communist Party could operate legally again, it regained its electoral hold over the Donbas. In the first decade of the 2000s, the Party of Regions replaced it as a regional political machine. It also completed the ideological transformation that had been underway for some time: emphasizing the rights of Russian speakers over the previous class-based communist rhetoric. Around the time of the Orange Revolution, the Party of Regions pioneered the wide use of protestors-for-hire, who were often recruited from depressed mining towns of the Donbas and bused into the national capital when required. By the 2010s, it also used *titushky* (thugs for hire) to frighten its opponents. When the Party of Regions disintegrated in February 2014, its legacy of corruption and violence, long hidden by internal and external portrayals of the Donbas as a prosperous and politically significant region, was finally revealed.

Why did the armed conflict with the new Ukrainian authorities start in the Donbas and not in other eastern regions in the spring of 2014?

Since the Donbas had served as the main power base of ousted President Yanukovych and his Party of Regions, it seemed natural that this region would be alienated by the opposition's victory. Yet the local political elite's chagrin at sensing their imminent loss of power and privilege did not translate directly into an armed insurgency. A more complex causal mechanism came into play. The Donbas establishment and the Russian media had long cultivated an "ethnic" explanation of Ukraine's political divisions by associating civil society and democracy with Ukrainian nationalism, while the defense of Russian culture was linked to support for a paternalistic state rather than civil rights. Such connotations became entrenched in mass political culture on both sides of the conflict.

Yanukovych and the oligarchs used the language of protecting Russian culture in Eastern Ukraine pragmatically, as a way of preserving and legitimizing their rule. Yet it was also part of a greater post-imperial discourse embraced by Putin's Russia. When the EuroMaidan Revolution swept away the Yanukovych regime, Russian chauvinists took over the slogans they had prepared. Empire nationalists, who were often Russian citizens, flocked to the Donbas to fight for the idea, if not the actual restoration, of a greater Russia. The Russian state, which had just annexed the Crimea, supported them—covertly at first—but eventually it undertook the more overt measures of supplying arms on a large scale and recruiting servicemen "volunteers" to fight.

The conflict's external dimension was a decisive one, because only a minority of the Donbas population supported the idea of separation from Ukraine both before and after the fighting broke out. About a third of respondents were in favor, as attested by pre-conflict surveys conducted by Ukrainian pollsters. In December 2014, after the armed struggle began, an Oxford University polling team found 10 percent combined support for independence and/or joining Russia and 25 percent for autonomy within Ukraine, but over half of respondents favored retaining the status quo as Ukrainian provinces.[9] It took an external impetus and funding to mobilize the radical minority in the Donbas, but the shared ideology of the mythical "Russian world" as a Russian-speaking civilization extending beyond Russia's borders prepared the groundwork.

There is certain logic in why the Donbas had to become the battleground. After the EuroMaidan's victory in Kyiv, clashes between its supporters and opponents took place in several cities in the southeast, most notably in Kharkiv and Odesa. In both cities, mass rallies took place almost constantly throughout the winter and early spring of 2014, with one major square functioning as a local Maidan, and another as an anti-Maidan. In both cases, one side demanded the symbolic removal of the Lenin statue from the city center, while the other demanded that it be left in place. The situation became particularly acute after the change of power in Kyiv. The new government showed that it, too, was not immune to the "ethnic" framing of the conflict when on February 23 it pushed through parliament the abolition of the law on regional languages. This law was seen as justifying the continued predominance of Russian in the east. Acting President Turchynov announced on March 4 that he would not sign this bill, but it was too late: the new government provided its opponents with a perfect rallying call. Rumors about Right Sector militants "on their way" to any given eastern city also served as a mobilizing tool. Yet pro-Russian forces were not able to take control either in Kharkiv or in Odesa.

On April 6, 2014, about a thousand anti-Maidan activists in Kharkiv occupied the provincial administration building and the next day proclaimed the Kharkiv People's Republic, but the police quickly stormed the premises and re-established control over the city center. The interim cabinet in Kyiv appointed a reliable governor with old connections in the region; the local elites were in any case split on which side to take. The standoff in Odesa went on for longer, in part because of its proximity to the Crimea. It ended in a bloodbath on May 2, 2014, when a joint column of soccer fans and EuroMaidan activists clashed with a parade of pro-Russian forces in the city center. After the first casualties appeared, the fighting moved into the square where the anti-Maidan activists had set up camp. There, many pro-Russian activists took refuge in the abandoned trade union building and dozens died, apparently of smoke inhalation, when the building caught fire under circumstances that remain disputed. There were 48 casualties in the city that day, all but six on the pro-Russian side, and hundreds were wounded. Local police played an ambiguous role in the Odesa events and possibly even aided anti-Maidan protestors, but after the shock of May 2, the public wanted order restored. This allowed the new Ukrainian authorities to replace some elites, make deals with others, and consolidate their control over the region.

In contrast, in the Donbas the old ruling class and police leadership either fled or could not expect to keep their positions under the new government. Newly appointed officials could not re-establish control, even when they represented local business elites, because the entire fabric of regional political life was based on pro-Russian rhetoric now seized upon by the radicals. There was thus no way of quickly building a reconciliatory, pro-Ukrainian political model in the region. Moreover, all of this occurred under the shadow of Russia's openly hostile attitude toward the new Ukrainian administration and immediately after the annexation of the Crimea. Radicals on the ground felt that they could now appeal to Russia over the heads of the remaining, discredited Party of Regions functionaries and not even bother dealing with Kyiv's appointees. When the pro-Russian rebels started creating armed militias and proclaiming "people's republics" in the Donbas, there was no force there capable of stopping them, and the Russian border was close by.

What polities did the separatists create in the Donbas, and why did Russia not annex them outright, as was the case with the Crimea?

Pro-Russian rallies in the Donbas in March and April 2014 sometimes featured "elections" by acclamation of one of their own as "people's mayor" of the city or "people's governor" of the province. Soviet-style populist rhetoric was also apparent in the names of the polities that the separatists tried to establish. As a sign of developing coordination behind the scenes, on April 7 the pro-Russian activists occupying government buildings proclaimed "people's republics" in Donetsk and Kharkiv. In the first city, the heart of the Donbas, there seemed to be little resistance. If anything, lower-level functionaries and the police still on the ground seemed agreeable to following the Crimea's path. In contrast, in Kharkiv, which lies northeast of the Donbas, the Ukrainian authorities quickly reasserted their control.

But there remained another province in the Donbas, with its capital in Luhansk. On April 11 the United Command of the Army of the Southeast—and that was the first time most people heard about such an army—issued an ultimatum to the Luhansk provincial legislature to proclaim a people's republic within 10 hours and schedule a referendum on joining Russia. Actually, the rebels' three-way standoff with Kyiv's appointees and the remaining local elites in the province continued until the end of April, when the separatists finally managed to proclaim the Luhansk People's Republic and capture the provincial administration building on April 28 and 29, 2014.

Clearly, the events in Donetsk served as a catalyst for the pro-Russian victory in Luhansk, which ensued after a considerable impasse. Among the events that helped draw the battle lines were the first armed clashes between the "Donbas people's militia" and Ukrainian police and army units in mid-April, usually in connection with the rebels' attempts to take over police stations and military barracks outside their stronghold areas. It was also on April 28, 2014, that the West introduced a second round of sanctions against Russia in connection with the Ukrainian crisis, a decision that failed to prevent and perhaps even prompted the all-out capture of Luhansk.

Both of these self-proclaimed separatist entities followed the Crimean blueprint, holding snap referenda on separation from Ukraine on May 11, 2014. Their results were reported as 89.07 percent in favor of independence in Donetsk province and 96.2 percent in Luhansk province, with a turnout of 74 and 75 percent, respectively. The legitimacy of voting supervised by armed men and in the absence of access to official voter lists, which the Ukrainian authorities blocked, was questionable enough as it was, and it appeared even more dubious when the Donetsk authorities set about revising the results from 89.07 to 89.70 and back again to 89.07. Ultimately, the numbers game proved meaningless because Putin's Russia did not issue a response to the two republics' subsequent plea of acceptance, thereby derailing the Crimean scenario of speedy annexation.

On May 24, 2014, the Donetsk and Luhansk People's Republics announced their merger into the Federation of New Russia, a largely symbolic gesture seeking to capitalize on the currency of the term in Putin's historical lexicon. A month later, on June 24, the two polities proclaimed their confederation once more, this time within the very Soviet-sounding Union of People's Republics. All this feverish state building only suggested their uncertainty about the future—and about Russia's own intentions toward the Donbas after a quick victory failed to materialize.

Annexing the Donbas would have been a much more difficult and costly undertaking for Russia than the Crimean Anschluss. There was no ethnic Russian majority in the Donbas or relatively recent history of being part of the Russian SFSR. The Russian-backed militants did not control the entire territory of the two provinces, which did not have any natural borders comparable to the Black Sea around the Crimea. The Crimean precedent had already put the West on alert, resulting in much diplomatic chagrin for Russia and the initial rounds of sanctions. Besides, did Russia really need the incorporation of the Donbas for its grand strategic designs? A "frozen conflict" that would leave the self-proclaimed republics a thorn in Ukraine's side was probably more useful, among other things, for preventing Ukraine's potential accession to NATO.

In the summer of 2014, there were signs suggesting Moscow's intent to lend the self-proclaimed republics greater military support while at the same time preparing them for a longer existence in the political gray zone. In August some prominent separatist leaders, who were actually Russian citizens, such as Igor Strelkov (Girkin) and Aleksandr Borodai, were suddenly replaced by local figures, just as the Russian-backed forces went on a major offensive aimed at extending the area under their control. Yet the Russian authorities did not speak of absorbing the self-proclaimed republics in the Donbas; instead, they demanded that Ukraine empower the separatists politically without abandoning its responsibility to the region's population.

Years later the two "people's republics" remain in political limbo, with the Russian authorities emitting conflicting signals about their future. On the one hand, local elections (unrecognized by Ukraine and the international community) finally took place there in 2018, signaling that the status quo was to continue. On the other, in 2019 Russia intensified the process of awarding Russian citizenship to the local residents, which seemed to suggest that they would be able to escape to Russia should Ukraine end up taking back the occupied territories. For now, the leadership of the two self-proclaimed polities can only take comfort in being informally "recognized" by the other Russian-sponsored separatist enclaves in Moldova and Georgia.

Why did the Ukrainian army initially perform poorly compared to the pro-Russian forces in the Donbas?

Over two decades of corruption and neglect following the end of the Cold War left the Ukrainian army in shambles. What little money the state spent on its armed forces melted away in corrupt schemes without reaching the barracks, where the painted-over, old Soviet equipment simply rotted away. Most Ukrainian governments promoted generals and admirals based on the same criteria they applied to other functionaries and business associates—connections, loyalty, and financial gain—while paying little heed to military ability, training, or experience. As for rank-and-file conscripts, their composition reflected the ambiguous political loyalties of the population at large, and the majority of them tried to evade service.

After the first clashes with pro-Russian militants in the Donbas in April 2014 revealed the weakness and poor leadership of the regular army, Ukrainian volunteer battalions started forming alongside it. Some of them had their origins in radical right groups that came to prominence during the defense of the Maidan, such as Right Sector, while others were regionally based. Local patriotic oligarchs, most notably the new governor of Dnipropetrovsk province, Ihor Kolomoisky, reportedly funded the battalions. The arrival at the front of Ukrainian volunteers proved to be a double-edged sword. Although ideologically motivated and better supplied, they remained somewhat of an unruly paramilitary force. Some battalions were subordinated to the Ministry of the Interior, others to the military command, and others only to Right Sector. Cases of looting or abandoning positions without orders in some volunteer units did not help the public image of the campaign; in others, the use of neo-Nazi symbols as emblems only helped the Russian media to tarnish the Ukrainian civil-society revolution as a neo-Nazi coup. Militarily, the battalions were not capable of replacing a modern army. Moreover, the political ambitions of their leaders were bound to come to the surface, as they did in February 2015, when several battalions announced the creation of their alternative General Staff as a way of indicating their mistrust in the army command in the wake of recent defeats.

The Ukrainian army also faced a strong opponent. The original pro-Russian rebels in the Donbas were a mixed group of local separatist activists and disaffected military veterans cum Russian empire builders. As such, they possessed both ideological motivation and military expertise. A typical representative of this group, the Moscow-born Russian citizen and military-intelligence veteran Igor Girkin (nom de guerre: Strelkov) had been for years a participant in battle re-enactments in the Crimea, usually appearing in the uniforms of the tsarist or White army. In April 2014 he made the transition from leading fake imperial army formations to organizing real ones when his group trekked from the Crimea to the Donbas. Soon Girkin was fashioning himself into the commander of the Armed Forces of New Russia and minister of defense of the Donetsk People's Republic. However, in May 2014 he complained in a video address that he could not raise "even a thousand" local volunteers in Donetsk province to fight at the front.[10]

Whether or not Girkin's desperate appeal stirred anti-Ukrainian feelings among the Donbas residents, it was definitely heard in Russia. Beginning in June 2014, pro- Russian fighters in the Donbas began receiving heavy weapons, including tanks, from across the border. Underemployed war veterans from all over the former Soviet Union arrived in large numbers to take part in what was now a well-funded local war, supplementing empire builders, Russian Cossacks from the nearby Don region, and local Donbas activists. After the rebels shot down several Ukrainian army helicopters and aircraft, Kyiv lost control of its airspace. Yet the Ukrainian army recovered just enough to undertake a counteroffensive in July, briefly threatening both of the region's main cities, Donetsk and Luhansk. It was at this point that the Russian support of the rebels—in the form of money, war material, and personnel—escalated. In August 2014 the self-proclaimed republics miraculously matched and likely exceeded the Ukrainian forces in tanks and artillery, including the truck-mounted multiple Grad ("Hail") rocket launchers, apparently with an ample ammunition supply. The heavy weapons came complete with trained operators, who reportedly used drones to guide the Grad salvos. Russia consistently denied the involvement of its regular army units, claiming instead that the military personnel crossing into the Donbas did so as volunteers on contract.

In late August 2014, Russian-backed fighters went on the offensive, pushing the Ukrainian forces back from their two capitals and trapping thousands in a pocket in the town of Ilovaisk. The separatists also managed to reach the Azov Sea coastline south of Donetsk province, taking the port of Novoazovsk but stopping just short of the major port and industrial city of Mariupol. The September ceasefire did not last long, and fighting soon resumed near Donetsk International Airport, which Ukrainian units doggedly defended until January 2015. The fall of the airport, which by

then served as a symbol of new Ukrainian patriotism and heroic sacrifice, and yet another encirclement at Debaltseve in February 2015,
underscored the need for the Ukrainian side to re-evaluate its policy.
As another ceasefire was concluded the same month in Minsk,
Belarus, Ukrainian politicians pondered if their country could hope
for a military victory without both a reform of the army and Western
weapons to supply it.

Under what circumstances was the Malaysia Airlines passenger flight shot down over the Donbas on July 17, 2014?

The war in the Donbas was primarily a ground conflict until late May
2014, when a Ukrainian Air Force close air support Su-25 aircraft
delivered a rocket strike at enemy positions in Donetsk International
Airport. Beginning in June, with more military equipment arriving
from Russia or captured at Ukrainian bases in the region, the pro-
Russian rebels declared their intention to hunt the Ukrainian Air
Force. Accordingly, on June 14 they used two MANPAD missiles
to shoot down a large IL-76 military transport landing in Luhansk
International Airport. Forty Ukrainian paratroopers and nine crew
died instantly.

The Russian-backed rebels also used portable MANPADs to take
down several Ukrainian helicopters and low-flying Su-25s, but in
July suspicions emerged that they now possessed more sophisticated surface-to-air missiles with a longer range. On July 14 they
shot down an unsuspecting smaller An-26 military transport flying
at the "safe" altitude of 21,000 feet, although its crew managed
to eject. On July 16 pro-Russian fighters shot down an Su-25 and
damaged another, one of them possibly with a long-range surface-
to-air missile. After the An-26 incident on the 14th, the Ukrainian
authorities closed the airspace over the Donbas below 32,000 feet
to all commercial traffic, still leaving open the higher altitudes that
international airlines used. The government did not want to lose the
fees it collected for overflying its territory, and airlines had an interest in keeping the convenient routes available.

On July 17, 2014, Malaysia Airlines Flight 17, heading from
Amsterdam to Kuala Lumpur, crashed in the fields near the mining
town of Torez in Donetsk province, instantly killing all 298 people
on board. Only 40 kilometers from the Russian border, the depressed

mining town of Torez was deep inside rebel-held territory. Still keeping its Soviet-era name, which was given to it after the death of the French Communist leader Maurice Thorez, and with a Lenin statue proudly standing in front of the city hall, the town was now part of the self-proclaimed Donetsk People's Republic. According to international law, investigating the crash scene was the responsibility of Ukraine, but cooperation with the pro-Russian militia at war with Kyiv was required. In the end, both sides agreed to allow The Netherlands to take the lead.

It soon became apparent from examination of the debris that the aircraft was brought down by a missile. Satellite data helped US and German intelligence agencies identify the culprit, a Soviet-developed surface-to-air Buk mobile launching system fired from inside rebel-held territory. Buk is essentially a group of three trucks with mounted rockets, a radar, and a command post; it requires some level of professional training to operate. The rebels had just recently captured one such Ukrainian Army system in the Donbas, although the Ukrainian side claimed it was not operational. The Russian army has many such units in good condition. Wherever the Buk system came from, it was seen in the area in mid-July, both live and on satellite, before disappearing immediately after the airplane crash.

Since the Russian-backed fighters did not have an air force at the time, the Ukrainian military did not use proactive air defenses. In contrast, the rebels had a recent history of firing on Ukrainian airplanes, and in the days before the crash they had escalated their attacks into higher altitudes, previously considered safe. They had no reason to shoot down a foreign commercial airliner, but they likely mistook it for a Ukrainian aircraft. The missile strike on July 17 inspired a brief celebration on rebel social media sites, but all signs of it were erased after the true nature of the target became apparent.

Already in 2016, the four-country Joint Investigation Team led by the Netherlands concluded that the aircraft was shot down by the Soviet-made Buk surface-to-air missile fired from the separatist-controlled territory. The team subsequently traced the transfer of the Buk system from Russia, where it belonged to the 53rd Air Defense Missile Brigade stationed in Kursk. In 2019, the public prosecutor's office in the Netherlands began preparing for a criminal trial by charging in absentia the Russian and pro-Russian separatist military figures held responsible for the shooting down of Malaysia Airlines Flight 17.

How has the Ukrainian army performed since 2015?

February 2015 marked an important watershed in the conflict. That month brought a painful defeat at Debaltseve, where Russian and pro-Russian troops managed to encircle the Ukrainian forces, and the signing of the second Minsk agreement, which included an immediate ceasefire and a complicated road map to peace.

The fighting did not cease entirely but, rather, switched to an intermittent, low-intensity fire exchange that could escalate at any moment. Nevertheless, the Ukrainian side could regroup and reevaluate its performance. Since the Ukrainian army was now dealing with better-trained and -armed regular Russian army units, matching them in combat required a military reform—and the Poroshenko administration made this a priority. The Soviet-style conscript army of 18- to 20-year-olds was obviously inefficient and some of the volunteer regiments, sometimes difficult to control, even rejected the Minsk agreement. True, the defeats also produced some hardened units prepared to make a last stand, and the Ukrainian command now cultivated some elite detachments with higher morale. In the summer of 2015 these, together with volunteer units, managed to stand their ground during a massive enemy assault on the town of Marinka in the Donbas. The Ukrainian army also had the support of the country's numerous civilian volunteers, who collected funds for items ranging from boots to field hospitals.

The military reform started with the approval of a new military doctrine that finally designated Russia as the main strategic threat. The transition to a professional army, which previous governments had planned, had to be redesigned. The Ukrainian authorities first increased the conscription age to 27 in order to train a larger reservist corps, which could then be recalled for mobilization, if necessary. Then they stopped the deployment to the front of young conscripts aged 18 to 20—sending them to the trenches was not well received by society at large—and only dispatched those who volunteered for contract army service, usually older soldiers. Beginning in 2016, the new regulations allowed women to serve on contract, including in combat units. Some volunteer detachments were withdrawn from the front and dissolved; others were transformed into contract regiments within the armed forces or under the Ministry of Internal Affairs.

By the end of 2017, the Ukrainian army had reached its greatest numerical strength since the Soviet era: 250,000 men and women in uniform. The Poroshenko administration significantly increased salaries for contract soldiers and "de-Sovietized" the army's symbols by replacing Soviet insignia and names of detachments with those related to Ukrainian history. It also reoriented the military training toward Western models with the stated (if somewhat unrealistic) aim of fully implementing NATO standards by 2020. However, tens of thousands of Ukrainian soldiers have gone through the joint training program, which the United States, Canada, the United Kingdom, and some other European countries have been conducting since 2015 at a training field near the Polish border. An ever-increasing number of Ukrainian cadets and officers have been receiving an education or improving their qualifications at top Western military schools. In 2017, the Ukrainian command promoted to general the first officer from the new generation of military leaders who had never served in the Soviet army.

Between 2013 and 2018, Ukraine's defense and security budget increased by 53 percent to $4.8 billion.[11] In Soviet times much of Ukrainian industry had focused on military orders, and Ukraine remains to this day a major arms exporter with particular expertise in tanks and rockets, most of them modified Soviet models. It was relatively easy for the Ukrainian authorities to build up domestic arms production after they realized in 2014 that the only major ammunition factory was in occupied Luhansk. Beginning in 2015, the Western allies also stepped in with deliveries of non-lethal arms and, eventually, lethal ones as well, notably American-made Javelin anti-tank missiles in 2018.

Finally, in April 2018 the Ukrainian government ceased officially designating the war in the southeast as an Anti-Terrorist Operation, the name originally adopted in 2014 in order to allow holding elections and receiving international loans, which would have been impossible under martial law or after a declaration of war. One consequence of this previous designation had been an unclear chain of command, because anti-terrorist measures were technically the responsibility of the Security Service of Ukraine. When Poroshenko re-designated the war as an Operation of United Forces, this act placed in charge the military, which reported to him.

The mixed conscription-cum-professional army model allowed for a self-selection of patriotic professional soldiers to serve at the front line. Together with increased funding, training, and equipment, this created a force capable of engaging on equal terms the best Russian units on the opposite side. In 2017, the Ukrainian forces performed well during an escalation of fighting along the strategically important Svitlodar salient near Debaltseve. During late 2018 and 2019, the Ukrainian command pursued a campaign of small-scale, gradual advances into no-man's land to secure better defensive positions. In some cases, this changed the front line by a kilometer or more. However, by 2020 the Russian and separatist forces started fighting back vigorously to prevent such movements and recover some of these abandoned farmhouses-turned-forts.

Because of the Ukrainian army's transformation, already by 2016–2017 no international security expert could talk about the Russian army taking the Ukrainian capital in a week, as some had prognosticated in 2014. The war in the Donbas became a conflict of equals; it also became a standoff that could only be solved through international mediation and coordinated measures discouraging the aggressive behavior of Putin's Russia.

What has been the human cost of the armed conflict in the Donbas?

As of February 19, 2015, the official number of casualties in the Donbas war, as recorded by the United Nations Office for the Coordination of Humanitarian Affairs, had climbed to 5,793 killed (including 63 children) and 14,595 wounded (including 169 children). However, this UN agency relies on official government data, and many analysts believe that this figure is drastically underestimated. Earlier in February 2015, German intelligence estimated the real number of casualties in the Donbas at 50,000 people.[12] In the early days of the conflict, the Ukrainian army was apparently underreporting its casualties in open sources, and Russia quietly buried its "volunteers" who were returning from the Donbas in coffins. Both sides in the conflict have used heavy artillery frequently against targets located in or near cities and towns, although neither has acknowledged responsibility for the resulting civilian casualties, preferring to blame the strikes on the opposing side's provocations.

Keeping track of the number of casualties remained a challenge in subsequent years. In early 2020, the office of the UN High Commissioner for Human Rights estimated some 13,000 to 13,200 killed since the start of the conflict including 3,350 civilians, and total casualties including the wounded at between 41,000 and 42,000 people.[13]

Population displacement from the Donbas, which used to be a densely populated area, has also reached catastrophic proportions. By February 19, 2015, the number of officially registered Internally Displaced Persons (IDPs) in Ukraine passed the one million mark, reaching 1,042,066. At the same time, in February 2015 the Russian authorities also estimated some 900,000 Ukrainian refugees in their country, with 265,000 of them granted temporary shelter, a legal status that allows them to stay and receive some support, but which falls short of recognizing them as refugees under international law.[14] For its part, the Ukrainian government has also been reluctant to deem the conflict a war or to declare martial law even in the Donbas, primarily because doing so would disqualify Ukraine from receiving international economic assistance.

As the residents who fled the war-torn areas have attempted to rebuild their lives elsewhere, those who stayed have survived for weeks or months in buildings without water or electricity, risking death from artillery fire. Controversial Russian humanitarian convoys of trucks containing food supplies that the Ukrainian authorities have not always had a chance to inspect provide only symbolic relief for bigger cities, as do similar convoys of trucks sent from Kyiv by the Donbas's supreme oligarch-in-exile, Rinat Akhmetov.

The war led to the region's economic collapse, and the fleeing oligarchs who lost political control to radical pro-Russian nationalists left behind the lifeless carcass of what used to be the economic engine of the Donbas, its metallurgical and chemical industries. Even those enterprises that have not been damaged in fighting still face production stoppages caused by the breakdown of the region's commercial transportation network. The Ukrainian government ordered all institutions funded from the state budget to evacuate from separatist-controlled territories, and it stopped all money transfers there, including state pensions, which is the only type of pension currently available in Ukraine. Hundreds of thousands of retirees were forced to register elsewhere in the country in order to obtain their meager state pensions; some 200,000 failed to do so by the deadline. The war also made life difficult for Ukrainians elsewhere in the country, and especially those living on fixed incomes, as it led the national currency over a cliff in the winter of 2015.

Over the next several years Ukraine absorbed an estimated 1.4 million internally displaced persons, most of whom accepted that the war would not end in the near future and were thus forced to try to rebuild their lives elsewhere. A fragile "new normal" developed along the front line with many thousands of seniors from the self-proclaimed republics crossing monthly to the Ukrainian side to collect their pensions there. Death and injury from land mines have remained constant in the contact zone, and its residents faced the beginning of the COVID-19 pandemic in 2020 in the conditions of largely destroyed healthcare infrastructure.

7

THE WAR IN UKRAINE AS AN
INTERNATIONAL ISSUE

What sanctions did the West introduce against Russia, and did they work?

The United States, the European Union, and allied countries like Canada, Australia, and Japan introduced several rounds of sanctions against Russia in connection with its violation of Ukraine's sovereignty. The first round of sanctions was announced on March 17, 2014, the day after the Crimean referendum, and included visa bans and the freezing of financial assets in Western banks. It targeted a group of Russian and Crimean officials implicated in the annexation. The second round, starting on April 28, expanded the list of individuals to include some Russian companies with links to the Kremlin.

The escalation of the war in the Donbas led to a second round of sanctions in July 2014, which targeted entire sectors of the Russian economy. On July 17 and 31, the United States and the European Union, respectively, blacklisted several Russian energy companies and banks with majority state ownership, as well as defense contractors. The United States significantly widened this list on September 11. Targeted economic sanctions restricted access to Western debt markets and technology, specifically in oil exploration and defense-related industries. On February 16, 2015, the European Union expanded its list of blacklisted Russian individuals and businesses once again.

The third round of sanctions had a notable crippling effect on the Russian economy. The flow of foreign investments ceased at once, Russian banks were cut off by Western creditors, and the ruble tumbled. But the Russian authorities appeared to hold fast, insisting that the sanctions could actually benefit their country by promoting self-sufficiency. Russia reciprocated in March 2014 with individual sanctions against some US officials, but more important was its August embargo on agricultural exports from all countries participating in the West's sanctions. This ban hurt EU members in particular.

Although the sanctions undermined the economic security of the Putin regime, public support did not wane, at least in the short run. The state media hammered home the message that the West was trying to bring Russia to its knees, thus associating economic hardships with the external threat, rather than Putin's aggressive foreign policy.

It was the declining price of oil—from US$100 a barrel to US$60 between June and December 2014—that dealt the last blow to the Russian ruble. In December the ruble went into a freefall, leading to a run on banks, panic-buyers flooding grocery stores, and the withdrawal from the Russian market of cars and other valuable commodities that Western companies did not want to sell for rubles. The government's desperate attempts to prevent an economic disaster coincided with the renewal of negotiations about the conflict in Ukraine that led to the second Minsk truce of February 2015.

Western leaders have indicated in their statements that a continued peace in the Donbas could lead to the lifting of some sanctions. However, their full retraction, even in an optimistic scenario of future developments in the Donbas, is problematic because the original Western sanctions were tied to the Russian seizure of the Crimea, and President Putin has stated in the strongest terms possible that he will never consider returning the peninsula to Ukraine. In March 2015 he even alluded to Russia's nuclear arms as a guarantee of the Kremlin's newly gained control over the Crimea.[1]

In the following years, the United States and their allies continued extending their sanctions against Russia and imposed new ones, notably in connection with the Russian interference in the US elections of 2016, the construction of the Kerch Bridge connecting the Crimea with Russia, and the 2018 incident at the Strait of Kerch. The sanctions were a major factor in the Russian financial crisis (2014–2017) and caused systemic changes in the Russian economy, especially affecting its access to Western funding and advanced technologies. In 2019 the US sanctions derailed a major Russo-German gas pipeline project, Nord Stream 2.

Did Western diplomatic mediation assist in the de-escalation of the conflict in the Donbas?

The West first attempted to mediate when the clashes began in April 2014. Meeting in Geneva on April 17, the foreign policy chiefs of the European Union, the United States, Ukraine, and Russia agreed on a statement calling for a halt to the violence, disarmament of all illegal paramilitary formations, and initiation of a process for constitutional reform. Undefined in the text, the latter was a reference to the de-centralization of power in Ukraine, which would give more power to the regions. Both Ukraine and Russia found this treaty wanting, and neither side applied efforts toward its implementation. In addition, Russian decision-makers were uncomfortable with the American presence at the table and complained about the interests of the Donbas not being represented. The so-called "Geneva format" proved unpro-ductive, and the military showdown ensued in the Donbas.

When a number of world leaders arrived in Normandy, France, in June 2014 to celebrate the anniversary of D-Day, a brief meeting on the margins of these celebrations established a new diplomatic format: the heads of state of Germany, France, Russia, and Ukraine. The "Normandy format" involved rare meetings but more regular telephone consultations, as well as meetings of the foreign ministers of the four countries.

With prodding from the Normandy group, the conflict's direct participants also entered into negotiations under the aegis of the Organization for Security and Cooperation in Europe (OSCE). The talks took place in Minsk, Belarus, where Ukraine was represented by former president Leonid Kuchma; Russia by its ambassador to Ukraine; and the two breakaway republics by their leaders. The latter had no official status and neither did Kuchma, at least not on paper, precisely because the Ukrainian authorities did not want to legiti-mize the separatists by sending an official plenipotentiary. It was in Minsk that the first ceasefire was signed on September 5, 2014, in the wake of a successful counteroffensive by the pro-Russian forces. The agreement also called for the release of all hostages, a prisoner of war exchange, an amnesty for arrested separatists, and the removal of heavy artillery from a 30-kilometer-wide buffer zone between the sides. Ukraine also promised to pass a law on self-government in some districts of the Donbas, which it later repealed when the ceasefire failed.

The first Minsk agreement collapsed as intense fighting at Donetsk International Airport broke out in December. The fall of the airport, the last Ukrainian-held point in the environs of Donetsk, which acquired a Stalingrad-like status in the Ukrainian media, underscored the impossibility of winning the war by military means. This event coincided with the deepening economic crisis in Russia and intense Western diplomatic pressure for peace. The Normandy group also realized by then that it needed to be directly involved in negotiating any prospective settlement. On February 11, 2015, German Chancellor Angela Merkel, French President François Hollande, Russian President Vladimir Putin, and Ukrainian President Petro Poroshenko arrived in Minsk for a marathon 17-hour negotiating session that lasted all night and which resulted in the second Minsk agreement. They did not sign it, however, leaving this task to Kuchma and his negotiating partners, who also held a simultaneous meeting in Minsk.

Minsk II called for an unconditional ceasefire supervised by the OSCE starting on February 15 (Putin bargained for the delay on behalf of the pro-Russian forces, which were hoping to liquidate the large Ukrainian pocket around the railway hub of Debaltseve). Ironically, then, the nominal peace agreement was followed immediately by intensified fighting that ended only on February 18 with a Ukrainian withdrawal. Only afterward did the two sides start decreasing the intensity of fire and, later in February, withdraw heavy weapons from the contact line as specified by the agreement. Both sides also pledged to exchange all POWs, grant amnesty to prisoners, and enable the delivery of humanitarian aid to the region. Occasional firefights continued at some points along the frontline, but in late February 2015 a day could go by without reported losses on either side for the first time since the previous summer.

Experts saw as more problematic the long-term road map to peace specified in the agreement. According to this plan, Ukraine pledged to restore the law on self-government in the Donbas and specify the exact area it covered. It also promised to resume financial transfers to the Donbas, including pensions. The weight-iest promise of all, however, was decentralization of power in the form of a constitutional reform by the end of 2015. On the other hand, the Donetsk and Luhansk People's Republics—and implic-itly Russia, operating on their behalf—agreed to some conditions that they are unlikely to implement: the withdrawal of all foreign military troops and mercenaries and the restoration of Ukrainian control over the state border with Russia. Ukraine, Russia, and the breakaway republics started arguing almost immediately about the exact meaning and sequence of these steps. They disagreed in particular on what the agreement meant by local elections in the Donbas: was it a restoration of the Ukrainian political system, or a legitimation of the two republics, neither of which is mentioned in the agreement's text?

What is the Steinmeier Formula, and why did it become a stumbling block in the peace process?

The second Minsk agreement of February 2015 was signed in the heat of battle, just as it became clear that the Ukrainian forces had suffered a major defeat in the Debaltseve pocket. Minsk II mandated an immediate ceasefire followed by the withdrawal of heavy artil-lery from the front line and POW exchanges. But it went beyond that. Like the first Minsk agreement of 2014, it charted out a tenta-tive set of measures that could bring about a peace settlement in the region. Building on a proposal put forward by then French President François Hollande and German chancellor Angela Merkel, this set of far-reaching measures included a provision for local elections in the area not controlled by the Ukrainian government, granting it special status within Ukraine, the resumption of Ukraine's social payments to the region, the withdrawal of all foreign troops, and the restora-tion of Ukrainian control over the Ukrainian-Russian border in the Donbas. However, the very nature of the Ukrainian state would also have been changed by a constitutional reform enshrining decentral-ization. The exact meaning and sequencing of these measures were left unclear at the time. The negotiations in Minsk took place in the so-called Normandy Format, with the leaders of France, Germany, Russia, and Ukraine making important decisions in principle, but the details being left to a "tripartite working group," meeting separately and comprising representatives of the two so-called people's republics and Ukraine's special representative, the former President Kuchma. The "protocol" that this group produced—the only document listing the proposed measures—carried significantly less weight than the verbal agreements of the Normandy Four, and Russia was not even a signatory.

Minsk II resulted in a de-escalation of fighting in the Donbas, although low-intensity fire exchanges along the front line never really ceased. It soon became clear that the belligerents had no intention of following up on the long-term measures agreed on at Minsk. For Poroshenko, Minsk II was a difficult decision taken at a moment of military disaster. Some volunteer detachments at the front refused to accept it. In March 2015, when the president pushed through the Ukrainian parliament a law granting special status to the occupied areas of the Donbas (at least, in theory), Russia criticized it as unacceptable, because it made the implementation of the special status contingent on the regional elections being conducted according to Ukrainian legislation and under international monitoring. Conversely, Ukrainian patriotic forces saw it as a betrayal. Poroshenko's own party bosses had to explain to the rank and file that the law was no more than a signal to the West that Ukraine was not rejecting the peace process. Uncertainty also reigned on the other side of the front. Russia tried to test the waters by having the leaders of the two "republics" threaten to hold elections right away, which would allow them to take control of the peace process. However, the representatives of France and Germany intervened with Russia to shut down this opening. The measures proposed at Minsk could be interpreted as either the restoration of Ukrainian control over the Donbas or the legitimation of the two "people's republics." Since neither side felt that it had the means to enforce its preferred interpretation, both refrained from implementing any measures while awaiting changes in the international situation.

Following renewed fighting in the Donbas during the summer of 2015, the then German Foreign Minister Frank-Walter Steinmeier first spoke in the fall of that year about sequencing the initial steps in the peace process. His plan consisted of implementing the

Ukrainian law on the region's special status on a provisional basis at 8:00 P.M. on the day that local elections were held there, according to Ukrainian legislation and under international monitoring. After the OSCE confirmed that the elections were free and fair, the law on the region's special status would come into force permanently. The subsequent summits of the Normandy Four approved this solution in principle, but for years no document was signed, cementing the commitment of the belligerents to proceed with the implementation of what became known as the Steinmeier Formula. The Ukrainian position in the final years of the Poroshenko presidency was based on the reasonable argument that no free and fair elections in the occupied Donbas would be possible before the withdrawal of all Russian troops and the resumption of Ukrainian control over the border. Of course, Russia denied the presence of its troops to start with, thus revealing its failure to take the Minsk agreements seriously. Nevertheless, the Putin administration tried to damage Poroshenko's standing in the West by arguing that Ukraine refused to implement the Steinmeier Formula.

After he came to power in Ukraine in 2019, President Volodymyr Zelensky wanted to demonstrate his commitment to the peace agenda by reactivating the Normandy process. Apparently, his advisors did not see formalizing Ukraine's commitment to the Steinmeier plan as politically damaging. This was done in October 2019, not by signing a single document, but by submitting to the international moderator of the tripartite "working group" separate letters from Kuchma and representatives of the "people's republics," stating that they all accepted the agreed-upon text of the Steinmeier Formula. The text did not include the former Ukrainian conditions about the withdrawal of foreign troops or resumption of control over the border.

The signing led to mass protests in Ukraine. Zelensky's opponents accused him of betraying national interests, and some provincial legislatures even passed declarations condemning the agreement. Switching quickly into damage-control mode, Zelensky resorted to the old Poroshenko line about the importance of Russia's military withdrawal and Ukrainian border control. He also promised a new Ukrainian law on the breakaway regions' special status, which would reflect these demands better.

What role has the Organization for Security and Cooperation in Europe played in monitoring the conflict?

The Minsk agreements did not create a dedicated monitoring mechanism for the peace process in Ukraine. Instead, the Normandy Four came to rely on the existing international organization, the Organization for Security and Cooperation in Europe (OSCE), for information about what was happening in the Donbas. The OSCE was founded during the Cold War, when the two opposing camps attempted in the mid-1970s to establish basic international and humanitarian values on which they could agree. Because of the bipolarity during the Cold War, the United States and Canada were among the founding members of what was originally called the Conference on Security and Cooperation in Europe. Following the collapse of communism in Europe, the OSCE reinvented itself as an intergovernmental organization tracking the state of democracy and security in Europe. It provides a platform for international observers monitoring elections and documenting armistice violations in long-term armed conflicts.

In Ukraine, the OSCE played an important role in election monitoring during the Orange Revolution of 2004–2005. Unhappy with the revolution's outcome and the OSCE's activities in the former Soviet republics more generally, in 2007 President Putin accused the organization of promoting Western strategic interests there. Russia then started developing its involvement with the OSCE, hoping to influence the organization's reporting from the region and its resulting decisions.

The OSCE established its Special Monitoring Mission in Ukraine in March 2014 on the invitation of the new Ukrainian authorities. From an early contingent of about a hundred international monitors (plus Ukrainian technical personnel), within a year the mission's size increased to some 500 monitors and, as of April 2020, it consisted of 750 unarmed civilian monitors from 45 states; some 600 of them were stationed in the Donbas.[2] Russia has prevented OSCE monitors from entering the Crimea.

The mission played an important role in the war's initial years by helping to undermine Russia's official pretense of non-involvement. In 2015 and 2016 particularly, the mission reported numerous cases of Russian military personnel and equipment crossing the border into the Donbas, being directly involved in the fighting there, and even sending soldiers' remains back to Russia. There were cases of Russian and pro-Russian paramilitaries detaining OSCE monitors and of Russian troops shooting down OSCE drones over the Donbas.

In later years, however, the OSCE mission faced criticisms in Ukraine. The mandate of a Special Mission is not limited to observing the situation on the ground; monitors are also supposed to facilitate the delivery of humanitarian aid and help establish dialogue between warring factions. It is in this latter capacity that the OSCE mission sometimes crossed the line between recording facts and fraternizing with one side in the conflict. Ukrainian sources have reported that monitors allowed pro-Russian fighters to use their cars, painted white with OSCE markings, and attended the wedding of a separatist warlord—facts the mission has acknowledged with regret. The Ukrainian media has also aired more far-reaching claims about observers deliberately turning a blind eye to Russia's military actions or even feeding data about the location of Ukrainian units to enemy artillery posts.

It is not widely known in the West that a significant share of the OSCE monitors in Ukraine are Russian citizens and that some of them have military backgrounds (which is also true of Western monitors). Most countries involved in staffing this special mission send only a token number of observers, but the Russian representation is consistently one of the largest, and some post-Soviet states closely allied with Russia also send their monitors. In at least one known case in 2015, a Russian monitor was forced to resign after the media revealed his service record in Russian military intelligence. In 2018 the mission reported a security breach when an employee allegedly provided the Russian Federal Security Service with details concerning some monitors' personal lives and financial situations.

In October 2018 the long-serving deputy head of the OSCE Special Monitoring Mission in Ukraine, the Swiss Alexander Hug, who was about to leave his position in Ukraine, gave an interview to the influential US magazine and news resource *Foreign Policy*. When asked about the Russian presence in the Donbas, he began his answer with the unfortunate sentence, "If the question is what we have seen on the ground, we would not see direct evidence." Nevertheless, he went on to describe all kinds of direct and indirect proof of Russian involvement his monitors had recorded. But the Russian media had a field day with Hug's opening statement, trumpeting that this was an acknowledgment of Western and Ukrainian lies about the Donbas and conveniently ignoring the rest of the interview. At Hug's urging, *Foreign Policy* removed the offending sentence "as it did not convey his intended point of view," but the incident only underscored the hybrid nature of the war, in which the belligerents fight over interpretations as much as they do over the control of territory.[3] To many Ukrainians, the scandal merely confirmed their suspicions about widespread pro-Russian sentiment among OSCE monitors.

How should the results of the 2014 presidential and parliamentary elections in Ukraine be interpreted?

As soon as President Yanukovych escaped to Russia in February 2014, the Ukrainian parliament scheduled preterm presidential elections for May 25, 2014. The leaders of the EuroMaidan Revolution hoped that the snap elections would legitimize their victory and unify the country, a task that became even more urgent during the three months before the elections, when Russia annexed the Crimea and fighting in the Donbas broke out.

With the Party of Regions in disarray, the EuroMaidan forces did not face any significant opposition. Early polls indicated three prominent politicians from the same camp emerging as the main contenders: the chocolate tycoon and long-time opposition supporter Petro Poroshenko; Yulia Tymoshenko, fresh out of prison and eager to regain political ground; and the retired heavyweight boxing champion Vitali Klitschko, a Russian-speaking democratic reformer with no ties to the old regime, who was seen by many as a long-awaited third force in Ukrainian politics. However, Klitschko soon withdrew from the race and endorsed Poroshenko after revelations emerged that he had a German residence permit, thus disqualifying him from the presidency. Perhaps more important, Klitschko offered Poroshenko, who did not have his own political machine, the support of his party, the aptly named Ukrainian Democratic Alliance for Reform, or UDAR, which means "punch" in Ukrainian. Klitschko instead stood in Kyiv's mayoral elections, which he won easily. After concluding this alliance, Poroshenko took a clear lead in the polls all the way to the elections.

On election night, May 25, 2014, Poroshenko won in the first round with 54.7 percent of the vote. With the war in the Donbas on their minds, voters likely wanted to put a commander-in-chief in place as soon as possible, without going into a runoff. Poroshenko also appeared more moderate and thus more acceptable to the pro-Russian forces in the Donbas than Tymoshenko, who ended up a distant second with only 12.81 percent. Voting did not take place in the Crimea, or in most of the Donbas region, thus further diminishing the chances of the Party of Regions; amidst internal turmoil and the expulsion of several popular politicians, the party's nomination went to the former governor of Kharkiv, Mykhailo Dobkin, who scored a meager 3.03 percent. On the other hand, radical Ukrainian nationalists did not do well either: Oleh Tyahnybok, head of the Freedom Party, received 1.16 percent of the vote and Dmytro Yarosh of Right Sector a paltry 0.70 percent.

Russia initially called the preterm presidential elections illegitimate but in the end changed its position and recognized the outcome. The threat of escalating Western sanctions was a major factor behind this reversal, but the Kremlin was also interested in a dialogue with Kyiv, admittedly from a position of power, that could help achieve Russian aims in the Donbas without accepting financial responsibility for the region. However, Poroshenko proved an unwilling partner for such deals. His strategy vis-à-vis Russia was to involve the West as a third partner, which could both provide mediation and apply pressure on the Kremlin.

Poroshenko, whose team was finding it difficult to work with Prime Minister Yatseniuk from Tymoshenko's Fatherland Party, hoped to consolidate his hold on power during the preterm parliamentary elections. But Yatseniuk held a strong position by virtue of his control over funding to the regions, while the president's constitutional responsibility for foreign affairs and the military increasingly became a liability in light of the difficult war, which also demonstrated the limits of international diplomacy. In July 2014 the coalition in the parliament collapsed, triggering preterm parliamentary elections within three months.

The president had hoped that his new mega-party, the Petro Poroshenko Bloc, which now included Klitschko's UDAR, would obtain enough votes to form a cabinet without Yatseniuk and other Tymoshenko people. However, it did not help that in

August and September 2014 Ukrainian forces suffered some of their worst defeats in the Donbas. Yatseniuk skillfully sidelined his ambitious mentor Tymoshenko to create his own party, the People's Front, which adopted militant rhetoric calculated to contrast with the president's perceived ineptness. The People's Front promised to build a "European wall" on the Russian border and included in its party list some volunteer battalion commanders. As sitting prime minister, Yatseniuk was also well positioned to influence provincial bigwigs, who could deliver the votes. In any case, the People's Front defied poll projections to emerge as the winner among party lists in the elections held on October 26, 2014. Yatseniuk's party received 22.12 percent of the vote, beating out the Poroshenko Bloc with its 21.82 percent. A total newcomer, the Self-Reliance Party, led by the mayor of Lviv, who is close in ideology to European Christian Democrats, ended up in third place with 10.97 percent, highlighting disillusioned voters' continued search for new faces in politics. Yulia Tymoshenko's emasculated Fatherland Party barely crossed the required 5-percent threshold.

With the Crimea and much of the Donbas not participating, the Communist Party for the first time ever was not represented in the Ukrainian parliament, having obtained just 3.88 percent of the vote. The remnants of the Party of Regions consolidated into the Opposition Bloc (9.43 percent), which was to become the only real opposition in the new parliament. Buoyed by the war, Ukrainian radical nationalists did better than in the presidential elections, but they still failed to cross the threshold. Freedom ended up just short of it, with 4.71 percent, and Right Sector was further behind, with 1.80 percent.

In addition to those elected on the party lists, the other half of the seats were filled by first-past-the-post winners in electoral districts. There, the Poroshenko Bloc made up for its loss, surpassing People's Front as the largest faction in the parliament. A few other parties also managed to have their candidates elected this way, including Freedom and Right Sector, but not the Communist Party. The behind-the-scenes struggle between the president and the prime minister ended in a draw, forcing their parties to work together more closely. In the winter of 2015 the growth of voter disillusionment with the EuroMaidan coalition was fueled by the ongoing conflict in the

Donbas, the collapse of the hryvnia, and the unpopular austerity measures.

What was the composition of the new Ukrainian government after the EuroMaidan Revolution, and what were its first steps?

Parliament approved the new cabinet in the aftermath of the EuroMaidan Revolution, on February 27. The night before their confirmation by the parliament, the incumbent ministers went to the Maidan seeking a symbolic popular mandate. Indeed, in many respects it was a revolutionary government, as it included several prominent Maidan activists in its ranks, such as the new minister of culture, the actor Yevhen Nishchuk. The broad, pro-EuroMaidan parliamentary coalition guaranteed the government's confirmation, but only two parties delegated their members to serve in the cabinet: six ministers represented Tymoshenko's Fatherland Party, which was increasingly controlled by Yatseniuk, and three came from the ranks of the radical nationalist Freedom party. An equal number of ministers, nine, had no party affiliation. Yatseniuk himself became prime minister in a nearly unanimous confirmation vote.

Inheriting an almost bankrupt country, Yatseniuk referred to his cabinet's tasks as a "kamikaze mission."[4] He had in mind the political cost of painful reforms that the International Monetary Fund (IMF) had requested in exchange for a substantial financial bailout, but the warlike metaphor acquired a new meaning almost immediately. The cabinet had barely enough time to unveil its program, featuring closer links with the European Union, economic reforms, and a complete rebuilding of the corrupt justice system, before the Russian takeover of the Crimea took place, followed by the war in the Donbas. For the next year the government operated in a state of emergency, trying to keep the economy afloat while funding the war.

However, in April 2014 the IMF approved a US$17 billion loan to Ukraine with US$3.2 billion made available immediately. The Ukrainian government promised to carry out deep structural reforms and fiscal tightening, which could not really be implemented during the war. The ongoing devaluation of the hryvnia, however, resulted in the partial fulfillment of the IMF's main demand: deep cuts to the state's social expenditures, such as pensions and subsidies.

In July 2014 the broad parliamentary coalition collapsed, ostensibly because of disagreements over military expenditures and budget cuts, although it appears that the prime minister and the president were looking for an opportunity to revamp the cabinet and renew parliament through snap elections that such a crisis would trigger. Indeed, Yatseniuk stayed on as caretaker prime minister. The war in the Donbas escalated during the three months prior to the elections, and the economic crisis deepened. The government did not have any internal means to fund the war effort, other than by printing more money and initiating a fire-sale privatization of remaining state assets, although the latter did not proceed very far and was likely more of a declaration of intent in order to satisfy Western creditors.

It took the Ukrainian parliament a month after the elections of October 26, 2014 to form a new coalition, which now relied on cooperation between the Poroshenko Bloc and Yatseniuk's new party, the People's Front. These two forces took the most influential portfolios in the new cabinet, with some less important ministries reserved for the three minor coalition partners: Self-Reliance, the Radical Party, and Tymoshenko's debilitated Fatherland. The Ukrainian leadership also took the unusual step of recruiting three foreigners not implicated in the dirty business of Ukrainian politics to run the ministries with the greatest potential for corruption. Natalie Jaresko, an American investment banker of Ukrainian descent, became minister of finance, the Lithuanian banker Aivaras Abromavičius was confirmed as minister of economy and trade, and the former minister of health of the Republic of Georgia, Alexander Kvitashvili, took over the same portfolio in Ukraine.

The new cabinet was sworn in on December 2, 2014, just as the first Minsk ceasefire collapsed and fierce fighting resumed in the Donbas. During the next two months, the hryvnia went over a cliff, causing the population to empty supermarket shelves. The government desperately needed the next installment of the IMF loan, but it was only after some painful military defeats and a second Minsk agreement in February 2015 that it could push through some austerity measures, making the funding possible. On March 2 the parliament approved measures that would see household energy bills triple and also reduce some categories of state pensions. The IMF immediately disbursed US$5 billion with another US$5 billion promised within a year, an announcement that halted the hryvnia's free-fall. Yet, all sides understood that Ukraine needed a lasting peace to start serious economic reforms.

How should one evaluate Petro Poroshenko's tenure as president (2014–2019)?

Poroshenko scored an easy victory in the first round because voters saw him as best qualified to lead the country in a time of war. Once the war was over—which seemed possible at the time—he would be qualified to initiate major reforms. A former foreign minister and an experienced player in Ukrainian politics, as an oligarch he also knew the rules of the game within the Ukrainian business community. However, nothing went according to plan. The war became a perennial reality, and Poroshenko's connection to the old system became a liability.

The Ukrainian political system gives the head of state exclusive control over foreign, military, and security affairs, along with the prerogative to nominate ministers in these fields. Everything else is technically the responsibility of the prime minister and the cabinet selected by the parliament. In practice, Ukrainian presidents usually get involved in all major decisions and are seen as responsible for everything from military defeats to corruption to the decline in book publishing. In recent decades, they have often managed eventually to install prime ministers from their own parties.

Poroshenko's honeymoon with Ukrainian voters did not last long. As explained elsewhere in this book, in late 2014 and early 2015 Ukrainian forces suffered major setbacks at the front, forcing Poroshenko to accept an ambiguous peace plan that was potentially disastrous for Ukraine as part of the second Minsk agreement. These events also undermined his reputation in the very fields constituting the president's prerogative. Cooperation between the Poroshenko Bloc and the People's Front did not go well, but this turned out to be a blessing because the cabinet headed by Arsenii Yatseniuk from the People's Front ended up being blamed for all the economic troubles caused by the war. Yatseniuk pinned his last hope on the highly publicized project of building a "European wall" along the Russian border, but it too became an embarrassment when the public discovered that only a small section was built and all the money had disappeared.

As the People's Front approval rating dropped to below 2 percent, Poroshenko launched the slow and painful process of reforming the country in wartime. In April 2016 he began collaborating with the new Prime Minister Volodymyr Groisman, who represented the Poroshenko Bloc. The People's Front stayed on as a partner in the coalition, but Poroshenko's people now had the upper hand in the cabinet. This development gave Poroshenko more power, but also made him more responsible for the outcome of the reforms.

In a relatively short time Poroshenko managed to transform a conscript army, suffering from decades of neglect and corruption, into a trained and well-armed professional fighting force capable of holding its ground in the Donbas. This was accomplished by exempting young conscripts from contract-only frontline service while maintaining conscription. He also dissolved some volunteer formations and reorganized others into regular army units. On the international scene, Poroshenko proved a skillful negotiator, who worked well with Ukraine's Western partners. He understood when procrastination could be in his country's best interests, delaying the implementation of the long-term provisions of Minsk II, which went beyond de-escalation and humanitarian issues. The president also rightfully took credit for the 2017 introduction of visa-free travel to the European Union, an important sign for Ukrainian citizens that their most recent revolution had not been in vain.

At home, Poroshenko should be credited for working closely with citizen activists and foreign advisors on making government affairs more transparent. The public electronic register of government procurements at all levels allowed for civic supervision over what had been a major source of corruption. The introduction of obligatory electronic declarations of assets by all parliamentarians and most public servants offered, at least in theory, a mechanism for detecting the misuse of power for personal gain. The creation of a dedicated agency to investigate corruption, as well as a formally independent prosecutor's office to press charges in such cases, at first seemed to be a viable plan for combating corruption, of which the existing justice system was part. But the establishment of a special court for corruption cases could not be pushed through the parliament until 2018, and it did not start working under Poroshenko.

The reforms did not proceed easily, and ambassadors of Western countries often had to act as intermediaries between civil society and the government. They even showed up in parliament on days when crucial legislation was to be voted on. In the second part of his term, Poroshenko often played the middleman, explaining to the West why certain measures could not be passed or implemented yet. It became increasingly clear that he practiced the traditional style of politics in which the accommodation of power groups and the symbiosis of business with politics remained the norm. Most foreign reformers invited after the EuroMaidan Revolution left soon after the system rejected them. Only the US-born and -educated acting Minister of Health, Ulana Suprun, soldiered on between 2016 and 2019, trying to build a comprehensive insurance-based healthcare system in Ukraine modeled on British and Canadian examples.

Ironically, the Ukrainian public at large gave Poroshenko (or Suprun) little to no credit for the generally successful first stage of the medical reform. Nor did it appreciate the decentralization reform or the introduction of a helpful "single window" principle in citizen interaction with the state bureaucracy. His army reform and efforts to curb corruption also did not register as much as they should have. The public focused instead on Poroshenko's confectionary empire, which operated a factory in Russia until 2017; his registration while in office of an offshore company in Cyprus; and the persistent claim in some media—later shown to apply only to 2015—that his personal wealth had increased as a result of the war.

The president's initiatives in the cultural sphere also proved divisive. The 2015 "decommunization" legislation led to the widespread removal of Soviet monuments and street names, the latter often renamed in honor of radical Ukrainian nationalist heroes of the totalitarian age. The public outside of Ukraine's western regions was not always receptive to this rapid turnaround, which also neglected to condemn the legacy of Russian imperial policies under the tsars. The creation, late in Poroshenko's term, of a new Orthodox church independent from the Russian one but recognized by the Patriarch of Constantinople, was often interpreted as part of his re-election campaign. The transfer of parishes to this new church lost much of its initial impetus after Poroshenko's electoral defeat.

Going into the presidential election of 2019, Poroshenko found himself facing low approval rankings linked to the prevalent perception of stalled reforms and a deteriorating standard of living. He decided to make "The army, the language, and faith" the slogan of his campaign, betting on the possibility that the country at war would support a more patriotic incumbent with a proven record of building strong armed forces. However, his campaign stumbled from the start, never really gaining traction outside of the capital, the western regions, and his home ground—the latter also the center of his confectionary business.

As Poroshenko's desperation increased, two incidents sealed the fate of his campaign. In November 2018 the Russian coast guard fired on and captured three small Ukrainian navy boats trying to pass through the Strait of Kerch separating the Black Sea from the Sea of Azov. The two Ukrainian gunboats and a tugboat were being transferred to the Ukrainian port of Mariupol on the Sea of Azov, a procedure that had taken place in the past with no incident, following a notification of the Russian side. The two sides disputed whether the notification was sent this time, and more generally Russia's right to control shipping through the Strait of Kerch, which Russia started claiming after its annexation of the Crimea. In any case, opening fire on Ukrainian ships, ramming one of them, and capturing them all together with their crews raised alarms around the world, as an attack on foreign navy ships was a classic *casus belli* (an incident starting a war or making war an appropriate response). It also fit the UN definition of military aggression.

Poroshenko responded by declaring martial law for 60 days, which would have given him widespread powers and made campaigning impossible for other candidates, but parliament and Western stockholders balked. In the end, parliament approved only a watered-down martial law for 30 days, applying exclusively to regions bordering on Russia and complete with Poroshenko's assurances that the authorities would not use more extreme powers, such as confiscation of property or limitation of personal freedoms. Instead of spurring Ukrainians to unite around the commander-in-chief, Poroshenko's response to the incident at the Strait of Kerch exposed his vulnerabilities.

A corruption scandal erupting just a month before the first round crushed Poroshenko's last hopes. Journalists exposed an outrageous scheme to smuggle used parts from Russian tanks and armored personnel carriers into Ukraine and sell them at exorbitant prices as new. Poroshenko's long-time business associate, who was serving as deputy secretary of the Council of National Security and Defense, reportedly aided and abetted his son and a group of other state officials in running this scheme.[5]

After coming a distant second in the first round, Poroshenko organized the passage of a long-awaited bill on the status of the Ukrainian language that made it mandatory for all public-sector employees. This law, which somehow had not been among the president's priorities for the previous five years, helped to turn the page after the corruption scandal and consolidated the patriotic electorate around Poroshenko. The language law was likely being saved for a projected runoff battle against a pro-Russian candidate, but under the circumstances Poroshenko used it to solidify his support leading into the parliamentary elections of 2019, in which he returned to parliament at the head of a small faction.

What were the results of the anti-corruption policies during the Poroshenko presidency?

When he came to power in the aftermath of the EuroMaidan Revolution, Poroshenko rightly saw corruption as one of the greatest social ills and a major cause of the revolution. In this, he had the strong support of Ukraine's increasingly vocal civil society and the country's Western partners.

The early years of his presidency saw some important breakthroughs in the fight against corruption. One was a public-private initiative to make state procurements—a major source of corruption in Ukraine—transparent by releasing full information on the Internet. Originally designed by an alliance of Ukrainian NGOs and international organizations, a system called ProZorro was then transferred to state ownership and became operational in 2015. (*Prozoro* is Ukrainian for "transparent," but the spelling with a double "r" used in the system's name also references Zorro, the intrepid masked avenger.) Thanks to this open-source electronic system, the details of every new tender and government contract have become easily accessible to journalists and the public at large.

Another notable achievement of Poroshenko's early years in power was the creation of a state register of electronic declarations.

The new anti-corruption law of October 2014 envisaged the obligatory electronic declaration of assets for mid- and upper-level state servants, as well as parliamentarians and police—including in all cases their immediate family members. The Ukrainian bureaucracy and some groups in parliament did everything they could to derail this project. This included the last-minute refusal of a state information-security agency to certify the system, as well as false claims made by some politicians that their declarations had been compromised. Still, the European Union made the introduction of electronic reporting a precondition of visa-free travel to Europe, which had been Poroshenko's major political aim at the time. The system finally became operational in the fall of 2016, and the Ukrainian media had a field day covering a spectacular display of largely unexplained wealth in many declarations, as well as some ridiculous efforts by politicians, known for flashing enormously expensive watches from the windows of their luxury cars, to declare almost no earthly possessions.

The story of the state electronic register of declarations also revealed the limitations of Poroshenko's war on corruption. The law introduced these obligatory declarations in order to enable special state agencies to investigate the sources of unexplained riches or attempts to conceal them. But there were few dismissals from public service and even fewer prosecutions resulting from the filings. As a result of a media outcry in late 2016, Poroshenko's own party and its allies suffered just as much public embarrassment as the opposition. They remained, by and large, part of the old system, in which people went into politics to build or protect their business interests or those of their sponsors. The electronic register was rendered toothless in February 2019, when Ukraine's Constitutional Court conveniently annulled as unconstitutional the Criminal Code's article about illicit enrichment.

It is also telling that from the very beginning both Poroshenko and Ukraine's Western partners saw the solution to curbing corruption in the creation of dedicated investigative and judicial institutions— in essence acknowledging that the existing justice system was part of the problem. In 2015 the Ukrainian government established the National Anti-Corruption Bureau as a separate national investigative agency, as well as the Specialized Anti-Corruption Prosecutor's Office, which could indict suspects. The latter was conceived as fully independent of the Prosecutor General's office in matters of oversight and appointment, but the Ukrainian parliament tried to amend the legislation by placing the anti-corruption prosecutors at all levels under the control of the Prosecutor General and chief prosecutors in the regions. The European Union, which helped design this reform, threatened to withhold the promised visa-free regime and, in the end, the Specialized Anti-Corruption Prosecutor's Office was established as an independent department in the Prosecutor General's administrative structure. This prolonged affair saw the head of the EU's mission in Ukraine consulting with citizen activists before making demands on their government—a signal that the EuroMaidan Revolution had not changed the habits of Ukraine's political class.

It took Ukraine's Western partners even longer to push through the third component of the proposed dedicated structure: the High Anti-Corruption Court of Ukraine. Although this court was envisaged as part of the judiciary reform of 2016, the Ukrainian parliament delayed the passage of the requisite bill until mid-2018, disregarding numerous warnings from the European Union and the International Monetary Fund, among others. The judges and their immediate family members received around-the-clock security protection, and the International Advisory Board was granted the right to veto the appointment of judges. The High Anti-Corruption Court finally started its work in September 2019, several months after Poroshenko's electoral defeat.

In the short run, the National Anti-Corruption Bureau maintained its independence thanks to support from the civil society and international bodies, while the Specialized Anti-Corruption Prosecutor's Office engaged in traditional politicking. In 2018 its head was recorded coaching suspects on how to avoid corruption charges, but he refused to resign, as the US ambassador had suggested publicly. Ukrainian experts see the National Anti-Corruption Bureau as a promising institution, but the Specialized Anti-Corruption Prosecutor's Office as blocking its work.[6] Regardless of the tense relations between the two, in the absence of a specialized and truly independent court, few cases could be brought to trial.

When Poroshenko campaigned for re-election, he cited data from Transparency International as proof that under his watch Ukraine did make some progress in combating corruption: between 2013 and 2018, Ukraine rose from the 144th position to the 120th on the Corruption Perception index.[7] But the 120th position out of 180 nations was still very far from where ordinary Ukrainians expected to be; the two countries immediately above and the three countries below Ukraine in the table were all located in sub-Saharan Africa, not exactly a beacon of political and economic transparency. As with other Poroshenko reforms, Ukrainian voters did not examine his actual record on fighting corruption but voted based on their gut feeling that things were still being run the same old way.

What were the consequences of Ukraine's Association Agreement with the European Union?

Since President Yanukovych's last-minute reversal on concluding this agreement was the last straw that unleashed the revolt, the new Ukrainian authorities sought to sign it as quickly as possible. The Association Agreement does not offer Ukraine a clear accession path to the European Union, as many media commentators have assumed. Its tangible benefits for Ukraine include free trade with the European Union and, at some unspecified point in the future, visa-free travel for Ukrainian citizens. In the long run, the treaty committed Ukraine to aligning its legislation and production standards with that of the European Union, a process to be supported by Western funding.

The Russian government objected to Ukraine's agreement with the European Union on ideological and geopolitical grounds, but advanced an economic argument as its primary reservation. Because Ukraine also had free trade with Russia, European goods could enter Russia through Ukraine with no tariffs being collected on either border. Expressing concern over lost revenues and damage to the economy, Russia threatened retaliatory economic measures. The European leaders paid attention, not so much because of this threat, as because Russia had just annexed the Crimea. As a result, Ukraine and the European Union took the unusual step of dividing the Association Agreement into two parts, general political and economic, and then signing each part separately. In order to provide symbolic closure to the EuroMaidan Revolution, Prime Minister Yatseniuk went to Brussels on March 21, 2014, to sign the mostly declarative political clauses.

Seeing that the Russian-sponsored war in the Donbas had flared up anyway, President Poroshenko signed the contested economic part of the Agreement on June 27, 2014. When the Ukrainian parliament ratified the treaty, the president rhetorically framed the vote as his country's "first but very decisive step" toward future membership in the European Union.[8] The economic provisions were to come into force in November 2014. In mid-September, however, after the first Minsk agreement promised to stop fighting in the Donbas, Ukraine and the European Union agreed to placate Russia by postponing the implementation of free trade until the end of 2015. Instead, the European Union unilaterally removed tariffs on Ukrainian goods, thus hoping to support the Ukrainian economy, while Ukraine continued to collect duties on European imports.

In the end, Ukrainian exports to the European Union did not increase much because few Ukrainian producers could meet the high EU standards, and those who could were already present on the European market. The shrinking Ukrainian economy and war damage in the Donbas did not help either. Visa-free travel also failed to materialize in the year after the treaty. Moreover, after the second Minsk agreement in February 2015 reduced the intensity of fighting in the Donbas, EU representatives announced their intention to hold trilateral talks with Ukraine and Russia on ways of implementing the Association Agreement's economic clauses, which would address Russia's concerns.

What assistance has the United States provided to Ukraine since 2014?

The victory of the EuroMaidan Revolution in 2014 and the simultaneous commencement of Russian aggression against Ukraine redefined the nature of American support for this strategically important nation. Since the 1990s, the bulk of US assistance to Ukraine was aimed at promoting economic and governance reforms, as well as supporting humanitarian causes. The FREEDOM Support Act of 1992—FREEDOM standing for Freedom for Russia and Emerging Eurasian Democracies and Open Markets—defined the main parameters of this American effort and, since the late 1990s, Ukraine, alone among the post-Soviet states, has been its largest beneficiary.

A significant part of US support consisted of loan guarantees and targeted funding for economic development projects. Ukraine also received substantial financial support from international institutions such as the International Monetary Fund and the World Bank, in which the United States and its allies exercised significant influence. Only a small share of Western funding went to army reform in Ukraine.

All this changed in 2014. Consistent American political support of Ukraine's sovereignty within its internationally recognized borders became the most important aspect of bilateral relations. The Obama and Trump administrations, as well as Congress and the Senate, delivered on this promise, which often involved leading by example the more reluctant European allies. Unambiguous American condemnation of the Russian invasion and the annexation of the Crimea, as well as the subsequent imposition of sanctions on Russia, constituted just the kind of political support for which the new Ukrainian authorities had hoped. At the same time, the United States, together with such allies as the United Kingdom and Canada, changed the structure of their respective assistance programs for Ukraine by beefing up their security and military-assistance components.

American support for Ukraine's economic development and political reforms remained significant, constituting on average $380 million per year between 2015 and 2018. But the amount of military support between 2014 and June 2019 was just as impressive, with an estimated total of $1.5 billion. The United States has supplied the Ukrainian army with such essential military equipment as command-and-control systems, counter-artillery radars, and field hospitals. While the Obama administration stopped short of extending this list to lethal weapons, under Trump the State Department approved in 2018 the sale to Ukraine of 210 Javelin anti-tank portable missiles complete with launchers.[9] Although these are reportedly stored away from the front zone, American- and Canadian-made sniper rifles have been distributed to the troops. The delivery of the Javelins had major symbolic significance. Ukraine does produce a similar anti-tank weapon of its own, the RK-3 Korsar, but the arrival of Javelins signified that American support for Ukrainian sovereignty was now on a whole different level. The

Javelins also act as a deterrent of sorts in the conflict, which in its early stages saw the widespread use of Russian tanks.

Another major component of the American contribution to Ukraine's defensive capabilities has been training. Since 2015, the United States, the United Kingdom, and Canada (with smaller contributions from other European allies) have been operating a major military training program at the Yavoriv training field near the Ukrainian-Polish border, far away from the Donbas. Tens of thousands of Ukrainian soldiers and officers have gone through this intensive program. The United States has also led the Western effort to support the reform of the Ukrainian military and security fields. Together with other allied and partner countries, US troops participate in regular small-scale military exercises in Ukraine, Rapid Trident for the ground forces and Sea Breeze for the navy. These annual events help advance the training of the Ukrainian troops, and they also act as a deterrent to Russia's potentially more aggressive moves in the region. Finally, in the wake of Russia's aggression in 2014, the United States started providing vital intelligence and cybersecurity support to Ukraine.

Presently, crucial sectors of the Ukrainian economy and defense rely on American support, which also serves an important symbolic function by encouraging Ukrainian reformers and deterring possible further Russian aggression. Cutting off or delaying US aid in the middle of the ongoing war in the Donbas could seriously weaken the Ukrainian defense capabilities and reform programs. Doing so would also send a confusing message to US allies in the region and beyond.

Did the Ukrainian authorities meddle in the 2016 presidential election in the United States?

The breaking point in the EuroMaidan Revolution came unexpectedly for President Victor Yanukovych and his Party of Regions. The president only had time to pack his most valuable possessions before escaping from his residence outside Kyiv on the evening of February 21, 2014. There was no time to get rid of any potentially compromising paperwork; the staff at the residence simply dumped numerous paper files into the nearby river, where journalists found them floating the next day. The other leaders and administrative officers of the Party of Regions had even less time to escape from the capital. They were fortunate, however, in that the opposition did not think promptly about collecting evidence of the old regime's criminal misdeeds. The revolutionary crowds took some decorations and equipment as souvenirs, and some offices were set ablaze.

Two years later, in May 2016, the Ukrainian public found out about the existence of a large ledger (dubbed in Ukraine "a farmer's barn-book") with hand-written entries detailing secret expenses of the Party of Regions. It came as no surprise that this powerful and thoroughly corrupt political machine had a "black" ledger for bribes and other illegal payments, but Ukrainians were stunned to find out that it was kept in writing and the recipients or intermediaries actually signed in the last column. The notebook reportedly covered the period of 2007–2012, and the total expenditures amounted to approximately US$2 billion. The black ledger contained the names of numerous ministers, parliamentarians, judges, members of the Central Electoral Commission, political commentators, and journalists. Some of their signatures have since been authenticated, granting the black ledger certain credibility.

Whoever kept the ledger for two years was clearly waiting for the right moment to reap political or financial benefits from it. In the Ukrainian political and justice systems, the records' chief value lay in the political damage they could do rather than in the uncertain possibility of anyone getting convicted. Some pages had possibly already been "cashed" by then, as it was difficult to confirm the completeness of the records and some pages were made public separately both before and after the surrender of the ledger to the Ukrainian authorities. The initial announcement in May 2016 came from two well-known investigative journalists, Serhii Leshchenko (since 2014 a member of the parliament representing Poroshenko's party) and Sevgil Musaieva, although they only had several pages in their possession. It was the freshly fired deputy head of the Security Service of Ukraine, Viktor Trepak, who simultaneously handed in the bulk of the ledger to the authorities. General Trepak had served in high positions under both Yanukovych and Poroshenko and had extensive contacts among security-service officers. He never explained how the folder had come into his possession, but the timing of its release was clearly connected to his firing rather than any developments in the United States. Trepak's subsequent media interviews focused on his revelation of the corrupt nature of Ukrainian politics both before and after the EuroMaidan Revolution.

When the news broke in Ukraine, the public likewise focused more on the Ukrainian politicians who were implicated, especially the ones still prominent in public life. The then head of the Central Electoral Commission, Mykhailo Okhendovsky, was the only one to be officially charged, although in the end his case did not go to trial, as was common in cases of political figures. In early June, Leshchenko testified at the National Anti-Corruption Bureau, but then the summer began and with it, the dead season in Ukrainian politics. In mid-August Leshchenko broke some sensational news that was immediately confirmed by the head of the National Anti-Corruption Bureau: The black ledger also listed the American lobbyist and political consultant Paul Manafort. He was well known in Ukraine as a long-serving advisor to Viktor Yanukovych and the Party of Regions. Manafort was credited with rebuilding Yanukovych's image inside Ukraine after his defeat in the Orange Revolution of 2004–2005, as well as making him more acceptable to American decision makers during his tenure as president from 2010. Little was known at the time about his role during the EuroMaidan Revolution; subsequently, messages allegedly hacked from his daughter's phone in 2017 seemed to suggest that he had proposed a violent scenario to end the revolution after a staged provocation,[10] but he was also involved in early attempts to rebuild the pro-Russian forces into a viable opposition after the EuroMaidan Revolution. Not only did Manafort work for the discredited Yanukovych and other pro-Russian forces in Ukraine but also he had known connections to Russian oligarchs. His account in the black ledger was also one of the largest, with a total of US$12.7 million recorded between 2007 and 2012. (Two prominent businessmen who sat in parliament as members of Yanukovych's party signed as intermediaries on these disbursements.)

For all the right reasons that patriotic Ukrainians had to dislike Manafort, the timing of Leshchenko's revelation was highly suspicious. Since June 2016 Manafort had been the manager of Trump's presidential campaign, and the release of any compromising material on him was bound to harm it. It is also telling that the announcement came from someone better known as a controversial investigative journalist than a politician, although the head of the Ukrainian anti-corruption agency conveniently confirmed Leshchenko's words right away, adding that a name in the ledger in and of itself did not prove anything. The ever-present factionalism in Ukrainian politics and Leshchenko's reputation as a loose cannon cast some doubt on conspiracy theories presenting this affair as Ukraine's state policy of interference in the US elections. But even if one accepts the view that the Ukrainian authorities sought plausible denial by allowing Leshchenko to break the story, Manafort's transgressions were very real, and concealing this information about his entries in the black ledger would have constituted interference as well, benefiting the Trump camp. The Poroshenko administration found itself in a predicament, and its strategy of issuing only a limited confirmation of Leshchenko's story from the technically independent National Anti-Corruption Bureau was likely the safest choice. Doing so meant leaving this matter up to the American justice system.

It has since been revealed that the Federal Bureau of Investigation (FBI) began investigating Manafort in connection with his work for Yanukovych back in 2014; other US agencies opened investigations into his activities in 2016, based in part on his communication with Russian agents. As soon as Manafort joined the Trump campaign in March 2016, Alexandra Chalupa, the Ukrainian American consultant working for the Democratic Party on relations with ethnic communities and a former White House staffer, alerted the Democratic National Committee to Manafort's problematic connections in Ukraine and Russia. Chalupa then focused on investigating Manafort's record in Ukraine. She acknowledged involving in her search some unnamed Ukrainian investigative journalists. According to the investigation by *Politico* magazine, Chalupa also discussed this matter at Ukraine's embassy to the United States. Whether she received any research assistance from the embassy's staff is disputed; the embassy would only confirm the fact of the meetings rather than any help in investigating Manafort. Chalupa herself soon became the target of hacking attacks and break-ins, which she blamed on the Russian security agencies.[11] In any case, her (and Leshchenko's) role in the Manafort affair was over, because the US justice system could work directly with the Ukrainian agencies. In June 2016 the FBI signed a memorandum of understanding with Ukraine's National Anti-Corruption Bureau, which enabled their cooperation in the investigation of international crimes related to corruption and money laundering.

It is difficult to blame the fall of Manafort on a conspiracy concocted by the Ukrainian government—he was convicted by a US court based on evidence from various international sources rather than the unconfirmed entries in the black ledger of the Party of Regions. If anything, it appears that the Ukrainian authorities were trying to distance themselves from the Manafort scandal by leaving a muckraking journalist to continue as the main spokesperson on this issue. It certainly was not a coherent state-coordinated campaign, as in the case of the Russian interference in 2016. Unlike Russia, Ukraine had little at stake in the 2016 elections because it enjoyed bipartisan American support, but a lot to lose if it were to be implicated in any wrongdoings. Yet, there was one important, if largely symbolic, aspect. To the Ukrainian public, Manafort came to represent the "wrong" side of America, one that was willing to cozy up to the Yanukovych regime and was open to various corrupt deals. His fall thus became the American echo of the EuroMaidan Revolution, Ukraine's fight for freedom and dignity.

What do we know about the involvement of Joe Biden and his son Hunter in Ukrainian affairs?

As a US senator, Joe Biden has cultivated an interest in European affairs and, more specifically, in the Soviet Union and its successor states. Between 2001 and 2009 he served three times as chairman of the Senate Committee on Foreign Relations. Biden's foreign policy experience was one of the reasons that Barack Obama picked him as running mate in 2008.

As vice president between 2009 and 2017, Biden visited Ukraine six times, sometimes making a brief stop on a larger tour of Europe or the United States' strategic allies in Europe, the Caucasus, and Central Asia. The Obama administration saw Ukraine, together with the Republic of Georgia, as the two keystone states in the region; both also experienced Russian aggression. To Ukrainian politicians and the public at large, Biden's frequent visits symbolized American commitment to building a strong, independent Ukraine free of corruption and rule by cronyism. During one trip to Ukraine, in February 2014, Biden witnessed the revolution on the Maidan entering its crucial stage. All of this made him popular with patriotic Ukrainians, who realized nonetheless that their fight for freedom enjoyed bipartisan support in the United States. The late Republican senator John McCain also visited often and spoke even more strongly in support of the EuroMaidan; there is now a street in the Ukrainian capital named after him.

Because Ukraine had developed by the early 2000s into a kleptocracy, a thoroughly corrupt state with most public servants at all levels involved in various embezzlement schemes, Western support of Ukraine had to take unorthodox forms. The United States and its allies often found themselves supporting Ukrainian civil society against its own corrupt political class. As explained elsewhere in this book, Ukraine's Western partners routinely had to force the Ukrainian political elites into accepting important reforms by making them a condition for receiving a major loan from the IMF or visa-free travel to the European Union. Because their states were now major stakeholders in the fight for reforms in Ukraine, ambassadors of the major Western countries showed up in the Ukrainian parliament on the dates of crucial votes. Rather undiplomatically, they would also speak publicly about the need to remove certain corrupt Ukrainian officials, as the US ambassador did in March 2019, when the Chief Anti-Corruption Prosecutor was taped advising suspects on how to avoid corruption charges.[12]

In this context, Biden's micro-management of Ukrainian politics was nothing out of the ordinary. When an independent Ukrainian parliamentarian with KGB and Russian connections released to the public in May 2020 audio clips from 2015 and 2016, purported to be from Biden's (and then Secretary of State John Kerry's) phone calls with President Poroshenko, there was nothing there even close to the "favor" Trump asked of Zelensky in July. What stood out in these tapes was how closely the United States was involved in forcing the various Ukrainian reformist parties to work together, as well as in pushing through major anti-corruption measures. Although the tapes confirm the well-known story of Biden making US$1 billion in American loan guarantees conditional on the removal of the then

Prosecutor General Viktor Shokin in 2016, Biden never denied this and, in fact, spoke repeatedly of this episode.

Although Poroshenko saw Shokin as a reliable ally, the Ukrainian public disagreed, giving him a stunning negative rating of 73.2 percent in a February 2016 poll.[13] By then, the US ambassador, EU representatives, the IMF, and leading Ukrainian anti-corruption groups denounced Shokin for blocking decisive anti-corruption measures and the much-needed reform of the prosecution system. His own deputy resigned because of the alleged corruption and politicking in the Prosecutor General's Office. Biden's 2016 ultimatum to Poroshenko was thus completely in line with the opinion of Western diplomats and the Ukrainian public. Shokin was forced to resign, not because he was investigating the wrong people, but because he was not investigating them with sufficient vigor. Nobody in Ukraine protested his removal.

Until Trump raised this issue in his phone call with Zelensky in July 2019, the Ukrainian public knew nothing about Hunter Biden and his Ukrainian connection. After Trump and Giuliani suggested that Shokin's ouster had been motivated by his investigation of the Burisma gas company that had employed Biden's son, Hunter, as a board member, this matter became widely discussed in Ukraine— and investigated by the National Anti-Corruption Bureau. A large natural gas company owned by an oligarch associated with the Yanukovych regime, Burisma was vulnerable after the EuroMaidan. While serving as minister of the environment before 2012, its oligarch owner issued exploration and extraction permits to his own gas company. In April 2014 Burisma hired the American lobbyist and investment advisor Hunter Biden to serve on its board as a specialist on corporate governance. Of course, this lucrative job, which included a salary of up to US$50,000 per month and none too onerous duties, had everything to do with his family name. Nepotism is an important part of post-Soviet business culture, but it is difficult to imagine a large Ukrainian company run by people so naïve as to believe that they could buy the "protection" of a US vice president this way. The more likely reason was a kind of name-dropping intended to make enemies think twice before going after a company for which the son of a US vice president considered it appropriate to work. At the same time, the company also hired the former president of Poland, Aleksander Kwaśniewski. In other words, Burisma was trying to create the image of a "clean" and well-connected company rather than buying actual immunity from prosecution. The National Anti-Corruption Bureau confirmed that at some point Burisma had indeed been investigated by the Prosecutor General's Office, but the investigation concerned the company's actions between 2010 and 2012, well before Hunter Biden came on board. It was also dormant in 2016, when Joe Biden pushed for Shokin's ouster. Neither in 2016 nor later did the Ukrainian authorities document any wrongdoing on the part of Hunter Biden. After Trump and Giuliani put forward their own version of events, Shokin tried to return from political oblivion by claiming that his dismissal had been connected to the investigation of Burisma, but no documents or recordings have surfaced in support of this interpretation. The sensational release of the "Biden Tapes" in Ukraine in May 2020 ultimately flopped because nothing in the clips posted on the Internet supported the conspiratorial version that Trump and Giuliani promoted.

How can one explain the sweeping victory of Volodymyr Zelensky and his party in the Ukrainian presidential and parliamentary elections of 2019?

Only four months before the March 2019 presidential election, the Ukrainian political scene looked familiar. President Poroshenko was seeking re-election on a pro-European integration platform, and the strongest opposition figure was the ideologically similar Yulia Tymoshenko, who remained critical of Poroshenko's record on reform. Weakened by the Russian occupation of the Crimea and parts of the Donbas, where their most reliable voters lived, the pro-Russian opposition could not mount a united campaign or agree on a single candidate. Poroshenko and Tymoshenko had been in politics for nearly two decades, as had Yuri Boiko, the higher polling of the two pro-Russian candidates. The only thing that seemed unusual was the exceptionally low support for these familiar political figures. Ukrainians appeared tired of them all.

All the calculations and strategies that these main players had developed for the campaign were confounded on New Year's Eve, when the popular comedian Volodymyr Zelensky announced on television his intention to participate in the election. Zelensky represented the direct opposite of establishment candidates—he had zero political experience and the mien of an honest everyman. A successful entrepreneur, he rose to fame as the star of an unpretentious Russian-language comedy television show, but he also possessed the Charlie Chaplin–like charisma of a "little man" refusing to accept this world's injustices. The latter came out clearly in a television series called *Servant of the People*, where Zelensky played a lowly history teacher who accidentally becomes the president and attempts to build a more equitable Ukraine. The runaway success of this series gave Zelensky and his supporters the idea of transitioning into politics, and early secret polling showed that he could do very well in an election. Zelensky's open acknowledgment of being Jewish did not hurt his popularity at all, contradicting the stereotype of Ukrainian anti-Semitism.

By the beginning of March, Zelensky's candidacy came to dominate the polls, leaving all others to fight over a place in the runoffs. Shrewdly, he and his advisors delayed until the last moment the release of any platform, which meant that voters ascribed to him the intentions of his popular television persona. Zelensky did not speak against the Ukrainian language and culture but downplayed such issues by stressing that peace and reforms had to take precedence. He managed to undercut his main rivals by attracting voters from across the ethno-linguistic spectrum—both Ukrainian- and Russian-speakers, who, for quite different reasons, felt disillusioned with Poroshenko and his traditional opponents. Meanwhile, Poroshenko had to use all his considerable powers as president and oligarchical owner of two television channels to secure second place in the race. He campaigned on the slogan, "The army, the language, and faith," but even during the de facto war with Russia, such a narrowly national-patriotic program appealed to only a small sector of the electorate. Poroshenko's unsuccessful attempt to introduce martial law after the Russians captured Ukrainian navy boats in the Strait of Kerch in November 2018 undermined his posture as commander-in-chief. Erupting just before the election, a corruption scandal over military acquisitions involving his longtime business partner, then serving as deputy chairman of the Council of National Security and Defense, made the president's slogans about the army ring hollow.

Thirty-nine candidates were on the ballot on March 31, 2019, but Zelensky enjoyed a clear lead in this crowded field, receiving 30.24 percent of the vote. Poroshenko came a very distant second, with 15.95 percent, followed by Tymoshenko with 13.40. The top ten included two mutually antagonistic candidates from the pro-Russian opposition; taken together, their share of the vote would have been 15.82 percent. For all the talk in the Western media about the alleged influence of Ukrainian right-wing groups, the candidate from their flagship Freedom Party received only 1.62 percent. Going into the run-offs, Poroshenko attempted to recruit the supporters of other candidates, but he could not overcome his remarkably high negative rating—the share of voters prepared to vote for anyone but him. When the country went to the polls again on April 21, 2019, Zelensky won easily, with 73.22 percent compared to Poroshenko's 24.45.[14] The incumbent carried only the western province of Lviv, a traditional stronghold of nationalism and, ironically, the electoral district comprising Ukrainian citizens living abroad.

Following Zelensky's astonishing success in the spring of 2019, parliamentary elections were scheduled for October. However, his advisors hoped to leverage the president's current popularity, and Zelensky dissolved parliament on his inauguration day, thus triggering snap elections for July. His party was a very recent creation. Zelensky campaigned for president without having his own party, although polls had demonstrated strong support for a hypothetical populist force, and the party name Servant of the People had been registered proactively in 2018. The work of creating a party and selecting its candidates for the parliamentary election was done hurriedly during May and June of 2019. The overwhelming majority of the candidates were younger people with little political experience, but who had worked for NGOs or studied in the West. The party leadership consisted of Zelensky's circle of entertainment-industry lawyers and managers, together with a few former bureaucrats and trusted political commentators. Sensing the nature of his political appeal, Zelensky promised that the party would not ally in the future parliament with either Poroshenko or the pro-Russian opposition. An alliance with Yulia Tymoshenko was apparently considered, but Zelensky's advisors quickly understood that they could capture some of her voters by imitating her populist rhetoric. Soliciting Tymoshenko's support would have meant giving her and her people their share of high appointments and potentially would have proven unnecessary. Thus, Zelensky's party announced that it would not include in its list any candidates who had served previously in parliament. This anti-establishment message held its appeal on election day.

In the election held on July 21, 2019, Servant of the People won an outright majority in the parliament by securing 254 seats of 450, and for the first time in the history of independent Ukraine, the winning party did not need to join any coalitions. The pro-Russian opposition, now organized as the tandem of the Opposition Platform and the new party For Life, came second with 43 seats; followed by Tymoshenko's Fatherland with 26, the Petro Poroshenko Bloc with 25, and the new party Voice with 20. It is telling that the Servant of the People won in both colleges: it received 124 seats of the 225 awarded based on the nationwide vote for party lists and 130 seats of the 199 in the first-by-the-post territorial electoral districts. (The total number of the latter was also 225, but 26 were in areas not controlled by the Ukrainian authorities.)[15]

The success of Zelensky's party led to attempts by others to emulate his approach. For example, For Life (with the connotation of "for a good life" rather than pro-life) was established by the pro-Russian businessman-cum-television personality Vadym Rabynovych in order to capture voters not enthused by the gloomy-looking Boiko. Similarly, a rock singer popular with patriotic youth, Sviatoslav Vakarchuk, created Voice to appeal to those younger voters disillusioned with Poroshenko. It was widely expected that Voice would enter a close alliance with the Poroshenko Bloc, but instead it was courted by Servant of the People as a potential coalition partner. In the end, however, their alliance was informal and short-lived.

How can one evaluate President Zelensky's first year in power?

When he was campaigning for the presidency, Zelensky relied on broad populist statements rather than a realistic program. This encouraged expectations among his voters of an immediate peace with Russia, a complete overhaul of Ukrainian politics, an easy victory over corruption, and a radical improvement in their standard of living. In contrast, his opponents sounded a note of concern. They tried to present him as a puppet of the oligarch Ihor Kolomoisky, owner of the television station where Zelensky worked as a co-median and producer, issuing a warning over the possibility that Zelensky would seek to conclude peace with Putin at any cost. The public pressure on Zelensky proved helpful during his first year in office (May 2019–May 2020).

The Zelensky administration was composed almost entirely of new faces, which at first seemed to satisfy the public's demand for a new political class. However, some high-profile resignations during the first year indicated that not all the president's friends from the entertainment industry would become efficient and discreet state officials with a clear understanding of national interests. At the same time, Zelensky's complete overhaul of the cabinet after only six months showed that he was worried more about his approval ratings than about giving his ministers, who not so long ago had been introduced to the public as young, Western-educated professionals, a chance to produce results. In general, the emphasis on new faces in politics produced ambivalent results. In addition to some skillful managers generating promising ideas, a lack of qualifications and strategic thinking were also apparent among the members of the first cabinet that Zelensky's party formed under Prime Minister Oleksii Honcharuk (August 2019–March 2020) and the second one under Prime Minister Denys Shmyhal. Many observers rejoiced at the re-tention in the Honcharuk cabinet of Poroshenko's last finance min-ister, Oksana Markarova, but decried the presence in both cabinets of another survivor from the Poroshenko era, the powerful Minister of Internal Affairs Arsen Avakov, a skilled political showman with his own agenda.

Some of Zelensky's initial moves were intended for public con-sumption, such as the bold proposal to carry out lustration of all the officials and parliamentarians from Poroshenko's time, as though Ukraine's real problems had started after the EuroMaidan. Ukraine's Western partners disapproved of this suggestion, and it was shelved quickly. However, criminal investigations of Poroshenko and some of his allies were opened and their summons for questioning highly publicized.

Zelensky's attempts to end the war in the Donbas also became controversial, and many experts felt that scrutiny of his actions by the patriotic opposition prevented some costly mistakes. At first,

Zelensky focused on convening a meeting of the Normandy Four, which would show his acceptance as a statesman by both the West and Russia, as well as demonstrate to the domestic audience the renewal of the peace process. However, Putin insisted on troop disengagement in several crucial sections of the front, which resulted conveniently in the Ukrainian army's abandonment of some controlling positions. These were to become neutral zones, but in some cases the enemy tried to move in.

Zelensky also recklessly accepted another of Putin's demands, which Poroshenko had avoided wisely for years: acceptance of the Steinmeier Formula requirement that Ukraine grant autonomy to the occupied areas without the prior removal of Russian troops. Mass protests erupted throughout Ukraine in October 2019, after Zelensky authorized the Ukrainian representative to commit to the formula. The president hastily retreated to Poroshenko's position that no elections could take place there given the presence of Russian troops and the absence of Ukrainian control of the border. Prisoner exchanges, which came to include any civilian prisoners claimed by the opposing sides, also failed to bolster Zelensky's reputation as a peacemaker. Putin preferred to highlight the role that the pro-Russian Ukrainian politicians played in the exchanges and, on Russia's demand, Ukraine had to include in the exchanges its own policemen who were under investigation for killing protestors in 2014, which caused indignation among Maidan veterans.

Zelensky did get his Normandy Four summit in Paris in December 2019, even if it turned out to be a purely symbolic event without major breakthroughs; in all other respects, his foreign policy increasingly resembled Poroshenko's.

In the sphere of domestic policy, Zelensky tried to prove wrong those who accused him of being Kolomoisky's puppet and suspected that his agenda was limited to the realignment of the existing power groups. Using his party's parliamentary dominance after the July 2019 elections, he pushed through some remarkable pieces of legislation, which many previous Ukrainian leaders had talked about at election time but conveniently forgot about once they were in power. These included the law on presidential impeachment, the removal of parliamentary immunity from prosecution, and land reform.

The latter was particularly significant because it finally removed the prohibition on the sale of land in the countryside—a communist legacy that favored oligarchs, as major agricultural businesses could rent land much more cheaply than having to purchase it (and paying a sales tax to the state). It was also easy for their political allies to sell the ban to the public by using populist language of the sacred Ukrainian soil that could be bought by foreign interests. If implemented properly, the land reform could potentially rejuvenate the Ukrainian economy and fill government coffers.

Finally, Zelensky tried hard to distance himself from Kolomoisky, who returned from abroad apparently expecting a turn of fortune. Nevertheless, under the watchful eye of Ukrainian civil society and the country's Western partners, the Zelensky administration did not do what many commentators had expected: reverse the nationalization in 2016 of Kolomoisky's Privat Bank, the county's largest bank, or pay the oligarch a massive amount in compensation. The government took over the bank in 2016 because Kolomoisky had allegedly been trying to bankrupt it through fraudulent lending schemes, and the authorities then spent some US$6 billion stabilizing the bank. In May 2020 the Ukrainian parliament passed a law preventing former owners of insolvent and nationalized banks from reclaiming them. The IMF made the passing of such legislation a key condition for the resumption of its loan program to Ukraine, which was expected to provide US$5 billion with $3.5 billion disbursed before the end of 2020.

Ukraine entered the period of the coronavirus pandemic in reasonably good financial shape but also with an unfinished healthcare reform, which the Zelensky administration was considering halting. To compensate for this and to account for the return of many Ukrainian temporary workers from some of the European countries that were hit hardest by COVID-19, the Ukrainian authorities tried to institute quarantine measures that were stricter than elsewhere. At least in the short run, Ukraine has managed to limit the scale of the pandemic, although the damage to the country's economy remains to be evaluated. As Zelensky marked the first year since his inauguration with a well-attended press conference held in May 2020 in a public park in Kyiv, opinion polls indicated that he was still the most popular politician by far in Ukraine.

*How did the Zelensky administration react to the attempts
to embroil Ukraine in American politics?*

Before the scandal surrounding President Trump's July 25, 2019,
phone conversation with President Zelensky exploded in the world
media in September 2019, the Ukrainian public was blissfully unaware of their leadership's difficult position vis-à-vis the US president. Few Ukrainians noticed the June 2019 revelation in the media
that Trump's lawyer Rudy Giuliani had used the services of two
Russian-speaking American businessmen, Lev Parnas and Igor
Fruman, to establish contacts with Ukraine's prosecutor general and
his predecessor in this position in late 2018. To Ukrainians, Giuliani's
search for compromising information on Joe Biden was nothing
out of the ordinary, because for decades Ukrainian politicians had
exploited the country's justice system in order to undermine their
rivals' reputation, if not to imprison them. The office of prosecutor
general has consistently ranked near the bottom among Ukrainian
state institutions as measured by public trust. Prosecutor General
Viktor Shokin (in office 2015–2016 and reportedly eager to coop-
erate with Giuliani in 2018) was widely seen as obstructing the fight
against corruption. This position became openly politicized under
Yuri Lutsenko (in office 2016–2019), Ukraine's first prosecutor general without a law degree and one of Poroshenko's worst hiring
mistakes. In other words, the Americans were doing what ordinary
Ukrainians would expect from their own politicians.

Zelensky, however, had been swept to power on a wave of popular discontent with precisely such backroom politicking. His
hastily assembled team had few experienced political hands, but its
members understood the need to project an image of transparent
governance. Before the March 2019 election Zelensky's campaign
managers were unaware of the difficult problem in US-Ukrainian relations they were about to inherit from Poroshenko. When Giuliani
first contacted Prosecutor General Lutsenko about the Bidens and
alleged Ukrainian interference in the 2016 presidential election,
one can safely assume that President Poroshenko knew about this
and likely authorized Lutsenko to meet with Giuliani in person in
New York in January 2019. Moreover, Poroshenko himself met with
Giuliani twice in early 2019. The Ukrainian president retroactively
acknowledged the meetings but avoided questions about what was

discussed there, other than American assistance with Ukrainian cybersecurity—a strange topic to discuss with a person holding no official position in the US administration. According to Parnas, Giuliani offered Trump's support for Poroshenko's re-election bid, complete with a visit to the White House, in exchange for an investigation into the Bidens and Ukraine's alleged role in 2016.

After Zelensky took an impressive lead in the first round on March 31, members of the Poroshenko team started fighting for their political survival. Prosecutor General Lutsenko, who had the lowest chance of remaining in office, took a desperate gamble by denouncing publicly the US ambassador to Ukraine, Marie Yovanovitch, for allegedly impeding his fight against corruption. In his trademark populist style, Lutsenko claimed that Yovanovitch had given him a "do-not-prosecute" list of Ukrainian officials—a statement he would eventually retract. Lutsenko intended to demonstrate his usefulness to Trump, but instead he alerted the Zelensky team to the conflicting signals from Washington. Trump's removal of Yovanovitch in late April 2019, right after Zelensky's sweeping runoff victory, put the American dilemma at the top of the new president's agenda.

It remains unclear when exactly Giuliani first contacted the Zelensky team and whether the level of American representation at the new president's inauguration was used as an incentive in these early contacts. In the end it was rather low, with the highest US official in attendance being the then Secretary of Energy Rick Perry. We know that Parnas and Fruman stayed in Kyiv for Zelensky's inauguration in early May 2019 and Giuliani himself acknowledged having planned a trip to Ukraine for the same month. However, he canceled it when the Ukrainian side refused to commit to his personal meeting with Zelensky. Meanwhile, the new Ukrainian administration remained shell-shocked by the American overtures, which bypassed the US embassy. Zelensky reportedly even digressed into discussing this conundrum during meetings devoted to energy issues. His advisors apparently asked senior Western diplomats whom they could contact in Washington to clarify how to treat Trump's personal envoys.

In late May, Zelensky appointed Andrii Yermak as his aide for foreign-policy issues, and it was this lawyer and film producer—rather than the Ministry of Foreign Affairs—who handled all the subsequent interactions of the President's Office with Trump's personal representatives and US officials pursuing a similar agenda, such as Special Envoy to Ukraine Kurt Volker and US Ambassador to the EU Gordon Sondland. The Ukrainians understood the impossibility, for political reasons, of taking sides in the forthcoming US presidential election. The Manafort case and Trump's reaction to Ukrainian involvement in it communicated this lesson loud and clear. Yet, the Ukrainian negotiators also found themselves trying to persuade Trump's representatives that they were no enemies of the US president, who appeared to have taken umbrage at their neutral stand. As Yermak would later tell the *Los Angeles Times*, he spent weeks during the summer of 2019 "attempting to reassure U.S. officials that the United States had no enemies in the Ukrainian leadership," all the while feeling "dismayed that [his] country had been dragged into Washington's political fights."[16] From the Ukrainian perspective, the stakes were higher than the withholding of $391 million in US military aid that summer; they felt they were under suspicion as possible enemies. This charge brought fears of being denied American moral and diplomatic support, as well as billions in IMF loans, and perhaps even being abandoned to face Russia's aggression alone.

The Ukrainian position remained consistent: a commitment to political transparency and investigation of all suspected cases of corruption, but without promises to fast-track or prejudge any cases of particular interest to Trump. Occasionally, the two sides could be left with different impressions of the outcome, as was the case after Giuliani's meeting with Yermak in Spain in early August 2019, when Giuliani felt he had secured the desired promise. That same month Volker and Sondland drafted a statement that they wanted Zelensky to make about his commitment to investigate the Bidens and the issue of Ukrainian rather than Russian interference in the 2016 US election, but the Ukrainian president never issued it.

This entire struggle went on in private, without the Ukrainian public being aware of what was happening behind the scenes. In September 2019, when the US media revealed the content of Trump's July phone call with Zelensky, the impact on the Ukrainian administration was mixed. The transcription did not present Zelensky as a strong leader or skillful statesman; he was playing up to Trump and shamelessly complimenting him, while belittling Ukraine's European partners. But Zelensky's stand reflected the vulnerable position of his country. The revelation of Trump's perverse demands on the Ukrainian government lifted a burden from Zelensky's shoulders. Now that Trump's requests had become public—triggering impeachment proceedings in the United States—the Ukrainian authorities no longer needed to fulfill them. Zelensky's popularity in Ukraine did not suffer as a result of the scandal.

Has the Ukrainian crisis sparked a new Cold War?

In the wake of the conflict in Ukraine, relations between the West and Russia are at their lowest ebb since the Cold War ended. Escalating political rhetoric on both sides, as well as the mutual use of diplomatic and economic sanctions, also reminds observers of the international tensions during the Cold War. Yet there are three important reservations to be made here.

First, books and articles about the "new Cold War" between Russia and the West started appearing years before the Ukrainian crisis. The first edition of *New Cold War* by Edward Lucas came out in 2008, and the Canadian journalist Mark MacKinnon published a book under the same title a year earlier.[17] Tensions have been growing since the first decade of the 2000s, when the newly empowered Putin administration embarked on a course of rebuilding a stronger Russia, which could challenge Western values and the unipolar world order that emerged after the Cold War.

The Kremlin reacted nervously to what it interpreted as US involvement in the Rose Revolution in Georgia in 2003 and Ukraine's Orange Revolution of 2004–2005. In both countries, the Russian military got involved in supporting separatist movements in 2008 and 2014, respectively. A similar Russian-supported breakaway state has existed within another Western-leaning neighbor, Moldova, since 1992: the unrecognized Republic of Transnistria, which still uses a Soviet-style coat of arms decades after the collapse of communism.

The Ukrainian crisis did not spark a new Cold War but, rather, manifested the escalation of tensions simmering ever since the Soviet Union fell apart, which was ultimately connected to that event. A peaceful solution in Ukraine in and of itself would not resolve the larger tensions between Russia and the West. In fact, peace in Ukraine is not an internal issue but an international one.

Second, the current tensions differ from the original Cold War in that they are neither global nor ideologically driven. The Putin administration is trying to find an ideological foundation for its brand of authoritarian state capitalism, but so far it has not been able to construct a coherent ideology out of Orthodox Christianity and Eurasianism, the latter representing Russia's "manifest destiny" of building a land empire encompassing two continents. The anti-Western rhetoric of the Russian state media is equally incoherent in that it combines attacks on liberal democracy with nostalgia for Soviet great-power status, but not for communism itself. Similarly, Russia can oppose American policies toward Venezuela, Syria, Libya, and Iran, but on geopolitical rather than ideological grounds. Furthermore, Russia does not have the capacity to involve itself in far-flung global conflicts in the way the Soviet Union did. The so-called near abroad, or the former constituent republics of the Soviet Union, such as Ukraine or Georgia, is a different matter.

Finally, the conflict in Ukraine did not rise to the level of a Cold War–era "proxy war" between the superpowers. Although Russia was involved directly, if covertly, in military actions in Ukraine, the United States was not. In the spring of 2015, when the conflict had been raging for almost a year, the Obama administration was still weighing the option of supplying Ukraine with lethal weapons, possibly hoping that the very discussion of such a possibility would serve as a deterrent to Russia and its clients in the Donbas.

Viewed from a longer historical perspective, it is clear that the crisis in Ukraine is only masquerading as ethnic strife. It is a conflict over what type of a state and society will develop in the post-Soviet political space, and a part of Putin's challenge to the unipolar world order that emerged after the Cold War. As such, the conflict can only be resolved in a wider international framework. Local peacemaking in Ukraine is a global issue.

How did the issue of election interference change the dynamics within the Russia-Ukraine-United States triangle?

Although the actual effect of Russian interference in the 2016 US presidential election remains unclear and Donald Trump's possible collusion with the Russian authorities hotly debated, the fact of the Russian state's interference is well established. Numerous US agencies confirmed the existence of a well-coordinated disinformation campaign involving coverage in the Russian state media, opinions promoted on social media by Russian-based troll factories, and hacker attacks with subsequent releases of the hacked information. The US intelligence agencies believed that a coherent campaign on this scale was likely approved personally by President Putin.

What is not so widely known is that some of these methods were originally tried during the Ukrainian presidential election of 2014. In 2017 Russia attempted an even more brazen intervention in the French presidential election, resulting in a stern warning from France. Russian disinformation campaigns follow a certain model and are usually calculated to support candidate(s) seen as more friendly toward Russia or to sow discord in the target countries. In the case of the 2016 presidential election in the United States, Russian efforts were clearly aimed at harming the Democratic Party and its presidential candidate, Hillary Clinton.

However, President Trump has denied all this and characterized Russian interference as a conspiracy theory contrived to explain Clinton's defeat. He attempted to use the Manafort case to argue that it was Ukraine, in fact, that interfered in the US elections in 2016 on the side of the Clinton campaign. As explained elsewhere in this book, evidence against Manafort was bound to emerge in Ukraine because of his considerable involvement with the old regime there and his numerous transgressions against Ukrainian and US laws. When it did become public, the news did not come from state agencies but from an outlier parliamentarian from the president's party, who was also a controversial investigative journalist. The next Ukrainian administration did not confirm Mr. Trump's claims. During his visit to Ukraine, Trump's personal lawyer Rudy Giuliani failed to secure the collaboration of any significant, mainstream political figures in the quest to undermine Joe Biden's candidacy in the 2020 US elections. When an independent pro-Russian parliamentarian released the so-called Biden Tapes following Giuliani's visit, the sensation fell flat, and the new Ukrainian administration avoided getting dragged into the American political struggles. Following this incident in May 2020, seven former US ambassadors to Ukraine issued a statement against the attempts to involve Ukraine in US domestic politics as advancing "a false and toxic narrative, one with no basis in the reality of US-Ukraine relations, in order to weaken the relationship between the United States and Ukraine and sow division within our two countries."[18]

Regardless of such a marked difference between Russian involvement and alleged Ukrainian interference, Ukraine did acquire in certain circles in the West the reputation of a place where one could always find compromising material on any visiting Westerner. Even more troubling for Ukrainians was the perception that the Trump administration was willing to whitewash the Russian disinformation war and, instead, present Ukraine as a troublemaker. American support of Ukraine against Russian aggression was also thrown into doubt in the summer of 2019 with the withholding of US$391 million in military assistance. As Ukraine enters the seventh year of the war in the Donbas, uncertainty about the positions and motives of its most important Western partner threatens to undermine security both regionally and globally.

NOTES

Chapter 1

1. See the photo album *Studentska revoliutsiia na hraniti*, ed. Oles Donii (Kyiv: Smoloskyp, 1995).
2. Marcel H. Van Herpen, *Putin's Wars: The Rise of Russia's New Imperialism* (Lanham, MD: Rowman & Littlefield, 2014), p. 4.
3. "Address by President of the Russian Federation, March 14, 2014," *President of Russia* (http://eng.kremlin.ru/transcripts/6889).

Chapter 2

1. Oleksandr Kramar, "Nas bulo 52 mln: De podilysia 6,000,000?" *tyzhden. ua*, December 24, 2012 (http://mobile.tyzhden.ua/Society/39402); "Naselennia Ukrainy," *Derzhavna sluzhba statystyky Ukrainy* (http://database.ukrcensus.gov.ua/MULT/Dialog/statfile_c.asp).
2. See the text of the 1996 Constitution as posted on the Ukrainian parliament's website: *Konstytutsiia Ukrainy* (http://zakon4.rada.gov.ua/laws/show/254%D0%BA/96-%D0%B2%D1%80).
3. See Taras Kuzio, *Ukraine: State and Nation Building* (London: Routledge, 1998), p. 158 ("Soviets"); Andrew Wilson, *The Ukrainians: Unexpected Nation* (New Haven, CT: Yale University Press, 2000), p. 219.

Chapter 3

1. In 1904 the founder of modern Ukrainian historiography, Mykhailo Hrushevsky, famously compared the historical relations between Kyiv and what became the Moscow region to those between Rome and barbarian Gaul. See Serhii Plokhy, *Unmaking Imperial Russia: Mykhailo Hrushevsky and the Writing of Ukrainian History* (Toronto: University of Toronto Press, 2005), pp. 108–10.

2. Serhy Yekelchyk, *Stalin's Empire of Memory: Russian-Ukrainian Relations in the Soviet Historical Imagination* (Toronto: University of Toronto Press, 2004), pp. 96–99.

3. Shaul Stampfer, "What Actually Happened to the Jews of Ukraine in 1648," *Jewish History* 17, no. 2 (2003): 218.

4. See Henry Abramson, *A Prayer for the Government: Ukrainians and Jews in Revolutionary Times, 1917–1920* (Cambridge, MA: Harvard University Press, 1999).

5. Bohdan Krawchenko, *Social Change and National Consciousness in Twentieth-Century Ukraine* (London: Macmillan, 1985), pp. 100, 148.

6. S. Kulchytsky, "Teror holodom iak instrument kolektyvizatsii," in S. Kulchytsky, ed., *Holodomor 1932–1933 rr. v Ukraini: prychyny i naslidky* (Kyiv: Instytut istorii Ukrainy NANU, 1995), p. 34.

7. Terry Martin, *The Affirmative Action Empire: Nations and Nationalism in the Soviet Union, 1923–1939* (Ithaca, NY: Cornell University Press, 2001), pp. 273–308.

8. Yekelchyk, *Stalin's Empire of Memory*, 48.

9. "The Righteous Among The Nations: Statistics," Yad Vashem (http://www.yadvashem.org/yv/en/righteous/statistics.asp).

10. Timothy Snyder, "The Causes of Ukrainian-Polish Ethnic Cleansing, 1943," *Past and Present* 179 (May 2003): 202.

11. Vasyl Ovsiienko, "Pravozakhysnyi rukh v Ukraini (seredyna 1950-kh–1980-i roky)," in Ye. Yu. Zakharov, ed., *Ukrainske hromadska hrupa spryiannia vykonanniu Helsinkskykh uhod* (Kharkiv: Folio, 2001), vol. 1, p. 31.

Chapter 4

1. For an in-depth analysis of how and why voters from different regions voted the way they did in 1991, see Valeri Khmelko and Andrew Wilson, "Regionalism and Ethnic and Linguistic Cleavages in Ukraine," in Taras Kuzio, ed., *Contemporary Ukraine: Dynamics of Post-Soviet Transformation* (Armonk, NY: M. E. Sharpe, 1998), pp. 60–80.

2. "Budapest Memorandums on Security Assurances, 1994," *Council on Foreign Relations: Primary Sources* (http://www.cfr.org/arms-control-disarmament-and-nonproliferation/budapest-memorandums-security-assurances-1994/p32484).

3. Zbigniew Brzezinski, "The Premature Partnership," *Foreign Affairs* 73, no. 2 (1994): 80.

4. Paul D'Anieri, "Ethnic Tensions and State Strategies: Understanding the Survival of the Ukrainian State," in Taras Kuzio, ed., *Democratic Revolution in Ukraine: From Kuchmagate to Orange Revolution* (New York: Routledge, 2009), pp. 19–20.

5. "30 Parishes of the UOC (MP) Moved to the Jurisdiction of Kyiv Patriarchate," *Religious Information Service of Ukraine*, December 8, 2014 (http://risu.org.ua/en/index/all_news/confessional/orthodox_relations/58421/).

6. Anders Åslund, *How Ukraine Became a Market Economy and Democracy* (Washington, DC: Peterson Institute for International Economics, 2009), pp. 107–8.

7. John Lough and Vladimir Dubrovskiy, "Are Ukraine's Anti-Corruption Reforms Working?" Chatham House: The Royal Institute of International Affairs, November 2018, p. 3 (https://www.chathamhouse.org/publication/are-ukraines-anti-corruption-reforms-working/2018-11-19-ukraine-anti-corruption-reforms-lough-dubrovskiy.pdf).

8. James T. Hitch III and Yuliya Kuchma, "Ukraine's New Anti-Corruption Law: Will It Really Stop Corruption in Ukraine?" *International Lawyer* 45, no. 3 (Fall 2011): 839–55, here 841–42.

9. See "Corruption Perception Index 2012," *Transparency International* (https://www.transparency.org/cpi2012/results), and Viktor Tkachuk, "People First: The Latest in the Watch on Ukrainian Democracy," *Kyiv Post*, September 30, 2012 (https://www.kyivpost.com/article/opinion/op-ed/people-first-the-latest-in-the-watch-on-ukrainian-democracy-6-313710.html?cn-reloaded=1).

10. See Margarita M. Balmaceda, *The Politics of Energy Dependency: Ukraine, Belarus, and Lithuania between Domestic Oligarchs and Russian Pressure (1992–2012)* (Toronto: University of Toronto Press, 2013).

Chapter 5

1. Timothy Snyder, "Ukraine, Russia, and the Central Significance of Civil Society," A lecture at Charles University, Prague, January 27, 2015 (https://www.youtube.com/watch?v=yoUkoGn7cRU); Ilya Gerasimov, "Ukraine 2014: The First Postcolonial Revolution," *Ab Imperio*, no. 3 (2014): 22–44.

2. Andrew Wilson, *Ukraine's Orange Revolution* (New Haven, CT: Yale University Press, 2005), p. 53.

3. Andy Cohlan, "Skin Growths Saved Poisoned Ukrainian President," *New Scientist*, August 7, 2009 (http://www.newscientist.com/article/dn17570-skin-growths-saved-poisoned-ukrainian-president.html#.VMnHiWjF9qU).

4. Andrei Illarionov, "Putin schitaet, chto chast Ukrainy dolzhna prinadlezhat Rossii," *Ukrainskaia Pravda*, January 10, 2015 (http://www.pravda.com.ua/rus/articles/2013/10/10/6999733/).

5. Dominik Arel [Dominique Arel], "Paradoksy Pomaranchevoi revoliutsii," *Krytyka* 9 (April 2005): 2–4.
6. Joint Statement by President George W. Bush and President Viktor Yushchenko, April 4, 2005, US Government Publishing Office (http://www.gpo.gov/fdsys/pkg/WCPD-2005-04-11/pdf/WCPD-2005-04-11-Pg557.pdf).
7. Mustafa Nayem, "Uprising in Ukraine: How It All Began," *Voices*, April 4, 2014 (http://www.opensocietyfoundations.org/voices/uprising-ukraine-how-it-all-began).
8. "Vid Maidanu-taboru do Maidanu-Sichi: Shcho zminylosia?" Kyivskyi mizhnarodnyi instytut sotsiolohii, February 6, 2014 (http://www.kiis.com.ua/?lang=ukr&cat=reports&id=226&page=1&y=2014&m=2).
9. "Russian TV Announces Right Sector Leader Led Ukraine Polls," Radio Free Europe/Radio Liberty, May 26, 2014 (http://www.rferl.org/content/russian-tv-announces-right-sector-leader-yarosh-led-ukraine-polls/25398882.html).
10. As suggested by Radoslaw Sikorski, the former Polish foreign minister and mediator in the talks between the Ukrainian opposition and Yanukovych, in his interview with the *Frankfurter Allgemeine Zeitung*, January 24, 2015 (http://www.faz.net/aktu- ell/politik/ausland/ukraine-konflikt-sikorski-putin-verlangte-einsatz-von-gewalt-13388656.html).
11. Paul D'Anieri, "The Last Hurrah: The 2004 Ukrainian Presidential Elections and the Limits of Machine Politics," in Paul D'Anieri and Taras Kuzio, eds., *Aspects of the Orange Revolution*, vol. 1: *Democratization and Elections in Post-Communist Ukraine* (Stuttgart: Ibidem, 2007), p. 169; Wilson, *Ukraine's Orange Revolution*, 183–89.
12. "Oliver Stone on Ukraine Protests: 'The Truth Is Not Being Aired in the West,'" *Hollywood Reporter*, December 30, 2014 (http://www.hollywoodreporter.com/news/oliver-stone-ukraine-protests-truth-760755).

Chapter 6
1. "Kto sprovotsiroval voinu v Donbasse?" *Korrespondent.net*, January 18, 2015 (http://korrespondent.net/ukraine/politics/3467784-kto-sprovotsyroval-voinu-na-donbasse).
2. "Putin: Kharkov, Donetsk, Lugansk, Kherson, Nikolaev, Odessa ne vkhodili v sostav Ukrainy," *Segodnia*, April 17, 2014 (http://www.segodnya.ua/politics/pnews/putin-harkov-lugansk-doneck-herson-nikolaev-odessa-ne-vhodili-v-sostav-ukrainy-513722.html).

3. David Kashi, "This Gallup Poll Shows Crimeans Had Very Different Ideas about Russia Last Year," *International Business Times*, March 17, 2014 (http://www.ibtimes.com/gallup-poll-shows-crimeans-had-very-different-ideas-about-russia-last-year-1561821).

4. "Dynamika stavlennia naselennia Ukrainy do Rosii ta naselennia Rossii do Ukrainy," Kyivskyi mizhnarodnyi instytut sotsiolohii, March 4, 2014 (http://www.kiis.com.ua/?lang=ukr&cat=reports&id=236&page=1).

5. Maksim Tovkailo and Margarita Liutova, "Raskhody biudzheta na Krym uzhe prevysili 100 milliardov rublei," *Vedomosti*, May 20, 2014 (http://www.vedomosti.ru/finance/news/26692171/100-mlrd-ne-hvatit#ixzz3Iqu5jG8P).

6. Bohdan Krawchenko, *Social Change and National Consciousness in Twentieth-Century Ukraine* (London: Macmillan, 1985), p. 42.

7. Hiroaki Kuromiya, *Freedom and Terror in the Donbas: A Ukrainian-Russian Borderland, 1870s–1990s* (Cambridge, UK: Cambridge University Press, 1998), p. 41.

8. Krawchenko, *Social Change*, 194, calculated from table 5.9.

9. See "Kto sprovotsiroval voinu na Donbasse," *Korrespondent.net*, January 18, 2015 (http://korrespondent.net/ukraine/politics/3467784-kto-sprovotsyroval-voinu-na-donbasse); and Paul Chaisty and Stephen Whitefield, "Support for Separatism in Southern and Eastern Ukraine Is Lower Than You Think," The Monkey Cage Blog at *Washington Post* online, February 6, 2015 (http://www.washingtonpost.com/blogs/monkey-cage/wp/2015/02/06/support-for-separatism-in-southern-and-eastern-ukraine-is-lower-than-you-think/).

10. "Strelkov prizval grazhdan DNR stat na zashchitu Rodiny," *Vzgliad*, May 18, 2014 (http://vz.ru/news/2014/5/18/687248.html).

11. Nan Tian, Aude Fleurant, Alexandra Kuimova, Pieter D. Wezeman, and Siemon T. Wezeman, "Trends in World Military Expenditure, 2018," *Stockholm International Peace Research Institute*, April 2019, p. 9 (https://www.sipri.org/sites/default/files/2019-04/fs_1904_milex_2018_0.pdf).

12. UN Office for the Coordination of Humanitarian Affairs, "Ukraine: Situation Report No. 28 as of 20 February 2015" (http://reliefweb.int/report/ukraine/ukraine-situation-report-no28-20-february-2015); *Frankfurter Allgemeine Sonntagszeitung*, February 8, 2015 (http://www.faz.net/aktuell/politik/ausland/ukraine-sicherheitskreise-bis-zu-50-000-tote-13416132.html).

13. Office of the United Nations High Commissioner for Human Rights, "Report on the Human Rights Situation in Ukraine, November 16, 2019 to February 15," (https://www.ohchr.org/Documents/Countries/UA/29thReportUkraine_EN.pdf).

14. "FMS: Okolo 265 tysiach ukraintsev poluchili ubezhishche v Rosii," *MK*, February 16, 2015 (http://www.mk.ru/politics/2015/02/16/fms-okolo-265-tysyach-ukraincev-poluchili-ubezhishhe-v-rossii.html).

Chapter 7

1. "Russia Was Ready to Put Nuclear Forces on Alert over Crimea, Putin Says," CNN News, March 16, 2015 (http://www.cnn.com/2015/03/16/europe/russia-putin-crimea-nuclear/).

2. OSCE Special Monitoring Mission to Ukraine, "Status Report as of 6 April 2020," *Organization for Security and Cooperation in Europe*, April 10, 2020 (https://www.osce.org/special-monitoring-mission-to-ukraine/449965?download=true).

3. Amy MacKinnon, "Counting the Dead in Europe's Forgotten War," *Foreign Policy*, October 25, 2018 (https://foreignpolicy.com/2018/10/25/counting-the-dead-in-europes-forgotten-war-ukraine-conflict-donbass-osce/); "Chto na samom dele uvidel Aleksandr Hug is OBSE na Donbasse," *StopFake.org*, October 29, 2018 (https://www.stopfake.org/ru/chto-na-samom-dele-uvidel-aleksandr-hug-iz-obse-na-donbasse/).

4. "Ukraine Premier Starts 'Kamikaze Mission' as Crimea Erupts," *Bloomberg*, February 28, 2014 (http://www.bloomberg.com/news/articles/2014-02-27/ukraine-premier-starts-kamikaze-mission-as-crimea-anger-flares).

5. Oleg Varfolomeyev, "Ukrainian President's Political Ally Implicated in Scandal over Murky Defense-Sector Supply Chains," *Jamestown Foundation's Eurasia Daily Monitor*, February 28, 2019 (https://jamestown.org/program/ukrainian-presidents-political-ally-implicated-in-scandal-over-murky-defense-sector-supply-chains/).

6. Oleksandr Holubov, "Vtrachenyi chas: Borotba z koruptsiieiu za prezydenta Poroshenka," *DW Ukraine*, March 15, 2019 (https://p.dw.com/p/3F0Lx).

7. "Poroshenko pokhyzuvavsia prohresom u borotbi z koruptsiieiu," *Ukrainska Pravda*, April 15, 2019 (https://www.pravda.com.ua/news/2019/04/15/7212267/). I have corrected 145th in the article to 144th as per the Transparency International data.

8. "Ukraine Ratifies Landmark Agreement with European Union," CBC News, September 16, 2014 (http://www.cbc.ca/m/touch/world/story/1.2767449).

9. Cory Welt, "Ukraine: Background, Conflict with Russia, and U.S. Policy." Updated September 19, 2019. Congressional Research Service Report R45008, p. 30 (https://crsreports.congress.gov/product/pdf/R/R45008).

10. Simon Ostrovsky, "Ukraine Lawyer Seeks Probe of Alleged Hacked Texts of Manafort's Daughter," *CNN*, March 11, 2017 (https://www.cnn.com/2017/03/10/politics/ukraine-manafort-hacked-texts/index.html).
11. Kenneth P. Vogel and David Stern, "Ukrainian Efforts to Sabotage Trump Backfire," *Politico*, January 11, 2017 (https://www.politico.com/story/2017/01/ukraine-sabotage-trump-backfire-233446).
12. "Posol SShA v Ukraini vyslovylasia za zvilnennia ochilnyka SAP Kholodnytskoho," *Radio Svoboda*, March 3, 2019 (https://www.radiosvoboda.org/a/news-yovanovych-holodnytskiy/29805179.html).
13. "Gontareva stala liderom narodnogo nedoveriia (issledovanie)," *Finance.UA*, March 5, 2016 (https://news.finance.ua/ru/news/-/370557/gontareva-stala-liderom-narodnogo-nedoveriya-issledovanie).
14. "Vybory Prezydenta Ukrainy 2019," *Tsentralna vyborcha komisiia* (https://www.cvk.gov.ua/pls/vp2019/wp300pt001f01=720.html).
15. "TsVK opratsiuvala 100% protokoliv," *Ukrainska Pravda*, July 26, 2019 (https://www.pravda.com.ua/news/2019/07/26/7221983/).
16. Tracy Wilkinson, "Ukrainian Official: We Tried to Correct Trump's 'Negative Impression,'" *Los Angeles Times*, October 6, 2019 (https://www.latimes.com/politics/story/2019-10-06/ukrainian-official-false-stories-threatened-us-ukraine-relations).
17. Edward Lucas, *The New Cold War: Putin's Russia and the Threat to the West* (New York: Palgrave Macmillan, 2008); Mark A. MacKinnon, *The New Cold War: Revolutions, Rigged Elections, and Pipeline Politics in the Former Soviet Union* (New York: Basic Books, 2007).
18. "Statement by Former US Ambassadors to Ukraine," *Atlantic Council*, May 26, 2020 (https://www.atlanticcouncil.org/blogs/ukrainealert/statement-by-former-us-ambassadors-to-ukraine/?fbclid=IwAR2EkxC_q1uI88ypDxYJ1_tCwLIIulrScagjZGFUZ-6vPQH6ORd6yjztFo0).

FURTHER READING

History of Ukraine

Katchanovski, Ivan, Zenon E. Kohut, Bohdan Y. Nebesio, and Myroslav Yurkevich. *Historical Dictionary of Ukraine*, 2nd ed. Lanham, MD: Scarecrow Press, 2013.

Kubicek, Paul. *The History of Ukraine*. Westport, CT: Greenwood Press, 2008.

Lindheim, Ralph, and George S. N. Luckyj, eds. *Towards an Intellectual History of Ukraine: An Anthology of Ukrainian Thought from 1717 to 1995*. Toronto: University of Toronto Press, 1996.

Magocsi, Paul R. *A History of Ukraine: The Land and Its Peoples*, 2nd ed. Toronto: University of Toronto Press, 2010.

Magocsi, Paul R. *Ukraine: An Illustrated History*. Toronto: University of Toronto Press, 2007.

Plokhy, Serhii. *The Gates of Europe: A History of Ukraine*. New York: Basic Books, 2017.

Reid, Anna. *Borderland: A Journey Through the History of Ukraine*, 2nd ed. New York: Basic Books, 2015.

Rudnytsky, Ivan L. *Essays in Modern Ukrainian History*. Edmonton: Canadian Institute of Ukrainian Studies Press, 1987.

Schlögel, Karl. *Ukraine: A Nation on the Borderland*. London: Reaktion Books, 2018.

Snyder, Timothy. *The Reconstruction of Nations: Poland, Ukraine, Lithuania, Belarus, 1569–1999*. New Haven, CT: Yale University Press, 2003.

Subtelny, Orest. *Ukraine: A History*, 4th ed. Toronto: University of Toronto Press, 2009.

Wilson, Andrew. *The Ukrainians: Unexpected Nation*, 3rd ed. New Haven, CT: Yale University Press, 2009.

Yekelchyk, Serhy. *Ukraine: Birth of a Modern Nation*. New York: Oxford University Press, 2007.

Ukrainian-Russian Relations

Kappeler, Andreas, Zenon E. Kohut, Frank E. Sysyn, and Mark von Hagen, eds. *Culture, Nation, and Identity: The Ukrainian-Russian Encounter.* Edmonton: Canadian Institute of Ukrainian Studies Press, 2003.

Kuzio, Taras. *Ukraine: Democratization, Corruption, and the New Russian Imperialism.* Santa Barbara, CA: Praeger Security International, 2015.

Miller, Alexei. *The Ukrainian Question: Russian Nationalism in the 19th Century.* Budapest: Central European University Press, 2003.

Molchanov, Mikhail A. *Political Culture and National Identity in Russian-Ukrainian Relations.* College Station: Texas A&M University Press, 2002.

Plokhy, Serhii. *Lost Kingdom: The Quest for Empire and the Making of the Russian Nation.* New York: Basic Books, 2017.

Plokhy, Serhii. *The Origins of the Slavic Nations: Premodern Identities in Russia, Ukraine, and Belarus.* Cambridge: Cambridge University Press, 2006.

Plokhy, Serhii. *Ukraine and Russia: Representations of the Past.* Toronto: University of Toronto Press, 2008.

Potichnyj, Peter J., Mark Raeff, Jaroslaw Pelenski, and Gleb N. Žekulin, eds. *Ukraine and Russia in Their Historical Encounter.* Edmonton: Canadian Institute of Ukrainian Studies Press, 1992.

Prizel, Ilya. *National Identity and Foreign Policy: Nationalism and Leadership in Poland, Russia, and Ukraine.* Cambridge: Cambridge University Press, 1998.

Procyk, Anna. *Russian Nationalism and Ukraine: The Nationality Policy of the Volunteer Army during the Civil War.* Edmonton: Canadian Institute of Ukrainian Studies Press, 1995.

Saunders, David. *The Ukrainian Impact on Russian Culture, 1750–1850.* Edmonton: Canadian Institute of Ukrainian Studies Press, 1985.

Schmidtke, Oliver, and Serhy Yekelchyk, eds. *Europe's Last Frontier? Belarus, Moldova, and Ukraine Between Russia and the European Union.* New York: Palgrave Macmillan, 2007.

Solchanyk, Roman. *Ukraine and Russia: The Post-Soviet Transition.* Lanham, MD: Rowman & Littlefield, 2000.

Szporluk, Roman. *Russia, Ukraine, and the Breakup of the Soviet Union.* Stanford, CA: Hoover Institution Press, 2000.

Yekelchyk, Serhy. *Stalin's Empire of Memory: Russian-Ukrainian Relations in the Soviet Historical Imagination.* Toronto: University of Toronto Press, 2004.

Post-Communist Ukraine

Arel, Dominique, and Blair Ruble, eds. *Rebounding Identities: The Politics of Identity in Russia and Ukraine.* Baltimore, MD: Johns Hopkins University Press, 2006.

Åslund, Anders. *How Ukraine Became a Market Economy and Democracy.*
Washington, DC: Peterson Institute for International Economics,
2009.
Åslund, Anders, and Georges De Menil, eds. *Economic Reform in Ukraine: The
Unfinished Agenda.* New York: Routledge, 2000.
Balmaceda, Margarita M. *On the Edge: Ukrainian–Central European–Russian
Security Triangle.* Budapest: Central European University Press, 2001.
Balmaceda, Margarita M. *Politics of Energy Dependency: Ukraine, Belarus, and
Lithuania Between Domestic Oligarchs and Russian Pressure, 1991–2012.*
Toronto: University of Toronto Press, 2013.
D'Anieri, Paul J. *Economic Interdependence in Ukrainian-Russian Relations.*
Albany: State University of New York Press, 1999.
D'Anieri, Paul. *Ukraine and Russia: From Civilized Divorce to Uncivil War.*
New York: Cambridge University Press, 2019.
D'Anieri, Paul J. *Understanding Ukrainian Politics: Power, Politics, and
Institutional Design.* Armonk, NY: M. E. Sharpe, 2007.
Dyczok, Marta. *Ukraine: Movement Without Change, Change Without Movement.*
Amsterdam: Harwood Academic Publishers, 2000.
Kuzio, Taras. *Ukraine Under Kuchma: Political Reform, Economic Transformation,
and Security Policy in Independent Ukraine.* New York: Palgrave
Macmillan, 1997.
Kuzio, Taras. *Ukraine: State and Nation Building.* New York: Routledge, 1998.
Kuzio, Taras, and Andrew Wilson. *Ukraine: Perestroika to Independence.*
New York: St. Martin's Press, 1994.
Marples, David R. *Heroes and Villains: Creating National History in Contemporary
Ukraine.* Budapest: Central European University Press, 2007.
Motyl, Alexander J. *Dilemmas of Independence: Ukraine after Totalitarianism.*
New York: Council on Foreign Relations Press, 1993.
Nahailo, Bohdan. *The Ukrainian Resurgence.* Toronto: University of Toronto
Press, 1999.
Plokhy, Serhii. *The Last Empire: The Final Days of the Soviet Union.*
New York: Basic Books, 2014.
Wanner, Catherine. *The Burden of Dreams: History and Identity in Post-Soviet
Ukraine.* University Park: Pennsylvania State University Press, 1998.
Wilson, Andrew. *Ukrainian Nationalism in the 1990s: A Minority Faith.*
Cambridge: Cambridge University Press, 1996.
Wolchik, Sharon L., and Vladimir A. Zviglianich. *Ukraine: The Search for a
National Identity.* Lanham, MD: Rowman & Littlefield, 2000.
Wolchuk, Roman. *Ukraine's Foreign and Security Policy, 1991–2000.*
New York: Routledge Curzon, 2003.

The Crimea and the Donbas

King, Charles. *The Black Sea: A History*. New York: Oxford University Press, 2005.

Kuromiya, Hiroaki. *Freedom and Terror in the Donbas: A Ukrainian- Russian Borderland, 1870s–1990s*. Cambridge: Cambridge University Press, 2003.

Kuzio, Taras. *Ukraine–Crimea–Russia: Triangle of Conflict*. Stuttgart: Ibidem, 2007.

Magocsi, Paul R. *This Blessed Land: Crimea and the Crimean Tatars*. Toronto: University of Toronto Press, 2014.

Marples, David R. *Ukraine Under Perestroika: Ecology, Economics, and the Workers' Revolt*. New York: Palgrave Macmillan, 1991.

Qualls, Karl D. *From Ruins to Reconstruction: Urban Identity in Soviet Sevastopol after World War II*. Ithaca, NY: Cornell University Press, 2009.

Sasse, Gwendolyn. *The Crimean Question: Identity, Transition, and Conflict*. Cambridge, MA: Harvard Ukrainian Research Institute, 2007.

Siegelbaum, Lewis H., and Daniel J. Walkowitz. *Workers of the Donbass Speak: Survival and Identity in the New Ukraine, 1989–1992*. Albany: State University of New York Press, 1995.

Swain, Adam, ed. *Re-constructing the Post-Soviet Industrial Region: The Donbas in Transition*. London: Routledge, 2007.

Wynn, Charters. *Workers, Strikes, and Pogroms: The Donbass-Dnepr Bend in Late Imperial Russia, 1870–1905*. Princeton, NJ: Princeton University Press, 1992.

Civil Revolutions and the Conflict with Russia

Åslund, Anders, and Michael McFaul, eds. *Revolution in Orange: The Origins of Ukraine's Democratic Breakthrough*. Washington, DC: Carnegie Endowment for International Peace, 2006.

Averre, Derek, and Kataryna Wolczuk, eds. *The Ukraine Conflict: Security, Identity and Politics in the Wider Europe*. New York: Routledge, 2017.

Bertelsen, Olga, ed. *Revolution and War in Contemporary Ukraine: The Challenge of Change*. Stuttgart: Ibidem, 2017.

D'Anieri, Paul J., ed. *Orange Revolution and Aftermath: Mobilization, Apathy, and the State in Ukraine*. Baltimore, MD: Johns Hopkins University Press, 2010.

Dyczok, Marta. *Ukraine's Euromaidan: Broadcasting Through Information Wars with Hromadske Radio*. Bristol: E-International Relations, 2016.

Judah, Tim. *In Wartime: Stories from Ukraine*. New York: Tim Duggan Books, 2017.

Kurkov, Andrey. *Ukraine Diaries: Dispatches from Kiev*. London: Harvill Secker, 2014.

Kuzio, Taras, ed. *Democratic Revolution in Ukraine: From Kuchmagate to Orange Revolution*. London: Routledge, 2009.

Kuzio, Taras. *Putin's War Against Ukraine: Revolution, Nationalism, and Crime.* Toronto: Chair of Ukrainian Studies, 2017.

Marples, David R. *Ukraine in Conflict: An Analytical Chronicle.* Bristol: E-International Relations, 2017.

Marples, David R., and Frederick V. Mills, eds. *Ukraine's Euromaidan: Analyses of a Civil Revolution.* Stuttgart: Ibidem, 2015.

Menon, Rajan, and Eugene Rumer. *The Conflict in Ukraine: The Unwinding of the Post-Cold War Order.* Boston: MIT Press, 2015.

Shore, Marci. *The Ukrainian Night: An Intimate History of Revolution.* New Haven, CT: Yale University Press, 2018.

Wilson, Andrew. *Ukraine Crisis: What It Means for the West.* New Haven, CT: Yale University Press, 2014.

Wilson, Andrew. *Ukraine's Orange Revolution.* New Haven, CT: Yale University Press, 2006.

INDEX